QUOCUNQUE
JECERIS STABIT.

Whichever way you try me I stand?

"However through the world they're tost,
However disappointed, crost,
Reverses, losses, Fortune's frown,
No chance nor change keep Manxmen down.

Upset them any way you will
Upon their legs you find them still,
For ever active, brisk, and spunky,
Stabit, Jeceris, Quocunque!"—OLD SONG.

MANX WORTHIES

MANX WORTHIES

OR

BIOGRAPHIES OF NOTABLE
MANX MEN AND WOMEN

COMPILED BY

A. W. MOORE, M.A.

DOUGLAS, ISLE OF MAN:

S. K. BROADBENT & COMPANY, LIMITED,

VICTORIA STREET.

1901.

FIRST PUBLISHED BY S. K. BROADBENT AND CO LTD 1901
THIS EDITION REPRODUCED BY THE PHOTO-LITHOGRAPHY
PROCESS BY THE MANX MUSEUM AND NATIONAL TRUST,
1971

PRINTED IN GREAT BRITAIN
BY ROBERT MACLEHOSE AND CO LTD
THE UNIVERSITY PRESS,
GLASGOW

Introduction

My main object in compiling this little book is to try and save from oblivion the names of as many as possible of those Manxmen who have done good service for their country. I believe that in so doing I have succeeded in showing that in proportion to its population, the Isle of Man has produced an unusually large number of able and distinguished men—such, for instance, as the Rev. Dr. Walker,* John Christian Curwen, M.P., Colonel Mark Wilks, the Rev. Hugh Stowell, Captain Quilliam, R.N., Captain Peter Heywood, R.N., Sir Mark Cubbon, K.C.B., the Hon. William Kermode, Professor Edward Forbes, and the Rev. T. E. Brown.

---

* Names given in order of date.

No doubt, too, some of the Manxmen* of the more remote past were equally able and distinguished, but, from want of adequate information, it is more difficult to form a correct judgment with respect to them.

Nor are there wanting living Manxmen who are equally deserving of these epithets. Many of the " Worthies " of whom I have given accounts in the following pages, are not, of course, men of equal calibre with those I have mentioned.

Moreover, I have also recorded the names of some who are chiefly remembered on account of their eccentricities, as having, in fact, been " characters." It is not necessarily the best man who is the best remembered. Many men have led most useful and blameless lives, and yet they do not afford interesting material for even the briefest biography. It is probable that

---

* It will be observed that I have been liberal in my use of the term "Manxman," including under it, for instance, not only such men as Sir Baldwin Walker, who, though not of Manx parentage, was born in the island, but also such men as Deemster J. F. Gill, who, though of Manx parentage, was not born in the island. I have, too, in a few cases, briefly referred to the descendants of Manxmen who have distinguished themselves in the countries to which their forefathers had emigrated.

many of my readers will think that there are names left out which should have been inserted. If so, let me at once point out that, with their assistance, any errors and omissions can be rectified in a second edition.

I wish also to point out that the comparative lengths of the notices given are, in most cases, regulated by the information available and not by the importance of the subject. The sources of this information have been so varied that it is impossible to indicate and acknowledge them all.

The more recent notices* have, with the permission of the editors, been taken mainly from the local newspapers, more particularly the " Isle of Man Times," the " Manx Sun," the " Mona's Herald," and the " Isle of Man Examiner." I have now to thank them for this permission, and, at the same time, to

---

* In accordance with the wish of the publishers, brief notices of "Worthies" who have died during the last twenty-five years are given. For obvious reasons these notices are written with less freedom than those which precede them in order of date; they are, in fact, what Mr Stead, in the " Review of Reviews," calls " appreciations." It has also been by wish of the publishers that I have inserted extracts from the obituary notices of my uncle, Archdeacon Moore, and of my father, W. F. Moore.

express my obligations to those who have
in any way assisted me in the compilation
of this book, which, I trust, may be accept-
able to all who love *Mannin Veg Veen* and
its sons and daughters.

A. W. MOORE.

CRONKBOURNE, JUNE, 1901.

CONTENTS

MANX WORTHIES

CHAPTER I.

The Church

WE begin our account of "Manx Worthies" with five bishops, the first four of whom were bishops of Sodor and Man.

HAMOND (? 1079-1095).*

According to the *Chronicle of Man*, "after William, in the days of Godred Crouan, Hamond, son of Jole, a Manxman, held the Episcopal See." This is all the information we have about him, unless we are to accept the theory that the chronology of the Chronicle is wrong, and that he is identical with a certain Wimund, elected Bishop of Man in 1134, who was afterwards ruler of the southern portion of Scotland, and who died about the year 1170; but this is more than doubtful.†

MICHAEL (? 1186-1203).*

The next to hold this position was MICHAEL, by race a Manxman, "a man venerable and pure in life, truly a gentle monk in deed as well as in dress . . . and he ending the closing day of life in a good old age, honourably lies buried at Fountains "‡ This charming little description in the *Chronicle* gives all that we know of him, except that we may feel sure—since Fountains Abbey is a Cistercian foundation—that he belonged to that order. The Rev. John Quine thinks that he was the builder of the chancel in St. German's Cathedral.§

---

* Date of episcopate.
† For particulars regarding this curious question, see "Diocese of Sodor and Man" (A. W. Moore), pp. 50-52.
‡ Translation of the *Chronicle of Man* by the Rev. John Quine, in an account of MICHAEL in the *Ramsey Church Magazine* for January, 1896.
§ *Ibid.*

WILLIAM RUSSELL (1348-1374).*

The third Manx bishop of the diocese, WILLIAM RUSSELL, Abbot of Rushen, was a notable man, and probably one of the ablest bishops that the island has ever had. He was elected by the clergy of Man " in the Cathedral Church of St. German, in Holm of Man, and was consecrated at Avignon by Pope Clement VI."† When in Italy, he obtained leave from the Pope to mortgage the Church revenues in order to pay the " great and burdensome outlay . . . for the successful carrying on of the affairs of the Sodor Church."‡ On his return he issued six canons, which were passed at a synod held in Kirk Michael in 1350. They may be summarized as follows : (1) If a clergyman dies, all his brethren, without any pretence or excuse, must attend his funeral ; and each must daily, for thirty days, celebrate mass for the dead. (2) God's Word is to be preached, children to be instructed, and the Sacrament to be administered on Sundays and Holy Days. (3) Churches and their books and ornaments are to be kept in good order. (4) All parish churches are to have a residence for a clergyman attached to them, especially those appropriated to the abbeys. (5) Foreign clergymen are only to officiate when they have given proof of their ordination and good character, and have received an authorization to do so. (6) At least one person from each house is to attend church on Sunday, under a penalty of three shillings and fourpence, unless a reasonable excuse is given.§ These stringent rules probably indicate a tightening of the Church's discipline. Mr Quine says : " The period seems to have been one of orderly and organised church life, of prosperity and extension . . . and from the canons we may infer a close strictness in the habits of the clergy."‖ Bishop Russell's influence had, no doubt, much to do with this state of affairs. He was buried in Furness Abbey.

JOHN DONKAN or DUNCAN (1374-1392).*

Except for the fact that he was a Manxman, nothing is known of his early life. It would seem that he belonged to the Benedictine order, and was a priest of the church of Camelyn, in the Diocese of Down, when he was, in 1367, appointed Archdeacon of that diocese by Pope Urban V. One reason for his appointment was that he was " skilled in Canon Law."** In 1834, he was elected Bishop of Sodor and Man by the clergy in their

---

* Date of episcopate.
† *Chronicle of Man.*
‡ *Manx Soc.*, Vol. XXIII., pp. 351-4.
§ Abstract from *Manx Soc.*, XVIII., pp. 188-193
‖ *Ramsey Church Magazine*, May, 1896.
** *Manx Soc.*, Vol. XXIII, p. 375.

Cathedral of St. German. This election was confirmed by Pope Gregory XI. JOHN DONKAN then went to Italy, and he was consecrated "at the Church of the Friar's Preachers, by the Cardinal of Palestrina, formerly Archbishop of Canterbury."[*] On his return journey, he was unfortunately captured and imprisoned at Boulogne, not being liberated till he was able to find money to pay a ransom. It was, consequently, not till the 25th of January, 1376, that he was installed in his own cathedral, when he received "many very great offerings."[†] We know nothing of his administration of his diocese, which, as regards Man at least, was then passing through a very troublous and unsettled period. It is, however, certain that he was a man of considerable ability, as well as influence, since we find him receiving important commissions from English kings. The first of these was in 1388, when Richard II. empowered him to treat with Godfrey, son of John, late Lord of the Isles, concerning various matters, and, in 1405, Henry IV. appointed him, together with Jenico de Artois, to conclude peace between his Irish subjects and the Lord of the Isles, between whom and the merchants of Drogheda and Dublin a sort of piratical war had been carried on. In 1392, he was translated to the Bishopric of Down. In 1401, he received from Henry IV. the office of Seneschal of his Liberty of Ulster, which seems a curious office for a bishop, but affords proof of the confidence the king had in him. He died in 1412, and was buried in his Cathedral Church of Down.

He is the last Manxman who has been Bishop of Man.

CHARLES CROWE (b. *circa* 1660, d. 1726),

is supposed to have been a son of the Rev. William Crowe, Vicar of Jurby from 1645 to 1690, and to have been born at the Nappin, in that parish. His grandfather was the Rev. Edward Crowe, Vicar of Lezayre in 1624. Edward's grandfather, William, was vicar of the same parish from 1603 to 1614, and his (Edward's) father, Silvester, was its vicar from 1614 to 1624. CHARLES CROWE went to Ireland, in 1680, in the humble capacity of amanuensis, He then became a teacher in, and afterwards head master of, St. Patrick's School in Dublin. He was afterwards chaplain to Laurence, Earl of Rochester, who was then Lord-Lieutenant of Ireland, and at the same time Rector of the parish of Coenab, in the Diocese of Leighlin and Queen's County. In 1702, he was promoted to be Bishop of Cloyne, being consecrated in Christ Church, Dublin. He seems to have been an estimable prelate, and to have conferred many benefits upon his diocese, among which may be mentioned his recovery for the see of the Manor of

---

[*] *Chronicle of Man*, p. 121.
[†] *Ibid.*

Donoghmore, containing 8,000 acres.   At his death, he left
nearly the whole of his property to the widows and orphans of
his clergy, and to educating a number of poor boys.   Nor did he
forget his native island.   By deed, dated the 9th February, 1718,
he, for the nominal sum of £40, and, " in consideration of his
respect and affection to the Isle of Man, more particularly to the
parish of Trinity, Lezayre, granted all and every the houses and
lands of right belonging to him in the said parish to the Rev.
Henry Allen, Vicar of the said parish, and his successors for
ever."*   Since Crowe, no Manxman, as far as we know, has been
elevated to the episcopal bench.

HUGH CANNELL   (*circa* 1585-1670),

is said to have been Vicar of Michael for the extraordinarily long
period of 61 years, between 1609 and 1670.   In 1626, he was made
assistant vicar-general, having been previously episcopal registrar, and was nominated by Bishop Phillips as one of a commission
for managing the diocese in his absence.   But his chief claim to
distinction is shown by the followng order by Governor Chaloner,
which was entered in the civil records in 1658 : " Takinge into
consideration that Sir Hugh Cannell, Viccar of Kk. Michael, his
livelihood, which is but little, and his parish greate, and that he
was   one   of   the   first   preachers   in   this . Isle,   and   the
first that taught the Manks to read the Scriptures in the Manks tongue,
and assistant to the late Reverend Father in God, John Phillips,
Bishop of this Isle in the translating of the Bible ; I doe by virtue
of that power and trust vested and reposed in me by his
Excellencie Thomas, Lord Ffairfax . . .   give and grant unto
the said SIR HUGH CANNELL during the pleasure of his said
Excellencie, the full sum of ffourteen pounds lawfull money of
England, to be paid half-yearly by even and equal porcons."†
Chaloner's statement that HUGH CANNELL was connected with
him in the translation of the Bible into Manx is repeated in his
history of the island, where he says that he assisted the bishop in
perfecting " that most laborious, most difficult, but useful work
. . .   in the space of twenty and nine years."‡   This is confirmed by Sacheverell,§ but Bishop Wilson, on the other hand,
says that the only translation made at that time was that of the
Prayer-Book.‖   All we can say is that no such translation of the
Bible has come down to us.   Another work attributed to SIR HUGH
CANNELL is a brief account of the diocese which was embodied in
a state paper endorsed by Archbishop Laud, in 1634.**

---

  * We learn from Bishop Wilson's Note Book that his widow gave £100
(Irish) for the widows and children of the Manx clergy.
   † *Lib Scacc.*
   ‡ *Manx Soc.*, Vol. X., p. 9.
   § *Ibid*, Vol. I, p. 91.
   ‖ *Ibid*, Vol. XVIII., p. 100.
  ** *The Manx Ecclesiastical Records.*

JOSEPH CANNELL (b. *circa* 1673).

We learn from a letter of Governor Sacheverell's, dated 1696, to the Archbishop of Canterbury, in which he dwells upon the misfortunes and poverty of the Manx Church, "that three of the hopefullest of our young men that ever the Island bred"* had left it because they were afraid that they would be compelled to accept three livings then vacant, which were worth only three pounds a year each. Two of these young men are unknown, but the third was JOSEPH CANNELL, who afterwards took the degree of M.A., and became rector of the united churches of St. Nicholas Coleabbey and St. Nicholas Olave in London. The only other fact that has been ascertained about him is that he preached a sermon on the 21st of March, 1708, about the "case of the Pretender," in the Church of St. Nicholas Coleabbey, in which he told the congregation what their "duty" was. The sermon, which was "printed and sold in London by H. Wills, near the water-side, for the benefit of the poor," has not been preserved, but it doubtless enjoined obedience to Queen Anne and abhorrence of the Pretender.

We next come to a number of excellent men, born between the years 1679-1735, all of whom came under the direct influence and teaching of the great and good Bishop Wilson.

WILLIAM WALKER (b. 1679, d. 1729),

was a son of Thomas Walker, of Lezayre.† Nothing is known of Thomas Walker, except that he died soon after his son's birth, leaving his widow in very straitened circumstances. Notwithstanding this, the lad's education was not neglected. That he was a zealous and eager student, the following anecdote will show : "When about twelve or thirteen years of age, he was employed as a servant in the family of John Stevenson, Esq., of Balladoole ; and in the harvest his business was to drive one of the cars,‡ which was used at that time for carrying home corn. The boy's passion for books began to show itself at this early period. One day in autumn, whilst sitting on his empty car, he took his book out of his pocket, and began to read with such profound attention that the horse, taking advantage of the inattention of the driver, and getting the halter off his neck, ran furiously down the lawn before the parlour windows. Mr Stevenson, standing at one of the windows, saw what had happened, and hastened to stop the progress of the horse. When he came up to the car, he soon perceived the occasion of the

---

* An account of the Isle of Man (Introduction). *Manx Soc.*, Vol. I.
† Ballaugh Register.
Low carts without wheels.

mistake. The little reader still had his book in his hand. This circumstance appeared to the master to mark the character of the boy; and, therefore, instead of rebuking him for his neglect, he turned round to him and said : " Since thou art so fond of reading, thou shalt have enough of it." Accordingly the next day he sent him to the Castletown Academy, where, by his diligence and good conduct, he made rapid progress in classical and academical learning, and, at a proper age, offered himself a candidate for the Holy Ministry.* He was ordained deacon by Bishop Wilson in March, 1700, being then just two years below the canonical age, and he appointed him to the mastership of the Douglas Grammar School at the same time. So highly did the bishop think of him that, when the Rectory of Ballaugh became vacant, he held it open for him until he was of age to be admitted to the priesthood, which was not for three years after this. In 1712, he was appointed vicar-general, and, from that time till his death, he was most intimately connected with the bishop, being " very high in his confidence and friendship; the chief of his fellow-workmen and fellow sufferers."† He entered heartily into his plans for building and beautifying churches, and himself contributed offerings to that end. In 1722, Bishop Wilson and his two vicar-generals—Curghey and Walker—were committed to Castle Rushen by order of Governor Horne, for declining to submit to his jurisdiction in appeals from the ecclesiastical courts. They remained there for nine weeks, employing their time in translating the Bible into Manx.‡ WALKER afterwards went to London several times in connection with the lawsuit which arose out of his imprisonment. The suit was ultimately decided in the bishop's favour. During one of these visits, Archbishop Wake conferred on him the degree of LL.D., being urged thereto, as Stowell says, by the zeal and ability with which he had pleaded his diocesan's cause.§ On his return home, when he saw his mother in the midst of the crowd that came to welcome him, " he dropped upon his knees to receive her blessing,"|| thus showing that, notwithstanding the honours conferred upon him, he had retained the simplicity of his character. He was evidently far above the rest of his countrymen in intellectual attainments, being no doubt the " one clergyman " alluded to by a contemporary observer as " indeed a man of letters."** In the following year he died, in the very midst of his usefulness and popularity, " to the great grief of all good men who had been witness to his great virtue."††

* Stowell's Life of Bishop Wilson, pp. 415-16.
† Keble's Life of Bishop Wilson, p. 151.
‡ The four Gospels, the Acts, and part of the Prayer Book are said to have been translated by them at this time.
§ Stowell, pp. 416-17.
|| Ibid, p. 417.
** Waldron. Manx Soc., Vol. XI, p. 16.
†† Keble, p. 696.

He possessed " a true judicial mind, an imperturbable temper, sagacity, and courage ever ready for emergencies, and the gift of sympathizing with all sorts and conditions of men."* Bishop Wilson, who preached his funeral sermon, closed it with the following words: "Would to God that every one who attends his funeral may leave the world with the same fair, unstained character."† In accordance with his will, he was buried in the chancel of his church, but, the walls of the chancel having been since then taken down, his tomb is now in the old church-yard. On it is an inscription written by Bishop Wilson. His mother, who survived him, wrote a ballad in Manx descriptive of his virtues and those of her other son. Of its 23 stanzas, it will suffice to quote the following:—‡

> Bannaght ny moght, scaa ny mraane hreoghe,
>   Fendeilagh cloan gyn ayr;
> Da ny hannoonee dreeym, nagh goghe
>   Veih treanee ghewill aggair.

> The poor's blessing, the widow's help,§
>   Guard of the fatherless;
> Supporter of the weak, he'd not
>   Bear from tyrants a wrong.

JOHN WOODS, Junior (b. 1695, d. 1740),

was a son of the Vicar of Malew of the same name. Bishop Wilson made him vicar-general in 1729, when he was only 34, which shows, either that he was a man of unusual ability, or that no one else among the clergy was competent or willing to take the post. The governor, however, refused to swear him in, stating that he had Lord Derby's positive orders not to do it. This being so, the bishop took the matter in his own hands, and ordered the required oath to be administered to him by the vicar-general, John Curghey. This was accordingly done, and the appointment was not afterwards disputed. At this time, JOHN WOODS was curate of Michael, there being no vicar, because Lord Derby had not only long delayed to fill the vacancy in that living, but declined to appoint WOODS to any living in his gift. In 1730, the bishop made him Vicar of German. From the following obituary notice in his "Episcopalia," it is evident that he thought very highly of WOODS: "This morning, after a two years' lingering sickness, died the reverend and worthy Mr. John Woodes, Vicar-General and Vicar of St. Germain's; a man of singular sobriety, integrity, veracity, probity, and piety."

* *Keble*, p. 705.
† *Ibid*, p. 707.
‡ Manx Ballads (A. W. Moore), pp. 202-7.
§ Literally " screen."

MATTHIAS CURGHEY (b. 1699, d. 1771),

was one of the Curgheys of Ballakillingan, and son of John
Curghey, Vicar of Braddan and vicar-general.   He was Vicar of
Lezayre from 1729 to 1761, and Rector of Ballaugh from 1761 till
his death.   He was also vicar-general.   He assisted in translating the Liturgy into Manx, and in revising the Pentateuch.
He also transcribed the Epistles, and, in connexion with the Rev.
James Wilks, the Gospels and Acts.   Archdeacon Mylrea, writing
to the Rev. Philip Moore about him, at the time of his death,
remarks : " Mr Curghey is indeed a public loss to Mona ; and a
particular loss to you in your arduous undertaking (the translation of the Bible into Manx).   .   .   .   He was certainly a man
of great candour, and a good Christian."[*]   In his reply, Philip
Moore speaks of him as his " learned friend and fellow labourer."[*]
His tombstone in Ballaugh Churchyard declares him to have been
" an humble, meek, pacific man, sound divine, learned and
exemplary."

THOMAS WILSON (b. 1703, d. 1784),

the only son of Bishop Thomas Wilson and Mary Patten, was born
at Bishop's Court, in the Isle of Man.   He seems to have been
educated by his father till he went to Christ Church, Oxford,
where he took his M.A. degree in 1727, taking the further degrees
of B.D. and D.D. in 1739.   He was, for many years, chaplain to
King George the Second, and Prebendary of Westminster.   He
was also Rector of St. Margaret's there, till 1738, when he was
appointed to the Rectory of St. Stephen's, Walbrook.   Several
pamphlets are attributed to him, one being " A Review of a
Project for building a new Square at Westminster," which he
strongly opposed.   His grievance seems to have been that the
proposed alteration would have entailed the destruction of his
prebendal house.   The scheme was, however, abandoned.
Another was " The Ornaments of Churches considered ; with a
particular view to the late decorations in the Parish Church of St.
Margaret."   Nothing is known of his work as a clergyman, but
he seems to have been a learned and worthy man.   He was a
benefactor to the funds of the Manx Church, and, during the time
of the famine in 1740 and 1741, it was chiefly due to his exertions
that corn was allowed to be exported to the island.   The initia-
tion of the clergy's " Widows and Orphans' Fund," in 1850, was
also due to him, and, in 1774, he, aided by some friends, purchased
the impropriate tithes of Kirk Michael, the proceeds of which
were devoted to the same object.

(Partly from the Memoirs of Bishop Hildesley, pp. 267-70.)

---

* Letter in the writer's possession.

PHILIP MOORE (b. 1705, d. 1783),

was the sixth son of Robert Moore, of Pulrose, and Catherine Kelly. He went to the Grammar School in Douglas, which had been founded by Bishop Wilson in 1706, its master, on his entrance there, being the Rev. Peter Lancaster. He was succeeded in 1717 by the Rev Anthony Halsall, with whom PHILIP MOORE continued till 1726, when he went to Bishop's Court to be examined for " an academic scholar's place "* by Bishop Wilson, who found him " fit."† In 1729, after some two years at the Academic School, Castletown, and a few months at Bishop's Court, where the Bishop prepared him for the ministry, he was ordained, and remained at Bishop's Court as chaplain till 1731, at a salary of £25. In 1731, he went to Marown as curate-in-charge, and, after being four years there, he was appointed chaplain of St. Matthew's, and Master of the Douglas Grammar School. He took to his educational duties with zest, having " an inherent love of teaching."‡ He was undoubtedly a good classical scholar, and " well read " generally. He was not ordained priest till 1739. The reason of this appears to have been that he refused to assent to the dogma that it was impossible that the heathen and the unbaptized could be saved. In 1751, he was appointed Rector of Ballaugh by the Duke of Atholl, whose chaplain he was, and he held this living with his other appointments, employing a curate to officiate there. In 1755, his beloved bishop, Wilson, whose chaplain he was, and to whom he was as devoted as to a father, died, and he preached his funeral sermon.§ With his successor, Bishop Hildesley, he was, as the numerous letters between them show, on terms of truly fraternal affection, but with the two bishops who followed he was altogether out of sympathy.

PHILIP MOORE will be chiefly remembered by the large share he had in the preparation of the Manx Bible. He translated part of the Psalms and Acts, and he revised the whole of the translations of the Old Testament made by the other clergy, as well as the second edition of the New Testament. But the work done by him which had the greatest influence upon his contemporaries was undoubtedly his teaching at the Grammar School in Douglas, and, as showing this, it may be mentioned that at his death all the clergymen but four at that time in the Manx Church had been educated by him. He was a remarkably good letter writer, his letters which have been preserved clearly indicating that he was possessed of a lively and somewhat sarcastic

---

* *i.e.*, For an exhibition, of which there were three or four.
† Bishop Wilson's Diary.
‡ Letter from the writer's grandfather, who was one of his pupils in his later years.
§ This sermon was published by Cruttwell in his Life of Bishop Wilson.

humour, combined with real kindliness of heart. It is, however, provoking not to find a single reference in them to any Manx custom, superstition, proverb or ballad, while they teem with classical quotations. He was buried in Kirk Braddan Churchyard, and there is a tablet to his memory at St. Matthew's.* Butler, in his Memoirs of Bishop Hildesley, speaks of PHILIP MOORE as being " well known in the literary world," and as being " eminently distinguished as the divine, the gentleman, and the scholar." † Referring to his conversation, he remarks that " prompted by an uncommon quickness of parts, and refined by study, it was at once lively, instructive, and entertaining,"‡ and, as to his correspondence, he says that it " breathed perhaps as much of original humour as can be met with in any writer who has appeared in public."

JAMES WILKS (b. 1719, d. 1777).

Nothing is known of his early life till 1742, when he was ordained by Bishop Wilson, and appointed Curate of St. German's, " with power to dispose of the Glebe and all other profits to the best advantage." As there was no school in that parish, he at once interested himself in the matter, and obtained a piece of ground near St. John's, where it was ultimately built. In 1745, he became vicar of the parish, and, in the same year, he was sent by the bishop to Dublin to obtain arrears of interest on some money left to the Academic Fund under Bishop Barrow's will, which had been invested in that city. His mission was successful, and his conduct of it received the bishop's approbation. In 1750, he was appointed episcopal registrar, and, in 1752, Vicar of Michael. He was very intimately connected with Bishop Wilson, who, in his later years, greatly depended upon him. As surviving curator of his will, to which he had been a witness, he carried out the bishop's instructions respecting his funeral.

He went to London in 1755, and again in 1756, in connexion with the chancery suit against the Earl of Derby for the recovery of the impropriate tithe. His diary of these journeys, and the business transacted during them, is of considerable interest. On his first journey, he dined with the Duke of Atholl, who asked him many questions about the island and the bishopric, and, a few days after, introduced him to Dr. Hildesley, Vicar of Hitchin, whom he had appointed to succeed Bishop Wilson. The bishop elect entered into a long conversation with him, and was much pleased with what he heard. In 1766, he undertook another journey to London, to assist in the defence of the clergy in the

---

* Now transferred to the new church.
† p. 186.
‡ p. 188.

dispute between them and the fishermen concerning the fish tithe, the latter having appealed from the decision of the governor, which was against them, to the King in Council. The governor's decision was, however, confirmed. On this occasion, he had an interview with the Archbishop of York, to whom he represented the deplorable state of the island, where there had been a very bad harvest; and he laid before him various proposals with regard to trade, which, he contended, would benefit the people, and in no way prejudice the revenue. The archbishop and the Bishop of Durham promised to do what they could, but it was late in the session, and Parliament was embarrassed with North American affairs, so nothing was done at that time. However, in the next year, an Act was passed for the encouragement of Manx trade and manufactures.

At this period there were disturbances and riots in London, caused by a constitutional struggle, in which John Wilkes was the most conspicuous character. JAMES WILKS was, consequently, often questioned as to his relationship to his namesake. Referring to this, he says: " For my own part I would wish, for the present, my name was any other than Wilks, for wherever I have occasion to tell my name I am stared at, and asked whether I am not a relative of the 'Great Wilkes,' as he is called." In 1769, he became one of the vicars-general, and in 1771 Rector of Ballaugh. On his appointment there, he and the Vicar of German perambulated a great part of the boundaries of their parishes, attended by a large number of parishioners, and fixed the limits in several doubtful places. He had taken part in the translation and revision of the Manx Bible, having translated Joshua and the Epistles, and he also translated part of the Liturgy.

In 1772, Bishop Hildesley died, and JAMES WILKS was left executor, together with the bishop's sister.

JAMES WILKS died in June, 1777, and was buried in the old churchyard of Ballaugh. On his tombstone is the following epitaph:—

Sleeping in Jesus.

Translated hence the good man never dies,

But like the day-star only sets to rise.

REV. JAMES WILKS,

Rector of this Parish and Vicar-General,

Aged 58 years.

Was buried June 21st, 1777.

Next to Philip Moore, JAMES WILKS may justly be considered the ablest Manx clergyman of his time.   Like him, he was the devoted friend and assistant of both Bishop Wilson and Bishop Hildesley, and like him, he was possessed of some literary power.* (An abstract of the account by Rev. S. N. Harrison in the "Manx Note Book," vol. iii., pp. 67-72.)

HENRY CORLETT   (b. 1735, d. 1801),

became an academic student in 1753, and was, in the following year, staying at Bishop's Court with the aged bishop, to whom he was a great comfort in his last illness.   So serious was then the difficulty of finding suitable men to become clergy, owing to the fear of losing the impropriate tithe, that the bishop was compelled to give CORLETT, though then only 19 years old, a licence, which was worded as follows : " We do tolerate† you to read the prayers and service of the Church as by law established, as also to read an Homily or some other practical or instructive book, as you shall be directed by the Vicars-General of the Isle for the time being, in such churches or chapels as you shall be desired by the said Vicars-General, to whom we require you to give all due obedience."   He was appointed Vicar of German in 1761 by Bishop Hildesley, and he held that living till his death in 1801. He was among the few clergy in the Isle of Man who showed any active friendliness towards the Wesleyan Methodists.   In 1775, he assured John Crook, one of the earliest preachers in Man, that he would give him the right hand of fellowship, and he desired him to make use of his house as if it were a brother's.   In 1777, he told John Wesley that he would gladly have asked him to preach, if it had not been that the bishop had forbidden him to do so, but, 21 years later, he seems to have fallen out with John Crook, and to have stated his intention of preaching against the Methodists.   In 1781, he greatly increased his congregations by preaching Bishop Wilson's sermons to them in Manx.   He translated the Book of Exodus into Manx, and superintended the publication of the " Christian Monitor " in the same language.

Bishop Wilson's pupils were followed by men who, in sadly decadent times, strove to emulate his example, and that of the scholarly and gentle Bishop Hildesley, in their devotion to duty, though their Church views were far removed from those of either of these bishops, they being decided " Evangelicals."

---

* See his account of "The Inhabitants of the Isle of Man and their Language" in the *Manx Note Book*, Vol. III, pp. 178-180.
† The word "tolerate," which is curious, shows that the bishop would evidently not have made such an appointment if he could possibly have helped doing so.

HUGH STOWELL, Senior (b. 1768, d. 1835), the third son of Thomas Stowell and Ann Brown (aunt of the Rev. Robert Brown), was born in Douglas. When quite a child, he fell into the harbour, being rescued from drowning by a sailor. Shortly after this, he went to the Grammar School at Ramsey, then conducted by the Rev John Crellin. Under his tuition, he "made a considerable progress in classical learning."*   He tells us that he was "by nature timid and bashful in the highest degree," that he "had a passion for retirement," that he looked back with great pleasure upon the time spent in reading with his mother, from whose example and precept he "early received deep impressions of religion," and that, almost from his infancy, his parents had decided to bring him up for the Church.   In 1801, he was removed to the Academic School at Castletown, the master of which was then the Rev. Thomas Castley, M.A., an able teacher and an excellent scholar.   In 1783, his mother died, an event which he terms the "first real affliction" of his life.   In 1786, he gained a scholarship worth £22, and this, added to £3 received by him annually for the tuition of three or four boys—he himself was only 18—made him the possessor of an income which, with his modest ideas, he considered a competency.   He then extended his hitherto almost exclusively classical reading to other subjects, and he tells us that "a new world of knowledge" opened to his view. He read metaphysics, mathematics, geography, philosophy, and divinity, which afforded him "daily fresh delight and improvement," while, for relaxation, he revelled in Shakespeare, Milton, Dryden, Pope, Young, Gray, and Thomson.   But his main object was to satisfy himself "of the truth and certainty of our Holy Religion," and to diligently prepare for Holy Orders. In April, 1791, he became a deacon.   Seeing that he was to develop into a singularly eloquent and forcible preacher, it will be of interest to give his account of the way in which he prepared his sermons :—" In composing my discourses, I have endeavoured to set the congregation before me and imagine myself personally addressing them on the subject of my text"; and, he continues, "this mode seems to connect the advantages of extemporaneous speaking with the benefit of careful premeditation and correct composition."   However this may have been, the testimony to the power of his preaching is unanimous.   The Rev. T. E. Brown says "he was a great preacher; wherever he filled the pulpit he filled the church," and the writer's father always declared that he was a more striking preacher than his more widely-known son, the Canon.   His first appointment was as curate to Vicar-General Moore, at Arbory, and, in the following year, in accordance with

* These and similar quotations are taken from a diary kept by him between 1795 and 1810, which has been kindly lent by Sir James Gell.

the request of the inhabitants of Douglas, he was appointed
Master of the Grammar School and Chaplain of St. Matthew's in
that town. On being admitted to Priest's Orders, in 1793, he
writes:—" This was an awful day to me. Never shall I forget
the strong emotions which I felt on the occasion, and I pray God
to imprint on my heart and memory the solemn vows which I then
took upon me." In 1795, eighteen resolutions for his future
guidance, of which the following are the most striking, are
recorded in his diary: — " To rise every morning during the
summer season at five o'clock; to spend half-an-hour in deep and
solemn devotion; to labour after further advancement in charity,
humility, and every other Christian virtue," and, he concludes,
" These resolutions I determine, by Divine Grace, to observe with
care and exactness." Does not the whole tenour of his life show
that he did so? Both as schoolmaster and chaplain he was
remarkably successful. The school had a yearly increasing
number of pupils, and his introduction of a Manx service and
sermon every Sunday attracted a large congregation. But his
strenuous labours, which, between 1799 and 1801, were added to
by " an uncommon scarcity, which had reduced, not only the
mendicants, but many of the labouring part of the town, to
extreme distress," proved too much for his never very robust
health, and so, in 1802, he asked to be moved to a country parish.
He was, thereupon, appointed Vicar of Lonan. Here, in 1808,
he established the first Sunday School in the island. At this
period of his life, he began writing the numerous religious
pamphlets, both in Manx and English, and the pious memoirs,
which he put forth from time to time. It was then, too, that he
corrected the edition of the Manx New Testament which was
issued in 1810. In 1818, he compiled a " Manx Spelling and
Lesson Book," and in 1819, his *magnum opus*, the Life of Bishop
Wilson, a pleasantly-written and interesting work, appeared. In
1824, he was transferred to Ballaugh, where he remained till his
death. He was asked by Bishop Ward, in 1827, to make a tour
in England for the purpose of soliciting subscriptions for building
churches in the island, and he gladly consented to do so. When
on this mission, he was everywhere received with admiration and
respect, and his efforts were rewarded by the receipt of a very
considerable sum. We should remember, too, that he was the
first, in the Isle of Man, to organize temperance societies on the
moderation system, the members pledging themselves to abstain
from spirits, but not from ale and wine. Let us now, as the
best means of estimating his character, quote the evidence of the
Rev. Thomas Howard, who knew him intimately, and of the Rev.
T. E. Brown, whose father was closely connected with him. The
former says : " Will not you, who fully knew his ' manner of life,'
bear testimony that he was an example in word, in conversation,
in charity, in spirit, in faith, in purity ; that he ' adorned the

doctrine of God our Saviour in all things,' and showed himself a pattern of good works? . . . His brethren in the ministry looked up to him as a model of ministerial faithfulness, of ardent, yet chastened zeal, of heavenly-mindedness, and of entire devotion to the duties of his high life"; * and the latter, after describing him as being " of short stature and homely," declares that he was " a man of God, a veritable saint," and he continues, " the fact is, there can be no doubt that in Mr Stowell we had an all but angelic presence, a heavenly-minded man and something more, a splendour and a power."† He also points out that he was an "Evangelical of the Evangelicals "‡ in the days before the Oxford movement, when they; headed by such men as Wilberforce, Venn, and Simeon, strove against a dead clergy and an irreligious laity."†

HUGH STOWELL is particularly interesting as having been the leader of this school of thought in the island, a school which was composed of such men as the Rev. Thomas Howard, E. Craine, R. Brown, J. Nelson, Joseph Qualtrough, W. Corrin, and J. L. Stowell, men, as the Rev. T. E. Brown says, " endowed with a singular elevation of tone and sentiment, combined with a depth of seriousness and sincerity."

JOSEPH STOWELL (b. 1772, d. 1801),

was the eighth son of Thomas Stowell and Ann Brown.‡ He was a delicate boy, with " an extraordinary capacity for learning, and a peculiar fondness for books." At an early age he was sent to be educated by the Rev. Philip Moore at the Grammar School in Douglas, where he quickly distinguished himself by his proficiency in grammatical learning. " His tutor," says his brother and biographer, Hugh Stowell, the Rector of Ballaugh, " who was an enthusiastic admirer of genius, conceived a particular partiality for him." On Philip Moore's death in 1783, he went to the Academic School at Castletown. Here, " after having obtained an accurate knowledge of the Roman and Greek classics, he entered on the study of mathematics with intense application." In 1792, he became tutor to the family of Governor Shaw. He is at this time described as being " a scholar of no ordinary attainments—one furnished not merely with classical learning, but with general and extensive information—well versed in ancient and modern history—intimately connected with the best authors in the English language—and no stranger to any of the departments of the *belles lettres*." During this period, he found time to study the insular records, and he drew up a prospectus of a history

---

* Funeral Sermon.
† *Ramsey Church Magazine.*
‡ There were 15 sons altogether.

of the island, which, unfortunately, never advanced beyond this preliminary stage. In 1794, he entered into Holy Orders, " with an ardent desire of promoting the glory of God and the salvation of his fellow creatures." In the following year, he left Governor Shaw, and opened a school in Castletown, which he conducted with great success till 1799, when he was appointed to the mastership of the Grammar and Mathematical Schools at Peel. There he laboured with equal success, but his health, which was never good, sank under the severity of the task which he had undertaken, and his death was hastened by an attack of typhus fever. Let us quote briefly from a contemporary account of him. The writer of it, after dwelling upon his remarkable talents and attainments, says : " In the pulpit, his eloquence was irresistible. Assisted by slight notes, he pronounced discourses which left an indelible impression on his hearers. The unaffectedness, the suavity, and the elegance of his manners captivated all who knew him. . . . But what gave the finishing grace to his character was that the qualities of his heart rivalled those of his head. Active in the service of his friends, and benevolent to the poor, he was in every respect an instance of example forcibly illustrated by precept."[*]

JOHN EDWARD HARRISON (b. 1784, d. 1858),

Was appointed Chaplain of St. Mark's in 1812, Vicar of Maughold in 1814, and Vicar of Jurby, where he remained for the rest of his life, in 1818. He will be chiefly remembered as an excellent Manx scholar, and for his great knowledge of Manx Folklore. Indeed, his store of local knowledge generally was a vast one. It is said that Archibald Cregeen (see Chapter V.) was greatly indebted to him for information with regard to the Manx language when he was compiling his dictionary, and it is certain that his death was a serious loss to the *Manx Society*, which had then just been formed.

THOMAS HOWARD (b. 1784, d. 1876),

was the son of Thomas and Catherine[†] (*née* Callow), widow of John Christian, of the " Flat," Maughold. His first teacher was the Rev. Henry Maddrell, who, between 1790 and 1803, was Chaplain at Ramsey. He then went to the Rev. Joseph Stowell's school at Peel, where he was " distinguished for his capacity and amiable disposition."[‡] He then went to St. Bee's

---

[*] " Monthly Magazine," September, 1802. (The above account is mainly taken from the " Memoirs of the Rev Joseph Stowell," by the Rev Hugh Stowell (1821).

[†] Catherine was born at Ballaglass in the same parish which belonged to her family.

[‡] Memoirs of Joseph Stowell, p. 91.

School, where he remained till 1803, when he received an ensign's
commission in the Royal Manx Fencibles.   The fact of his half-
brother, John Christian,* being a captain in his company, was
probably an inducement to him to join.   He served, during the
rebellion in Ireland, at Omagh, Coleraine, and elsewhere, being
both a great favourite with his brother officers, and much respected and beloved by the men.   But his quiet and peaceable
turn of mind, his delicate health, and the religious views with
which he was strongly imbued, all combined to render a military
career distasteful to him, and so he resigned his commission in
1806.   He at once began reading for Holy Orders, and was
ordained by Bishop Crigan in 1807.   His first appointment was
as Curate of Maughold.   After a very short stay there, he came
to St. George's as curate.   In 1809, he was admitted to Priest's
Orders, and, in 1810, he became Vicar of Braddan.   In 1832, on
the resignation of Benjamin Philpot, who had accepted the Archdeaconry and the Rectory of Andreas, he, at the urgent request of
his friends, took the Chaplaincy of St. George's.   He still retained
the title of Vicar of Braddan, and appointed the Rev. Robert
Brown as his curate there, giving him the full emoluments of the
living.   The Rev. Hugh Stowell having died in October, 1835,
THOMAS HOWARD was, in April, 1836, promoted to the Rectory of
Ballaugh. In 1868, he was prostrated by a severe illness, and,
though he recovered in a marvellous way, and his mental powers
were as clear as ever, his bodily health was so weakened as to
prevent his being able, except very occasionally, to attend to the
duties of his parish.   He was, however, fortunate in having a
most devoted curate and son-in-law in the person of the late Rev.
H. G. White, who was afterwards Vicar of Maughold.   In a
charming account of him in the *Ramsey Church Magazine*, the
Rev. T. E. Brown uses the epithets " wise, prudent, circumspect,
patient, loving," and, more especially, " courteous," in describing
his character ; and, in describing his appearance, he remarks that
" he was a singularly handsome man, though, perhaps, ' beautiful '
more aptly fits the type," and he continues, " Tall and shapely,
he had a most loveable countenance.   .   .   .   The whole face,
the gesture, were full of purity and perfect sweetness," and, he
adds, " you could not look on him without loving him."   He was
diligent and indefatigable in the discharge of his clerical duties,
being of a truly catholic spirit, though, at the same time, a
decided evangelical.   Cheerfulness was a prominent trait
in his character, in which gentleness and firmness were
blended to a remarkable degree.†   The conspicuousness of
the first might lead people to underrate his true manliness. Affec-

---

* Son of John Christian and Catherine Callow.
† The Rev T. E. Brown comments on the " tranquil radiance of his spirit"
(*Ramsey Church Magazine*).

tionate and charitable, there was in him a rare combination of Christian qualities. He was, indeed, the " beau ideal " of a clergyman, being quite the country parson depicted by Herbert and Goldsmith. He was considered a good preacher, and his sermons all breathed the spirit of genuine Christianity and fervent holiness. He published two series of these, which he entitled " Plain and Practical Sermons."*

ROBERT BROWN (b. 1792, d. 1846),

the only son of Captain Robert Brown and Jane Drumgold, was born in Douglas.† His father died at sea when he was a child. He was chiefly educated at the Castletown Academic School. He was both a learned man—his favourite study being ecclesiastical history—and a faithful pastor. Learning he loved with a surpassing ardour, and he assiduously and successfully cultivated the charm of a refined and graceful style. This was conspicuous in his sermons, which he composed and committed to memory, since, owing to imperfect vision, he was unable to read anything written with facility. ‡ With his Manx sermons, one of which he preached every Sunday, he took even more pains than with his English. These sermons were delivered in an exquisitely musical voice, " a voice steeped in delicacy, and vibrant with the most subtle tendencies."§ This, no doubt, contributed to his " magnetic faculty of affecting the strong, rugged natures which were in many respects so sharply contrasted with the delicacy of his own high-strung nervous temperament."|| In his church views he was a pronounced evangelical. Deeply in earnest, he was a simple and faithful preacher of the Gospel. It should be mentioned that he was a musician and a composer, two well known hymn tunes—" Braddan " and " Hatford "—being by him. He was also a poet. In 1826, he published a volume of poems, chiefly on sacred subjects, which are mainly distinguished by the vein of unaffected piety which runs through them. But his best poems, consisting of satires, published in the " Manx Liberal " newspaper, are now completely forgotten. His son, the late Rev. T. E. Brown, pronounces these poems to be " very good, good in the style of Dryden or Pope, with a marked leaning towards Byron," and he further remarks that "they were polished, witty, humorous,, metrically excellent, and marked by that classical turn of phrase and idea which is always unmistakeable."|| In

---

* The first in 1827, and the second in 1850.

† For genealogical details, see account of his son, the Rev T. E. Brown.

‡ For an interesting account of the way in which these sermons were composed, and for the charming biographical account by the Rev T. E. Brown, from which this notice is taken, see the *Ramsey Church Magazine*.

§ The Rev T. E. Brown at the Liverpool Meeting of the Manx Association n 1881.

|| *Ramsey Church Magazine.*

some respects they resemble the satires of his cousin, John Stowell, to which we refer elsewhere, but, unlike them, they are devoid of coarseness. He was head master of the Douglas Grammar School and Chaplain of St. Matthew's from 1817 to 1832, when he took charge of the Parish of Braddan for the Rev. Thomas Howard, his beloved friend. In 1836, he succeeded him as Vicar of Braddan, and he remained there till his comparatively early death ten years later.

WILLIAM CORRIN (b. 1795, d. 1859),

son of John Corrin, of the Croit, Arbory, and Ann Harrison, of Ballamoar, in the same parish, was educated at the Academic School, Castletown, by the Rev. Thomas Castley, and, after his death, by the Rev. Joseph Brown, becoming an excellent classical scholar. He was ordained by Bishop Murray in 1816, and, in 1818, he followed his late schoolmaster, Joseph Brown, who, in that year, had been appointed Vicar of Michael, as curate to the Rev. Robert Brown at St. Matthew's, Douglas. In 1825, he was appointed Vicar of Rushen, where he remained during the rest of his life. Up to 1850, he did his work in this large and important parish without any assistance, and so, since he never neglected any duty, it will be seen how hard a worker he was. On two occasions, especially, during this period, he had need of all his energy and devotion. One was in 1832, during the terrible outbreak of cholera, when, till he was himself attacked by it, he was constantly among the sick and dying; the other was in 1852, when the dreadful catastrophe of the explosion of the brig " Lily," on Kitterland, in his parish, gave him the care of a number of poor wounded men. We should mention that he was a total abstainer, and one of the originators of the movement in the island. An earnest and able preacher, both in English and Manx, he exemplified in his own life what he preached to others. A man of many sorrows, for his wife and several of his children preceded him to the grave, he was remarkable for his serene patience. Charitable, hospitable, a cheerful companion, a sage adviser, perhaps his most striking characteristics were his shrewd common-sense and his intense sympathy—a sympathy extended to all, whatever their careers and characters. He entered into the amusements of the young, who spent many happy days " In that old vicarage that shelters under Brada,"* and into the troubles of the old, and he took interest in the occupations of all, more especially of the fishermen, who formed a large part of the population of the parish. It is, perhaps, not generally known that he was the prototype of " Pazon Gale," in " Betsy Lee."

---

* Chalse-a-Killey (T. E. Brown).

This being so, the quotation of a few lines from that inimitable
poem will place the man before our readers as our own words
cannot do : —

> Now the grandest old pazon, I'll be bail,
> That ever was, was ould Pazon Gale.
> Aw, of all the kind and the good and the true
> And the aisy and free, ...
> And many a time he'd come out and try
> A line, and the keen he was and the spry !
>
> .   .   .   .
>
> He was a simple pazon, and lovin' and wise,
> That's what he was and quiet uncommon,
> And never said much to man or woman ;
> Only the little he said was meat
> For a hungry heart, and soft and sweet,
> Aye, many a time I've seen his face
> All slushed with tears and him tellin' of grace
> And mercy and that, and his v'ice so low.
> But trimblin'—aw, but we liked him, though.

He was offered the Rectory of Bride, a much better living, in
1847, but he refused it, saying that he was too much attached to
his parishioners to leave them, and how strong this feeling was is
shown by the fact that he desired the words : " He never left,
nor wished to leave the place " (Goldsmith) to be put on his
tombstone. He, like nearly all the Manx clergy of his time, was
a strong evangelical.

WILLIAM GILL (b. 1797, d. 1871),

son of Henry Gell,* Customs Officer at Peel, and Marcia,
daughter of the Rev. Henry Corlett, was ordained in
1820 by Bishop Murray, and was, in the same year, appointed
Government Chaplain at St. John's. In 1824, he became Curate
of Ballaugh ; in 1827, he went to Malew as curate-in-charge, and,
in 1830, he was presented to the vicarage of that parish by the
Crown, his being the first appointment after the purchase of the
Church patronage from the Duke of Atholl. This living he
retained till his death, 41 years later. To such an extent was he
devoted to his parish that he rarely preached in any church but
his own, and so ardent was his love for his home, and his native
island, that it was most difficult to persuade him to leave either
the one or the other. A most rigid disciplinarian, he was himself
a stranger to self-indulgence in any form. His fare was of the
simplest kind ; he was a total abstainer, being one of the first

---

* William changed his name to Gill. For a charming account of him see
the papers by the Rev T. E. Brown in the *Ramsey Church Magazine*.

leaders in the movement in the Isle of Man, and, even in his old age, he could not be persuaded to sit in an easy chair. By constant self-denial he was enabled, not only to give largely in his own parish, and to keep almost open house for the poor, and his friends, but, though his living was less than £200 a year, to send four of his sons to the universities and the fifth to the Manx Bar, besides educating his four daughters ; and then, as if this was not enough, he adopted two nephews, and reared and educated them from childhood.   As the records of his achievements will show, he was an indomitably hard worker.   Thus, his glebe, which, when he came, was merely a bog, was drained by him ; by the help of subscriptions, he erected a vicarage at a cost of £500 ;* rebuilt the parish schoolhouse, and built another schoolhouse in a mountainous part of the parish.   His schools were, indeed, his hobby—a parishioner of his remarking that he was " terrible for the schools."   But, while attending to the educational wants of his parishioners, he was specially earnest about their religious needs, his Sunday Schools being also the objects of his most tender and constant care.   Not content with these labours, he did most important work for the Church as organizer and secretary of the " Diocesan Association " in the provision of additional clergy, and he undertook the arduous task of editing the Manx-English portion of Kelly's Manx Dictionary, of assisting the Rev. J. T. Clarke in compiling the English-Manx portion of it, and of revising the whole for the press,† also of editing the Manx Grammar‡ originally published by the same author (Kelly), in 1804.   His official post as translator of the Acts of Tynwald into Manx entailed more labour than it does now, because the whole of the Acts were translated, not a summary of them as at present. It is no wonder that a man of his character, so endowed with singular judgment, moderation and charity, and with, moreover, a mind well cultivated by severe study and thought, should have been one of the leaders of the clergy, whose proctor he was, and that he had great influence for good.   In appearance, he was a tall, fine, muscular man.   In his views, he was, according to the Rev. T. E. Brown, " a doctrinal High Churchman," and, in this respect, he differed both from the men of his own day and those who followed him.

With CANON STOWELL, who comes next in order of date, there seems to be the beginning of a new school.   Quite as capable, though less scholarly, its members were, as a rule, more militant and enterprizing than most of their predecessors.

---

* The largest subscription he received towards this was £2.
† Published by the Manx Society in 1866.
‡   „   „   „   1859.

HUGH STOWELL, Junior (b. 1799, d. 1865),

the eldest son of the Rev. Hugh Stowell and Amelia Callow, was
born at St. Matthew's Parsonage, Douglas He was educated
during the earlier years of his life by his father, going afterwards
to the Castletown Grammar School, where he gained a scholarship.   In 1818, he matriculated at St. Edmund Hall, Oxford,
and took his B.A. degree in 1822, proceeding in due course to his
master's degree.   It is not recorded that he in any way distinguished himself during his undergraduate career. His title for
orders was the assistant curacy of an outlying chapel of the parish
of Sheepscombe, Rinswick, Gloucestershire.   In the following
year he accepted the curacy of Trinity Church, Huddersfield.
Here he remained till 1825, when he was appointed to the sole
charge of St. Stephen's, Salford. He had, by this time, become so
popular as a preacher, and so highly esteemed as a devoted and
hard-working pastor, that his parishioners, being afraid of his
accepting one of the many offers of preferment which he received,
built a church called Christ Church, with schools, for him, at a
cost of £31,000, which was opened in 1831.   In 1845, he was
appointed to an honorary canonry in the Cathedral Church of
Chester.   In 1851, shortly after the erection of Manchester into
an episcopal see, the bishop of that city appointed him one of his
chaplains, and, subsequently, rural dean of Salford.   During the
greater part of his life he continued to issue a number of religious
treatises.   Whatever his subject, he invariably dealt with it in
a practical and popular way.   Among his best known works are
" Tractarianism tested," " A Model for Men of Business," " The
Pleasures of Religion, and other Poems," and " The Peaceful
Valley."   In addition to these, many of his sermons,
lectures, speeches, and letters, mostly on subjects of theological
controversy, have been published, and he wrote a number of
hymns.   He was an earnest supporter of the evangelical body,
being militant and uncompromizing in his Protestantism.   He
was a staunch opponent of the Maynooth grant, and was one of
the first to agitate in opposition to the attempt to establish a
Roman Catholic hierarchy, his efforts having contributed largely
in bringing about the passing of the Ecclesiastical Titles Bill.
Whenever anything in the shape of a challenge was thrown out
to him by an opponent professing a different religious faith, he
was never backward in taking up the gauntlet on behalf of his
own creed.

When the great discussion arose in Manchester on the Education question, he took a prominent part in the contest between
the Biblical and Secular parties ; and it was mainly due to his
efforts that the latter was defeated.   In 1861, he took an
equally prominent part in connection with the " Manchester
Church Defence Association."   Canon STOWELL would appear to

us, in these more tolerant days, as being a man of narrow views, but he undoubtedly possessed very great power and ability. He was remarkable both as an orator and preacher, but there was a great difference between his platform and pulpit styles. On the platform he was fervent, vehement, flowing, and energetic, and always succeeded in carrying his audience with him. In the pulpit he was argumentative, persuasive, and deeply interesting. His ideas were always expressed in choice and poetic diction. He never lost the thread of his argument, and never became incoherent, though he always spoke extemporaneously.

Canon STOWELL was looked upon as a man of note, not only in Manchester and Salford, but in every part of England. In Salford he lent a helping hand to every good work, and there is no doubt that its prosperity was largely due to the excellent system of education which he had initiated; and, in England generally, the appreciation of him was shown by the way in which the various religious societies sought his assistance at their annual meetings.

An obituary notice of him in the " Manx Sun " speaks of him as " one of Mona's most distinguished sons," who, " by his piety and ability," reflected the highest honour upon her. The Rev. W. T. Radcliffe, who knew him well, writes of him as follows : " He was a man of noble presence ; an able preacher ; on the Protestant platform an orator of uncommon power."

JOSEPH CHRISTIAN MOORE (b. 1802, d. 1886),

was the eldest son of James Moore, of Cronkbourne, and Elizabeth Jeale. During his childhood he was delicate, and so, instead of going to school, he received private instruction from the Rev. Joseph Qualtrough, Chaplain of St. Matthew's, and Head Master of the Douglas Grammar School. When he was 16, he was sent to the Rev. W. H. Havergal, father of the well-known Frances Havergal, to be prepared for Oxford. He went there in 1823, being entered at St. Edmund Hall, and took his degree in 1827. His first and only curacy was at Measham, Derbyshire. After he had been there less than a year, his vicar died, and he was at once offered the living by the Marquis of Hastings. On accepting it, he promptly set to work to improve the condition of the parish. In a few years he had succeeded in building infant and national schools, and, after much labour in seeking voluntary assistance, he raised sufficient funds to thoroughly restore his church. Not content with this, he was largely instrumental in promoting church building in the parishes adjacent to Measham, he being rural dean for the southern part of Derbyshire. In 1842, he was offered and accepted the Archdeaconry of Man and the Rectory of Andreas. Here he soon found a warm friend in the bishop of the diocese, Vowler Short, his intercourse with whom he always spoke of as one of the most valued privileges of his life. It did not take him long, not only to gain the affection and respect of the parishioners of Andreas, but to make his presence felt in every part of the diocese. As at Measham, he was specially active in educational works, being wont to ride about the island paying surprize visits to the various schools, examining the children, and suggesting improvements in the methods of teaching. He was one of the most active and valued trustees of King William's College, and he also did good work as examining chaplain to the bishops. In church building he took a considerable part, and, during the later years of his life, he restored Andreas Church, and built the tower which is so conspicuous an object over the whole of the north of the island. He was not a party man in the sense of being a high or a low Churchman, though his views were decidedly of the evangelical type. He had an unmistakeable love of order, and a strong faith in the efficacy of prayer, being a man of deep personal piety. As a preacher he was forcible, thoughtful, and original. In social life he was truly hospitable, and very popular. His genuine wit and quaintness of speech were well known; and his sound common sense, whether in the pulpit or on the platform, in private conversation or in the discharge of his duties as member of the Council, gave him great influence. Unmarried, and, after the death of his father and mother, possessed of considerable means, he spent much more than the whole of his clerical income in charity. He had reached his 78th year before signs of declining health began to be seen in him, but he continued to discharge his duties for some two or three years longer, when he was compelled to resign them one by one.*

WILLIAM DRURY (b. 1808, d. 1887),

Vicar of Braddan. No account of him can be given, owing to his eldest son, the Rev. William Drury, Vicar of Burton-on-Trent, placing his veto upon it.

Fortunately this is of small consequence, as the memory of this excellent Manxman will remain in the hearts of his countrymen without assistance from any pen.

ROBERT LLEWELLYN CALEY (b. 1809, d. 1861),

son of Captain P. Caley, a retired army officer who lived in Castletown, went to St. John's College, Cambridge, where he took the degree of B.A. in due course. In 1837, he was elected

---

* An appreciative account of him, by the Rev T. E. Brown, has been published in his " Letters" (Sidney T. Irwin, 1900).

to the office of Precentor in Bristol Cathedral. The Bristol "Times," in an obituary notice, remarks that "theoretically and practically he was a good musician, and some of his compositions, especially a Sanctus and Kyrie which are published in Richardson's collection, were in frequent use in many of the English Cathedrals," and, in referring to his character, that "he was one whose gentle, genial, and kind nature, in which Christian simplicity and courtesy met, made him the object of affectionate regard to all acquainted with him."

JOHN QUALTROUGH (b. 1814, d. 1879),

was ordained deacon by the Bishop of Chester in 1837, and priest by the Bishop of Sodor and Man, James Bowstead, in 1839. His first curacy was that of St. Stephen's, in the parish of Lezayre. This he held from 1840 to 1847. He was then removed to a sole charge at St. Jude's, in the parish of Andreas, where he remained till 1859, when he was appointed Vicar of Arbory. In 1875, he became Rector of Bride. He was intimately acquainted with the language and character of his fellow countrymen, with whom he was a great favourite. When he was a curate, and during the greater part of his time at Arbory, he conducted regular services in Manx.* He was greatly esteemed for his kindly, upright, and manly character.

WILLIAM KERMODE (b. 1814, d. 1890),

a son of Thomas Kermode and Margaret Cowle, was born in Ramsey. He was educated at King William's College and Dublin University, being ordained deacon in 1839 by James Bowstead, Bishop of Sodor and Man, and priest in 1840 by Henry Pepys, his successor. After holding two curacies, he was, in 1843, appointed Chaplain of St. Paul's, Ramsey, where he remained for 28 years. During this time he attended with the utmost zeal, not only to the ministrations of the Church, but to the relief of the poor, and the alleviation of the sufferings of the sick. In 1840, he was mainly instrumental, in connexion with High-Bailiff Tellet, in forming the Ramsey "Health Association" for the preservation of the public health—an association which was practically the beginning of the self-government of the town. In 1849, he was foremost in suggesting sanitary precautions against cholera, and, in 1853, when cholera visited Ramsey for the second time, he tended the sick, and laid the dead in their coffins with his own hands. In acknowledgment of his devoted services, both at this time and in the education of the children of the town, he

---

* It is uncertain whether the last sermon preached in a parish church that language was by him or the Rev William Drury.

received a presentation of silver from the inhabitants of Ramsey.
In 1856, the Ramsey Sanitary and Medical Dispensary was instituted by him.   He built the present St. Paul's Parsonage on
a portion of the Claughbane estate presented by his father, con-
tributing one-third of the cost out of his own pocket; and he
restored and re-opened Ballure Chapel.   His devotion to duty
was in all respects so unremitting that it affected his health,
which rendered it necessary in 1871 that he should be removed to
the comparatively easy work of the parish of Maughold.   Here
he effected many improvements in the schools and vicarage, and
had a large share in obtaining an increase to the vicar's stipend
by the success of a suit which he brought against the Crown,
entirely at his own risk, for the recovery of the royalties of the
iron mine running under the glebe lands.   He held the
office of surrogate from 1847 onwards, while the confidence
reposed in him by his brother clergy was shown by the fact that
they elected him as their proctor to York Convocation in 1872,
and re-elected him to the same office in 1874, 1880, 1885, and
1886.   When Bishop Hill revived the office of rural dean, in
1879, he appointed WILLIAM KERMODE first Rural Dean of Peel.
In 1877, he left Maughold on his appointment to the Rectory of
Ballaugh, in which parish also he did much for the schools.   He
built the new and commodious rectory there, besides restoring
and re-opening the old church.   He was a zealous antiquarian,
being a President, and a very valuable member, of the " Isle of
Man Natural History and Antiquarian Society."   He initiated
a " Parish Book " for Ballaugh, in which he wrote a useful account
of the antiquarian remains in the parish, and a record of events
of special interest to its people.*   The Archdeacon (Hughes-
Games), when preaching at Ballaugh on the Sunday evening after
his funeral, said : " He was a man of much weight and dignity of
character;   unostentatious and unobtrusive;   always calm and
thoughtful;   always to be depended upon;   always the same,
wise, sagacious, and practical.   His influence amongst his brother
clergy was deservedly great; his counsel was always valued by
them.   He will be greatly missed by us; the Manx Church has
lost in him not only one of its most valued and useful servants,
but also one of its wisest and most experienced counsellors."

Bishop Bardsley, who preached in the morning, also spoke of
him in eulogistic terms, referring more especially to his eloquence
as a preacher.

JOHN HOWARD (b. 1817, d. 1892),

son of the Rev. Thomas Howard and Nessy Stowell, daughter
of Thomas Stowell, C.R., was educated at King William's

---

* This is a practice which should be more generally followed.

College.   Ordained in 1841, priested in 1842, he was for a
short time a master in his old school, and then served in curacies
in Liverpool, Castletown, and elsewhere.   In 1847, he was appointed Vicar of Onchan, where he remained till his death.   JOHN
HOWARD's character was a remarkable one.   He combined great
kindliness of heart and sweetness of disposition with a quick
temper and readiness to take offence.   This, with his equal
readiness to resort to physical force, frequently got him into
trouble.   He was noted for his physical strength and agility as
well as for the considerable mental ability which he showed both
as a preacher and a *raconteur*.   He had an ever-flowing stream
of excellent stories and was, consequently, a most entertaining
companion.   As a parish priest, he was distinguished by his
reverent performance of the church services—his singularly
beautiful voice being used with great effect—and for the genuine
sympathy and real love which he had for the poor.

JAMES SAMUEL POLLOCK (b. 1834, d. 1895),

son of Major Pollock, of the 43rd Light Infantry, was born at
Derby Castle, Douglas.   He took his B.A. and M.A. degrees at
Trinity College, Dublin.   In 1858, he was ordained by the
Bishop of Chester, and, in 1861, he became Curate of St. Paul's,
Birmingham.   From that time, nearly the whole of his life was
spent in mission work in that city, in which he was joined by his
brother, the late Rev. T. B. POLLOCK, whose name is inseparably
connected with his, as a partner in an invaluable and admirable
ministry.   This work was begun by them as assistants of the
Vicar of Holy Trinity, Bordesley, whose parish was in the very
poorest part of Birmingham ;   it was pursued with the utmost
enthusiasm and devotion, and, notwithstanding, or, perhaps,
largely because of, the persecution which they met with on
account of their ritualistic services, they obtained a most
remarkable success.   In 1881, through their exertions, and
largely also owing to their subscriptions—since the brothers spent
the whole of their not inconsiderable private means on their
churches, etc.—the magnificent church of St. Alban the Martyr
was erected at a cost of £20,000, and its district was created a
separate parish.   Since that year, they have also opened three
mission churches in the parish, with schools for 1,500 children,
and they have organized guilds, friendly societies, &c.   These
churches and institutions were conducted by three assistant
clergy, six lay readers, and four deaconesses, besides the brothers
POLLOCK.   It is estimated that, during their labours among the
poorest people in Birmingham, they raised no less than £100,000
for church purposes.   They were true and earnest Christians,
and did a great and noble work, which will not soon be forgotten
by the poor of Birmingham.

THOMAS HOWARD GILL (b. 1837, d. 1894), son of the Rev. William Gill, was educated at King William's College, and Trinity College, Cambridge, where he graduated as *senior optime* in 1859, and in the same year was ordained as curate to his father at Malew. In 1863, he was appointed Chaplain of St. Mark's, where, though only remaining two years, he repaired both the chapel and the parsonage. From 1865 to 1868 he was Rector of St. Jude's, Ancoats, when he re-built the parish church, and opened a fund for building a new church. In 1868, came his appointment to the important living of St. Margaret's, Whalley Range, a suburban district where the population increased from 5,000 to 30,000 during the thirteen years of his incumbency. Such a change naturally imposed a strenuous struggle upon the rector, by whose exertions, mainly, the single parish, with one church and school, was divided into four parishes, with four churches and schools. But all this imposed a terrible strain on his constitution, so that, in 1881, he was driven to accept a lighter charge at Trowbridge, in Wiltshire. Restored to health by this change, he was able to accept the arduous post of Chaplain of the Rue d'Agnesseau Church in Paris, in 1883. Here, in the words of Lord Lytton, in a farewell address to him, in 1890, " he found his church deserted and decaying, and he leaves it restored, substantially re-built, and thronged with worshippers." In addition to this, he, in 1888, founded the Victoria Home, at Neuilly, as a shelter for aged Englishwomen who had been left isolated in France, without sufficient means. At Tonbridge, where he was instituted in 1890, he pursued the same path of practical benevolence. During the whole of his career he had taken a great interest in educational problems, and had a fixed determination to maintain the Church's hold, not only upon the training of the young, but upon every department of the national life. Wherever he came to minister, he threw himself at once, and heart and soul, into organizing Church literary societies, social clubs, charities, and all like institutions. A strong and devoted son of the Church, he had the ability to devize and the power to carry out much for its benefit and advancement. He was a true man, as well as a true Churchman, and his virtues were broadly rooted in a genuine humanity.

No account of Manx clergymen would be complete without mentioning the families of ALLEN, COSNAHAN, and PARR.

THE ALLENS.

THOMAS ALLEN, the first member of this family to come to the island, was a clergyman who fled from Norwich during the Marian persecution, and settled at Castletown. He is said to have been the first Protestant minister here. His son, THOMAS, was government chaplain as late as 1622, and his great grandson, also THOMAS (b. 1625, d. 1660), was the first of five Allens who held the Vicarage of Maughold in succession. Then came Thomas's son, ROBERT, from 1660 to 1666. Robert's son, THOMAS (b. 1643, d. 1726), was vicar for sixty years. Bishop Wilson mentions him in his diary as "having been a diligent pastor, of a serious, grave, sober behaviour," and, in his funeral sermon, which he (the bishop) preached, he says: "This good man's life, as a Christian, has been unblameable; as a pastor for three score years, laborious and exemplary; always resident upon his cure, always content with his position."

In the following year his son, HENRY (b. 1677, d. 1746), who had been Vicar of Lezayre, was appointed to succeed him. His son, THOMAS (b. 1702, d. 1754), the last of the family who held an ecclesiastical appointment in the island, had been Curate of Andreas since 1739, and was appointed to Maughold on the death of his father. He was the author of two of the best "Carvals" in the Manx language. Henry's brother, JOHN, was Vicar of Michael, in 1734, but died in the following year.

THE COSNAHANS.

Nine members of this family, which has contributed several distinguished men to the service of the Manx State, served in the Manx Church. The first was JOHN, who was Vicar of Jurby in 1575 and of German in 1585. Four of them, except for a brief interval from 1656 to 1667, were Vicars of Santon, in succession, from 1614 to 1731, i.e., WILLIAM, from 1614 to 1618, JOHN, from 1618 to 1656, HUGH, from 1667 to 1691, and JOHN, from 1691 to 1731.

It is said the first JOHN was the only clergyman in the island who ventured, during the rule of Lord Fairfax, to baptize children according to the rites of the Established Church. The last JOHN was vicar-general. Bishop Wilson wished to appoint his son, of the same name, Vicar of Santon, in 1731, but Lord Derby declined. The bishop then made him vicar-general, while still a curate, and, a few days later, he appointed him to the Vicarage of Braddan, which was in his own gift. He held this living till his death in 1750. These three JOHNS, and HUGH, together with JOSEPH and JULIUS (see below), were all buried underneath what is called "the great broad stone" at Santon. John's son, JOSEPH, succeeded him as Vicar of Braddan, where he remained till his death in 1768. He translated the Second Book of Samuel into Manx. Finally, Joseph's son, JULIUS, was Vicar of Braddan in 1786, having previously been Curate of St. George's, but he died in the same year.

THE PARRS.

RICHARD PARR, bishop of Sodor and Man (1635-1644), was probably not a Manxman, but there can be little doubt that the two most conspicuous clergymen of that name, ROBERT and THOMAS PARR, were Manx by birth. They belonged to a Lancashire family, who were first officially connected with the island in the middle of the sixteenth century, when WILLIAM PARR was comptroller. Both ROBERT and THOMAS PARR were remarkable for the ease with which they accommodated themselves to the changes in public worship resulting from the establishment of the Commonwealth, and THOMAS was also remarkable for his quaint entries in the Malew Register.

ROBERT was Vicar of Malew from 1633 to 1640, and Rector of Ballaugh from 1640 to 1673. He was appointed vicar-general in 1646. It would seem that he was in sympathy with the rising against the Countess of Derby in 1651, since it was sworn in evidence, in 1662, that, when the Lezayre company of militia proposed to " sett a guard on him," he declared that they need not do so, " as he knew more of the risinge than they did."[*] He was evidently in good odour with the new regime, seeing that, in 1665, Deputy-Governor Cadwell writes: " I have received direcons from the Right Honourable Thomas Lord Ffairfax, Lord of this Isle, for the allowinge you MR. ROBERT PARRE, publicke preacher of this Isle. I expect your faithful care and diligence therein."[†] Mr PARR, on receiving this appointment, applied for an increase of salary, and, in response thereto, Lord Fairfax writes : " I am willing to allow MR. ROBERT PARRE, minister for preachinge[‡] to the people of the Island in Mankes or English, as he see best for the propagatinge of the Gospel, five pounds yearly."[§] In 1657, Governor Chaloner appointed him one of his examining chaplains, and, in his " Treatise of the Isle of Man," he mentions that he had received some assistance from him in elucidating the derivation of Manx place-names.[||] He was sponsor to the governor's son, James. Just after the Restoration he appears to have been equally in favour, since he was one of the four Manx clergy appointed by the ministers of Charles, Earl of Derby, to act as their substitutes in managing the Church affairs of the island. In 1661, however, he got into trouble for some unknown cause, for which he was confined in Peel Castle. On the 23rd of December in that year, he was released by order of

* *Manx Soc.*, Vol. XXVI., p. 17.
† *Lib. Scaccar.*
‡ *Ibid.*
§ *Ibid.* It should be explained that it had been the practice for the Earls of Derby to maintain two public preachers—one for the garrison and the towns, and the other for the country churches.
|| *Manx Soc.*, Vol. X., p. 17.

Bishop Rutter, " in respect of his health, and the near approach-
inge of these festivals."*

THOMAS PARR, Robert's brother, held the Vicarage of Malew
from 1641 to his death in 1695. He too, rendered himself accept-
able to the ruling powers during the time of Lord Fairfax, being
one of the commissioners appointed early in 1660 to examine Lieut.-
Hathorne, who had imprisoned Governor Chaloner in Peel Castle.
In consequence of his supposed sympathy with the rebels of 1651,
he was, in 1662, brought before the court which was then inquir-
ing into the circumstances connected with the rebellion of that
year. He stated that he " never had any knowledge of the
risinge,"† and that he had declined the oath tendered to him by
the conspirators. The chief record that he has left of himself
consists of the quaint and racy entries he made in his Church
Register. As Archdeacon Gill remarks : " Sir Thomas Parr has
so impressed his own character upon almost every page of the
book that it reads more like an autobiography than a Parish
Register, and the very self of the worthy vicar stands out vividly
before us. We picture him to ourselves as a somewhat pompous
personage, with a strong sense of his own dignity, and very jealous
of his official rights ; amusingly subservient to the higher powers,
at one time falling down on his knees with gratitude, as he records
the ' miraculouse pservacon ' of ' our right Honourable Lord ' the
Earl of Derby, and, at another, actually canonizing the newly-
appointed Bishop, Samuel Rutter, who landed at Ronaldsway, ' on
the 21st Sept., 1661, beinge St. Samuell's Day' ; easily accommo-
dating himself to the changes of government in Church and State,
expressing astonishment at the use of the Book of Common Prayer
at a marriage in 1654, yet hailing with evident pleasure the res-
toration of King Charles in 1660 ; delighting in sonorous and well-
rounded sentences, as when describing the proclamation of James
II. ' with great congratulacons and repeated acclamacons ' ; fond
of airing his Latin (such as it was) ; a bit of a quack doctor ; a be-
liever in witchcraft and astrology, careful to note the position of
the planets, the direction of the wind at the time of the birth of
one of his own children ; yet withal an honest, kindly, gossipy old
gentleman, who wins upon our affections while we laugh at his
foibles, and from whom we part at length with sincere regret."‡
There were several other members of this family in the Manx
Church. The three following were sons of Robert : CHARLES,
(b. 1644, d. 1684), who succeeded his father as Rector of Ballaugh
in 1673. In the latter year he was made vicar-general and died.
JOHN was Chaplain of Ballure in 1688, Vicar of Rushen from 1691
to 1700, and Rector of Ballaugh from 1700 to his death in 1723.

---

* *Lib. Scaccar.*
† *Manx Soc.*, Vol. XXVI., p. 22.
‡ *The Manx Note Book*, Vol. II., pp. 73-4.

Another CHARLES, perhaps a brother of Robert's and Thomas's, was Vicar of Lezayre.   In 1653, ROBERT, grandson of the first Robert, and son of the second, was Vicar of Lezayre from 1698 to 1713, and Rector of Bride and vicar-general from 1713 to 1729.

This ROBERT PARR was one of the only two clergy who were on Lord Derby's side in his dispute with Bishop Wilson.   In 1722, Lord Derby refers to this by noting that "Parr and Brightson" (i.e. William Bridson, Vicar of Marown) were "good" in a letter to the governor. In the following year, Robert Parr in writing of Bishop Wilson's party to Lord Derby says: "These are the patriots who under a colour of religion and the Church would have sacrificed your Lordship's Regalia [? regal powers] to their private disappointments or resentments.   From the power of such implacable mortals *Libera Nos Domine.**

---

* Loose papers, Knowsley.

CHAPTER II.

Nonconformity.

During its comparatively short history, Manx Nonconformity has produced a number of good and able men. Owing to the great difficulty of obtaining information, we are only able to refer to a few of them.

PHILIP GARRETT (b. 1771, d. 1842),

born at Douglas, was the son of a shipwright who was killed by a fall from a mast, when he was yet a boy. High-spirited, fearless, and fond of hazardous adventure, he was frequently in mischief. At the age of fourteen, he was bound as an apprentice to a shipbuilder in Liverpool, and proved himself so expert that he soon received sufficient wages to enable him to contribute to the support of his mother, then in very straitened circumstances, and to that of her younger children. It was not till he attained his twenty-first year that he felt any call to the Methodist ministry, of which he became so distinguished an ornament. As a first step towards his new vocation, he formed a class composed entirely of chimney sweeps, at that time a most abandoned and abject body. It soon appeared that the young shipwright had gifts as well as zeal, and that he was destined for a higher position and a wider sphere than that of a local preacher. PHILIP himself was with difficulty brought to the same conclusion, and, though he had shown great powers as a preacher, he did not consent to enter the ministry till 1799, when he received an appointment as probationer, without having offered himself as a candidate. He was at once appointed one of the ministers in the Aberdeen and Inverness circuit. In 1803, being recalled to England, he served, for the most part, in the

manufacturing districts of the north. It is impossible in such a
limited space to do justice to his manifold and successful labours.
It must, therefore, suffice to state that he became a real power for
good among working men. "His plainness of speech, quaintness,
wit, originality, simplicity, sympathy, gave him the *open sesame*"*
to their intellect and feelings. He was even more popular on the
platform than in the pulpit. "His straight-forward, idiomatic
way of speaking, his undaunted fervour in rebuking what he
thought to be wrong, combined with his almost frolicsome
humour, his cheery, genial, and winning ardour, and his sweetness, shrewdness, and simplicity made him respected and beloved
wherever he went."* Let us now try and depict his personal
appearance. He was a little below the middle height, round,
plump, and with a bright and healthy complexion. "There was
in his face and figure a strange blending of the comic with the
venerable. One could see at a glance that he was a character, an
original, in some respects an oddity."† We should also remember
that it was not only in the path of his ministry that PHILIP
GARRETT attained distinction. He was a diligent student of
astronomy, and had a "rare knowledge in the science of gnomics
and ingenuity in constructing every possible variety of dials."† In
1828, he published his "Easy method of constructing Mathematical
Tables ; including the Logarithms of Numbers, Lines, Tangents,
Secants, Versed Lines, &c., and their application to Trigonometry,
Geometry, Compound Interest, Geography, Astronomy, Dialling,"
the main feature of which is that all the tables are constructed
solely by the aid of the first four rules of arithmetic, without
algebraic signs or formulæ. In 1827, he published " A Digest of
the Minutes of the Methodist Conference," and, in 1829 and 1830,
his " Astronomical Sketches " appeared. When we remember
that the man, who not only wrote these and other books and
pamphlets, but mastered sufficient Hebrew and Greek to read the
Bible in those languages, was practically self-educated, we are
lost in admiration at his application and perseverance, as well as
struck by his natural abilities. These abilities, it may be mentioned, were also conspicuously displayed in his conversation.
"He was a famous talker. His brusque repartee, ...
grotesque presentation of powerful thought, apt anecdote, rele-
vant reminiscence, sudden and most effective pantomime, . . .
all this made PHILIP GARRETT the life of any congenial company
into which he might be thrown."‡ But when all has been said
about PHILIP GARRETT, it is his beautiful and sterling character
that constitutes his best claim to remembrance. " Its basis was

---

* *Methodist Magazine* (1877), pp. 66-67.
† *Ibid*, p. 67.
‡ *Ibid*, p. 124.

Christian simplicity, its most prominent features contentment, cheerfulness, and kindliness."*

The Rev. W. T. Radcliffe, who knew PHILIP GARRETT, writes of him as follows : " He was an able preacher and very popular ; a great genius in mathematical science. In the grounds of Woodhouse Grove School, near Leeds, is a sun-dial made by him which is a summary of marvellous knowledge in astronomy. He was singularly free from pride, and from the stiff and conventional, even in the pulpit. In one sermon preached in the Well-road Chapel, Douglas, he told his congregation of his recollection of the site of the chapel being a garden, and of the interest he took, as a boy, in the apples there."†

WILLIAM HENDRY STOWELL (b. 1800, d. 1857),

was the only son of William Stowell, a paper stainer in Douglas, and Ann Hendry. His father was a member of the Church of England, and a brother of the Rev. Hugh Stowell, Rector of Ballaugh (see p. 29). Chief among the teachers of WILLIAM HENDRY was his relative, the Rev Robert Brown (see p. 34). From him the young student gained those severe canons of taste which he never afterwards neglected ; from him also he acquired a poetic tendency."‡ In 1810, his father transferred his business to Liverpool. For a short time, WILLIAM HENDRY took part in it. But, in 1816, through the influence of the learned and eloquent Dr. Raffles, he was encouraged to prepare himself for the Congregational ministry. With this object he went to pursue his studies at a collegiate institution then just established under the Rev. Dr. Joseph Fletcher, at Blackburn. In 1820, though his college course did not terminate till the end of the year, he received an invitation from St. Andrew's Congregational Chapel, at North Shields, to become its pastor. He was ordained in the following February, and at once began his ministry there. He soon became remarkably popular. His earnestness, his natural eloquence, the freshness of his thought and style, all combined to place him in a position where he was looked up to by all parties and denominations as a singularly gifted preacher. It is said that, but for want of vocal power, he would have risen to the highest ranks as a pulpit orator. From first to last his career at St. Andrew's appears to have been characterized by painstaking study and unflagging ardour in every department of his work. In 1827, he was nearly drowned. As a result of this, and his habit of constantly overworking

---

* For full particulars see the *Methodist Magazine* for 1877, from which the greater part of the foregoing account has been taken.
† *Methodist Magazine* (1877), p. 67.
‡ Life of W. H. Stowell.

himself, he was troubled with increasing weakness in the throat and chest. He, therefore, in 1834, asked to be transferred to a less severe climate, and this was accomplished by his acceptance of the posts of President of the Congregational Theological College at Rotherham, and Pastor of the Church at Masboro'. His pastorate was most successful, he having added no less than 300 members to the Church. His work at the college, too, had great results. He so ruled and loved his students that they practically formed part of his family, and benefitted in the highest degree from his brilliant lectures and his vast erudition, especially in languages. "His great characteristic as a teacher depended upon the conscientiousness and extreme anxiety with which he . . . endeavoured to stimulate as well as to guide the thinking powers of his disciples."* In 1848, he had a severe illness, which reduced his strength so much that he had serious thoughts of resigning his offices, and, though he struggled on for a time, it became necessary for him to take a less arduous post. In 1850, therefore, he accepted the Presidency of the Countess of Huntingdon's College at Cheshunt. As regards his career there, one of his students writes: "Those who have looked into his writings, to become acquainted with his talents, and to gain an impression of his style, can form no adequate conception of that masculine intellect, that luxuriant fancy, that rare and glorious abandonment and that prompt and happy manner. To know him and appreciate him, one must have been with him in his moments of inspiration, to have caught the gems as he flung them about in profusion; or when his great heart was weighed down with some deep sorrow or serious reflection."† And again: "Every one was struck with the singular beauty of his expressions, and the chasteness of his composition. . . . His exegetical skill was sometimes of a high order."† He resigned his presidency in June, 1856, and, during the short remainder of his life, he resided for the most part in London, visiting his native island in the autumn of 1857. Dr. Stowell's scholarship was accurate, extensive, and varied. He was a good classic and an able theologian. With general literature, especially in the departments of history and ethics, he was well acquainted. He wrote several books, the first of which was on the Decalogue. The next, in 1849, was a treatise on the work of the Holy Spirit. It was immediately after the publication of this latter work that he received the degree of D.D. from the University of Glasgow. He published other books of less note, such as volumes of the Religious Tract Society, &c., and also wrote largely for the Press, being at one time editor of the "Eclectic Review," and he contributed articles to the "Biblical Review" and the "British Quarterly Review." (Abstract of a memoir by William Stowell, B.A., London, 1869.)

* Life of W. H. Stowell, p. 202
† *Ibid*, pp. 271-2.

WILLIAM THOMAS RADCLIFFE* (b. 1816, d. 1897),

born in Douglas, became a Sunday-school teacher, a visitor of the
sick, and a local preacher, at the age of 16. When 22, he was
called to the ministry. He was a well-read man, being thoroughly
conversant with the Hebrew Bible and Greek Testament, and
steeped in the theology of his own and other churches. The whole
of his ministerial life was spent in circuit work, and he discharged
the duties of a superintendent of a circuit, and of chairman of a
district, in a way which won the admiration and gratitude of all
who came in contact with him. In 1870, he was elected by nomin-
ation into the " Legal Hundred." A born administrator, intelligent, cautious, reticent, judicious, courteous, yet withal strong,
resolute, stern, he gave, and expected others to give, all diligence
and reverence to the work of God. He was a model pastor, and a
most earnest preacher of the Gospel. His sermons and speeches
were worked out with consummate care, and were delivered with
a stately eloquence and a gracious unction from which all artifi-
ciality was banished, and which made him one of the foremost
Methodist preachers and platform speakers of his own day.
Genial, full of quiet, but deep humour, the storehouse of his
strong memory filled with readings and reminiscences of early and
later Methodist preachers and circuit work, his conversation had
all the charm which can only be given by culture. He was a man
of a noble and commanding presence, and with a cultured and
gentle manner of speech. He was devoted to his native island,
about which, some years before his death, he wrote a charming
little book, entitled " Ellan Vannin," containing sketches of its
history, people, language, and scenery. (From the " Methodist
Magazine.")

HUGH STOWELL BROWN (b. 1823, d. 1886),

the second son of the Rev. Robert Brown (see p. 34) and Dorothy
Thompson, was born in Douglas, and, when between 8 and 11
years of age, he went to the Grammar School there, which was
then kept by the Rev. Thomas Stowell. His education at that
institution was of the most elementary character. At 11 years
of age he was taken from it to read to his father, who was then
threatened with blindness. In this way, he acquired a fund of
miscellaneous information which was afterwards of great use to
him. In 1839, he went to England to learn land-surveying,
and speedily obtained an appointment on the Ordnance Survey.
But he gave it up almost at once, and in 1840, we find
him in the London and Birmingham railway engine shop
at Wolverton. At this time he became a teetotaller and

* He was a connexion of Charles Bland and John Netten Radcliff
(see Ch. IV).

a Sunday-school teacher. By the end of 1843, he had decided
to go into the Established Church, and, in 1844, he went
to King William's College, where he studied very hard.
In 1846, he changed his mind, and, by the end of the
same year, he joined the Baptist Church. Some months later,
he was invited to preach in the Myrtle Street Chapel, in Liverpool, and, after a short period of probation, he was elected as its
minister. In this position he continued during the rest of his
life, filling it with the greatest ability and success. As regards
his preaching, his biographer says that it "was simple and admirably direct, with many a sparkle of quaint humour, with many a
homely proverb and epigram; not seldom touched with the honest
pathos of a big strong heart, and always ringing out clear and full
in generous enthusiasm for righteousness, and scorn and loathing
of everything that was mean and low."[*] He was listened to by
the least as well as by the best educated members of his congregation with the greatest attention and interest. A strong and
faithful, though not an emotional friend, he was ever ready to
help in real cases of distress. The progress of the congregation
under his charge was very remarkable. When he began, it had
239 members; and, in 1884, it had 849. But it was not only his
ordinary congregation that benefitted by his exertions. In 1854,
he began a series of popular Sunday afternoon lectures. He also,
in the summer evenings after chapel, addressed large audiences of
working people, numbering from three to four thousand. It was
chiefly through his exertions in these respects that many of the
labouring class were induced to place their money in the "Work-
man's Bank" established by his church in 1861. This institution
was the means of fostering habits of saving, being thus the
salvation of hundreds from intemperance and from poverty. In
1873, he visited the United States of America, when he recorded
his opinion that that country would have "a future of greatness
that has never been equalled in the history of the world."[*]
During the last ten years of his life his name as a preacher had
become a household word in Liverpool, and honours of various
kinds were bestowed upon him. Thus, he became President of
the Baptist Union, President of the Liverpool Branch of the Peace
Society, and Chairman of the Liverpool Seamen's Friendly Society.
He was greatly esteemed, not only by the members of his own
denomination, but by all denominations, so great was "the breadth
of his sympathies and the catholicity of his spirit."[†] Well might
his son-in-law and biographer say of him that few men "have left
behind them so fragrant a memory among so wide a circle of
friends,"[*] and his brother, the Rev T. E. Brown, declare that he
had "ringed him round" all his life "with moral strength."[‡]

---

   * Autobiography, with introduction and notes, by W. S. Caine, M.P.
   † Ibid.
   ‡ Letters, edited by S. T. Irwin.

Local Preachers.

We regret that we have been able to find out so little about the early Manx Wesleyan local preachers, of whom Wesley said : "I never saw in England so many stout, well-looking preachers together. If their spirit be answerable to their look, I know not what can stand before them."[*] "How strange," as the late Thomas Kelly remarks, "notwithstanding we have had Manx Methodists second to none in philanthropy and piety that so little has been written of them."[†]

One of the earliest was JOHN ELLISON, leader of the first class formed in Douglas. To conduct this he walked to and from the neighbourhood of Peel, where he lived. He preached during about sixty years, and, in extreme old age, when unable to stand, he did so sitting.

Contemporary, or nearly so, with him is WILLIAM FARAGHER, of Cooil-cam (b. 1762, d. 1855), who was on the Douglas and Castle-town circuit for upwards of 60 years. He began preaching at the age of 19, and was on the plan for 74 years. He died at the great age of 93, retaining his faculties to the last. He possessed a vigorous mind, and was a powerful preacher in the Manx language.

Other pioneers were ROBERT COWLEY, of Ballaugh; WILLIAM CORRIN, of Ballameanagh, Braddan, who was one of the committee which published the Manx Wesleyan Hymn-book; JOHN COWLE, (b. 1768, d. 1848), of Ballakaneen, Andreas; and JOHN COWELL, clerk of St. George's. It is said that JOHN COWELL had made it a condition of undertaking the office of clerk that, when he was required to preach, he should be allowed to provide a substitute. There is a story that, on one occasion, when Bishop George Mason preached a sermon against Methodists from St. George's pulpit, COWELL was in his place, and, when the bishop had finished, he gave out the following hymn, which he thought appropriate under the circumstances : —

> In vain, O man of lawless might,
>   Thou boast'st thyself in ill,
> Since God, the God in whom I trust
>   Vouchsafes his favour still.
> The wicked tongue doth sland'rous tales
>   Maliciously devise ;
> And sharper than a razor whet
>   It wounds with treacherous lies.

We are told that the next day the bishop took his revenge by rebuking JOHN COWELL for preaching, when he did not understand

---

[*] Rosser. "Wesleyan Methodism in the Isle of Man." p. 99.
[†] Of Clypston, from his lecture on *Illiam-y-Close*.

Greek or Hebrew, but JOHN retorted that he knew English and Manx well enough to make men understand that he was calling them to repentance.*

Of rather later date are—

WILLIAM COWLEY, generally known as "Illiam-e-Close," of whom, thanks to the late Thomas Kelly, of Clypston, we are able to give an account; STEPHEN, LACE, SAYLE, and KNEALE (H.K., of Regaby), who were, according to the Rev W. T. Radcliffe, "men of original gifts and much usefulness."† Then came ANTHONY LEWTHWAITE, JOHN CORLETT, JOHN CAIN, Ballashen, PATRICK CALEY and WILLIAM KELLY, of Sulby, THOMAS CAIN, of Ballacain, and, later still, WILLIAM JOUGHIN, of Grenaby, JOHN JOUGHIN, of Ballacrebbin, HARRY CUBBON, of Laxey, WILLIAM CLUCAS, of Glenrushen, PHILIP SKILLICORN, and THOMAS CRENNELL. (See also JOHN COWELL and HUGH GARRETT, in Ch. VII, and JOHN STEVENSON MOORE and EVAN CHRISTIAN, in Ch. IX).

WILLIAM COWLEY (d. 1848),

usually known as "Illiam-y-Close," or William of the Close, from the name of the estate in the parish of Marown, owned and occupied by him, was one of seven sons. He was small of stature, being only about five feet high. There is not much to be discovered about his boyhood. It is said that upon one occasion he attended a service conducted by William Faragher (Cooil-cam), having gone there for the purpose of ridiculing the preacher. Faragher took as his text, "O foolish Galatians, who hath bewitched you, that ye should not obey the truth," and one result of his sermon was the conversion of ILLIAM, who soon afterwards became a local preacher himself. His reputation as a preacher became very great, and, no doubt, his capability of making quaint, witty, and trenchant remarks had much to do with his influence. We may quote a few of these, as they are characteristic of the rough, wholesome humour often indulged in by Manx local preachers. On one occasion he called to see a man who was very sick, and who was well known to be a malingerer and back slider. On ILLIAM's getting up to go, the man said, "ILLIAM, would'st thou not better pray with me?" but ILLIAM replied, "Pray with thee! Thou has't far more need of a stick!"

On another occasion a man met him on one of his journeys, and said to him, "Where art thou going, ILLIAM?" "I am going to Baldwin to preach." "It is a wonder they don't send young men on such journeys," said the man; and WILLIAM replied, "I did not think I would have met such a fool on my journey; dos't thou

* From *The Isle of Man Times*, February, 1895.
† Ellan Vannin, p. 147.

think I am going to lose the ship at the mouth of the harbour?"
ILLIAM often rebuked others, but sometimes he got a rebuke himself—thus, a friend who heard him preach from the text, "Sell
all that thou hast, and give to the poor," and urge that every one
should do this, said to him afterwards, "If all sold, who would
there be to buy?" ILLIAM saw his error, and replied, "If I had
not a sermon going, I had one coming home." It is said that he
once remarked to the young women of his congregation, in the
course of his sermon, "There are as many ribbons in your bonnets
as would make a nest for a goose I have at home." A well-to-do
person passing the collection box in chapel without putting anything in, ILLIAM called out, "Hold the box to his nose until he
gets red in the face." One of his usual prayers after the sermon
was, "Lord help the people to take the grain and leave the chaff."

(Abstract of the account by the late Thomas Kelly, Clypston.)

The Quakers.

It is pleasant to think that, though the discipline of the Manx
Church was severe, and though she punished those who offended
against it with imprisonment, fines, and the stocks, no one has
ever, as far as we know, suffered martyrdom on account of their
religion in the Isle of Man. The only cases of persecution, which
may really be termed barbarous, were directed by her against a
few poor Quakers, in the 17th century.

We first hear of the Quakers in Lord Fairfax's time, when
the governor prohibited anyone from receiving them into their
houses, and the Quakers themselves from meeting "in the fields,
or any out-house, or other place on the Lord's Day."[*] They seem
to have lived, for the most part, in the parish of Maughold,
where their burial-ground, called Rhullick-ny-Quakeryn, is
situated. The chief among them were WILLIAM CALLOW, of
Ballafaile, JOHN CHRISTIAN, of Lewaigue, EVAN CHRISTIAN, and
EVAN KERRUISH. They were constantly imprisoned and ill-
treated for not paying tithes both before and after the Restora-
tion. In 1665, WILLIAM CALLOW (b. 1629, d. 1676), the only one of
whose life we know anything, and others, were banished
from the island. CALLOW appealed to the Duke of York (after-
ward James II.) and Prince Rupert, and obtained a letter from
the latter to the Earl of Derby, with a request that he should give
CALLOW leave to return to the island, and restore his property
there to him. The earl declined, stating that he would not have
the island infected with heresy, and, to a despairing letter ad-

---

[*] *Lib. Scaccar.*

dressed direct to him by CALLOW, he returned the same reply.
CALLOW then betook himself to London.   This we learn from
some notes by him in the pages of his Bible,* which are as
follows :   " I, WILL CALLOW, of Ballafayle, Manksman, who have
been banished out off the Ile off Man by the Bishops and Priests
for conscience towards God, above two years and three months
ffrom my deare wife and tender children, and have bought this
book the rate 8s 10d in London where I am now in Robert
Bridge's house in Hozier lane, coach builder, near Smithfield.   I
say this day being the first of the 11th month in the year 1667
as witness my own handwriting the day and year above said."
He then proceeds to give particulars of his birth and that of his
wife and of three sons and of six daughters.   In 1762, when
Charles II. issued his " Declaration of Indulgence," he and the
other banished Quakers were allowed to return to the island.
The notes in the Bible, which were continued by his son Robert,
tell us that he died in 1676.   He was interred in the burial-
ground which we have already mentioned.

The aforesaid ROBERT, together with his wife, ELINOR, and
others of the Quakers continued to suffer great hardships at
the hands of the bishop and clergy till the advent of Bishop
Wilson, who was loved and respected by them.

[Taken from the MSS. notes by John Smith, Quaker, who had
extracted them from " Besse " and other writers.]

---

* This belonged to the late John Christian Fargher, a descendant of William
Callow's.

CHAPTER III.

The Legislature.

Under the heading of "The Legislature," we have placed some of those who distinguished themselves in the executive and legislative work of the island. With regard to the members of the House of Keys, it must be borne in mind that their legislative labours were only a very small part of their life-work, but it is, probably, in most cases at least, the part which chiefly entitles them to public recognition.

The Council.*

The first of the members of the Council, in order of date, of whom we have any record, is

EWAN CHRISTIAN (b. 1579, d. 1656),

of Milntown, father of *Illiam Dhone*. He is more remarkable for the powerful position he attained in the island than for, as far as we know, any special ability he showed either as councillor or deemster. His position is especially referred to by James, the 7th Earl of Derby, in his diary, as follows :—" By reason of his eminence here and that [he] holdeth much of the same tenure of the straw . . . he is so observed that certainly, as I temper the matter with him in this, so shall I prevail with

---

* Under the heading of "Law" will be found the names of lawyers who also did good service as members of the Council, but whose chief claim to distinction is their legal ability.

others " ; * and he then proceeds to say about his family : " There
be many of the Christians in this country—but they have made
themselves chief here . . . by policy they are crept into the
principal places of power ; and they be seated round about the
country, and in the heart of it ; they are matched with the best
families ; have the best livings [that is, farms] ; and must not be
neglected."†

Though, after 1642, some of his sons and connexions‡ were
concerned in plots against the Stanleys, he appears, outwardly
at least, to have remained on good terms with Lord Derby, and
that he was trusted by him at this time is shown by the fact that
he held the post of Governor of Peel Castle.   He was appointed
deemster when only 26, and held that office till his death, a
period of 51 years.   During the last six years, however, his son,
John, acted as his deputy.   This has been the longest nominal,
though not actual, tenure of office as deemster.§   Between 1634
and 1636, he acted as Deputy-Governor of the island.

EDWARD (or EDMOND)|| CHRISTIAN (b. circa 1600, d. 1661),

the second son of the Rev. John Christian, who was Vicar of
Maughold between 1580 and 1625, played many parts in life.   He
was at one time a merchant adventurer, then a captain in the
Royal Navy, then Deputy-Governor of the island, Commander of
the insular militia, reformer, and patriot, or rebel.   His early
life was spent at sea, where, becoming the owner as well as the
captain of a vessel, he amassed a fortune under the auspices of
the " East Indy Co."**   We next find him at the English Court,
as one of the suit of the Duke of Buckingham, by whose influence
he was appointed to the " Bonaventure," frigate, of 37 guns.   On
returning to his native island in 1627, he at once attracted the
attention of its ruler, James, Lord Strange, who writes of him
as follows : " I was newly got acquainted with Captain Christian,
whom I observed soon to have abilities enough to do me service.
. . I was told . . [he] had already made himself a good fortune
in the Indies ; that he was a Manxman born ; but, which took most
with me, that when he offered his service it was on these terms—
that he would be contented to hold the staff until I chose another
    .   .   .   For the pay, he so little valued that, as he would be
content to do service without any, or as little of it as it pleased

---

* *Manx Soc.*, Vol. III., pp. 47-8.
† *Ibid*, pp. 49-50.
‡ William Christian and Deemster John Christian (sons), also Edmund
Christian (governor), and John Curghey.
§ The longest actual tenure has been that of 50 years, in our own time,
by the universally respected Sir William Leece Drinkwater.
|| He is sometimes styled Edward and sometimes Edmond.
** Chaloner, *Manx Soc.*, Vol. X., p. 8.

The Legislature

[me] . . . He is excellent good company; as rude as a sea captain should be, but refined as one that had civilized himself half a year at Court, where he served the Duke of Buckingham."* Such being CHRISTIAN'S qualifications, Lord Strange, in 1628, appointed him "lieutenant and captain,"† and "for some few years he," says his master, "pleased me very well," for he "had a quality of the best servant—that what I directed him to do, if it succeeded ill, he would take the same upon himself; and what happened well would give me the glory of it."‡ In 1633, while he held this office, he got into trouble with the Admiralty, on the accusation of Captain Thomas James, of H.M.S. "Lion's Whelp," for "trucking with a pirate." CHRISTIAN replied that the supposed pirate had shown him a commission which appeared to be in order, so that he had not detained him. This explanation does not seem to have been satisfactory to Sir Thomas Wentworth (afterwards Earl of Strafford), then Lord Deputy and Governor-General of Ireland, since, in a letter to the Admiralty, he says that there were further proofs against CHRISTIAN, and he remarks: "Surely so long as these pirates may make their return thither (to Man) as to a market overt for the vending of their stolen goods, they will hardly be beaten from their harassing and infecting this channel, and therefore again I beseech your Lordships that there may be a severe hand held upon him, and heavily to feel his transgression both towards his Majesty and the quiet and necessary convenience of his subjects in these parts."§ In reply to this, the secretary, Coke, writes: I will also give you account what order shall be taken with Captain CHRISTIAN, whose trucking with pirates and manner of inviting rather than apprehending such people is not to be endured."§ Shortly afterwards, in January, 1634, the Commissioners for the Admiralty sent an order to Lord Strange that "Captain CHRISTIAN fayle not personally to attend us at the Council Chamber in Whitehall upon Friday the 14th day of Ffebruarie next at the farthest."|| Lord Strange thereupon sent a messenger to Man, who reported that CHRISTIAN was "soe weak and soe farr spent in body by reason of his long and lingeringe sickness that he is in noe way able to travaile on horseback at all, nor in any other way, without eminent danger of his life."¶ This report was duly forwarded to the Admiralty by Lord Strange. who again sent for CHRISTIAN in April, when he was still "sick." Whether he ultimately went we do not know, but, as he stated that he "would not faile to wait on his Lordship as soone as

* *Manx Soc.*, Vol. III., p. 39.
† Knowsley Muniments.
‡ *Manx Soc.*, Vol. III., p. 40.
§ Admiralty Papers (*Manx Sun*, T. Talbot).
|| *Lib Scacc.*
¶ *Manx Soc.*, Vol. IX., pp. 140-1.

possiblie he could," he probably did. Nor do we know what the result of his interview with the Admiralty was, but it does not seem to have resulted in his disgrace with Lord Strange, because, though Ewan Christian held the deputy-governorship (probably merely as his substitute) between 1634 and 1636, he did not finally lose that office* till 1639, when he once more got into disgrace. He was, however, restored to favour, for the second time, in 1642, being, on the breaking out of the civil war in England, appointed "Sergeant-Major"† of the insular forces. But the earl soon found that he had " believed and trusted him too much," discovering, as it was stated in evidence at his trial, that he was the " adviser, counsellor, and persuader " of the people who came armed to Tynwald on the 24th June, 1642, threatening that they would pay no more tithes; and there is no doubt that he was the leader of the popular party. In the following May, there was a serious riot at Douglas, originated by the arrest of a man who had declined to pay tithes, which is also said to have been instigated by him. In June, 1643, Lord Derby arrived in the island, and, shortly afterwards, CHRISTIAN was arrested and imprisoned. He was kept some time in prison before his trial took place. On this, Lord Derby comments : " I believe many wonder thereat, as savouring of injustice. . . . But, in my own knowledge, he deserves what he hath, and a great deal more," and, he continues, " I believe such a course will be taken, that he shall groan under the burden of it. But whether it will reach his life, l know not; for his judges do pretend they want precedents."‡ On this, he shrewdly remarks : "And, indeed, in this country any offence will be excused, if of never so high a nature, provided he steal not sheep; and that because the judges be sheep masters."‡ Lord Derby evidently thought that, " if a jury of the people do pass upon him (being he hath so cajoled them to believe he suffers for their sakes), it is likely they would quit him,"§ so he deliberately altered the ordinary procedure, and instead of bringing him first before a jury, he had him tried by the Keys, whom he had probably terrorised. The trial began in December, when the chief charges brought against him were (1) That he had said that the Keys should be elected by the people; (2) That the deemsters should be chosen out of the 24 Keys, one by the lord, the other by the people, and that they should hold office for three years only ; (3) That he had encouraged the people to resist the payment of tithes ; (4) That he had endeavoured to

---

* He signed an Act of Tynwald in that capacity in 1637.
† This was the highest military rank in Man after that of the lord, who was colonel.   It does not in any way correspond to the rank so called at the present day.
‡ *Manx Soc.*, Vol. III., p. 52
§ *Ibid*, p. 53.

get Peel Castle into his power; (5) That he had urged the people to behave seditiously against the lord. With regard to these accusations, the first two exhibit CHRISTIAN as a patriot, since both the deemsters and the Keys had formerly been elected by the people; but we can well understand how revolutionary such ideas would appear in the days of the Stuarts. With regard to the third charge, it only shows that CHRISTIAN had imbibed the notions in vogue at that time. But the last two, especially considering his position of trust as commander of the insular forces, were very serious, and fully justify the finding of the Keys, on the 13th of December, that CHRISTIAN had "most seditiously and tumultuously behaved himself." Upon perusal of this finding, the governor and Council, "for the greate and manifest misdemeanors of the said EDWARD CHRISTIAN, do adjudge and censure him . . . in one thousand markes fine, and his bodie to perpetuall imprisonment, or until he shall be released by the Lord of the Isle."* This verdict probably disappointed the earl, who remarks, with reference to CHRISTIAN, that "it was safer much to take men's lives than their estates."† In November, 1651, he was released on the Parliament taking possession of the island. We hear nothing more of him till 1659. It is probable that he was so broken down by the effect of his long imprisonment as not to be able to take any part in public affairs. In October of that year he seems to have been implicated in a plot against Fairfax's governor, Chaloner, and so was again committed to Peel Castle in January, 1660. He remained there till September in the same year, when he was let out for a few days to plead personally in a suit, but was sent back again, and died there on the 19th January, 1661. Three days later he was buried in Kirk Maughold Church.

It will be remembered that one of the characters portrayed by Sir Walter Scott in "Peveril of the Peak" was called Edward Christian, and that he was depicted as a wretch of unbounded depravity. Deemster John Christian, of Milntown, wrote to Sir Walter protesting against this description, and he received the reply that "the Edward Christian of the isle is a mere creature of the imagination."‡

---

* Document in Rolls Office, signed by Council and Keys.
† *Manx Soc.*, Vol. III., p. 53.
‡ Introduction to "Peveril of the Peak." It may be mentioned that the "Historical Notices" of Edward and William Christian," which were "recommended" to Sir Walter by Deemster Christian, and were published by him in an appendix, attempt to vindicate their characters, but they are unfortunately full of inaccuracies. They were said to have been written by a Mr Marsden in 1823.

WILLIAM CHRISTIAN (b. 1608, d. 1663),

popularly known as "Illiam Dhone," (Brown William), was a younger son of Deemster Ewan Christian, of Milntown. Nothing is known of his early life. He was steward of the Abbey Lands in 1640, and a member of the House of Keys in 1643. In the same year his father presented him with the property of Ronaldsway, which he agreed to hold from the Earl of Derby on a lease for three lives, instead of by the old straw tenure. He and his family were, consequently, received into favour, and he was appointed to the then important office of "receiver." CHRISTIAN must have thoroughly gained the earl's confidence, since, when he (Lord Derby) left the island in August, 1651, to join the Royalist forces, he not only put him in command of the insular militia, but committed his countess, the famous Charlotte de la Tremoille, to his care. It is exceedingly difficult to ascertain precisely what part CHRISTIAN played in the subsequent transactions, since the only statements that remain to us are conflicting and obscure. We know that the countess, on hearing that her husband was a prisoner, made proposals to Parliament for the surrender of the island, in the hope of saving his life. We know also that CHRISTIAN, and some of the most influential Manxmen, suspected she had done so, and that they excited their countrymen against her by declaring that the countess intended to save herself by sacrificing them. This being so, we are not surprized to learn that, on the night on which the bearer of these proposals sailed, the insular militia, under CHRISTIAN'S command, rose, and attempted to seize all the forts. They succeeded as regards the smaller forts, but failed to take Rushen and Peel. Burton, Governor Musgrave's biographer, remarks that they plundered the earl's property, and ill-used all the English who fell into their hands. This statement, however, is uncorroborated. Musgrave demanded an explanation of the rising from CHRISTIAN, who replied that it was to procure the redress of certain grievances; and he added that the countess had sold the country into the hands of the Parliament. These grievances we know to have been connected with the 7th earl's action in depriving the people of their old system of land tenure, and there were also complaints of the free quarterage of troops upon them. It is said that an agreement was then entered into between CHRISTIAN and the governor to defend the island until satisfactory terms could be obtained, but, as both parties were negotiating with the Parliament, whose troops were now mustering for its capture, the agreement was, in reality, a mere pretence for the sake of gaining time. These troops arrived on the 20th of October, but, being delayed by storms, they did not land till the 28th. They had been assured by CHRISTIAN that they would not be opposed by the soldiers under his command.

On the 3rd of November, the countess, finding that she could not rely upon the fidelity of her soldiers, surrendered the castles of Rushen and Peel, and soon afterwards she left the island. In December, CHRISTIAN, and his brother John, the deemster, who were described in the Journals of the House of Commons as "two of the ablest and honestest gentlemen in the island," were summoned to London to be consulted about the Manx laws and other matters. He was continued in his office of receiver under Lord Fairfax, and, between 1656 and 1658, he also held the office of governor. In the latter year, James Chaloner, who had then been appointed governor, ordered his arrest on the charge of having misappropriated the revenues of the sequestrated bishopric, which Fairfax intended to be used for the support of the Grammar Schools, and for the augmentation of the stipends of the poorer clergy. This accusation does not seem to have been proved, and CHRISTIAN, through his son George, produced statements showing the substantial accuracy of his accounts. And yet it is curious that he should have fled to England without attempting to defend himself personally. It is not known where he spent the interval between 1658 and 1660. In the latter year, he "went to London with many others to have a sight"[*] of the king. His visit, however, was an unfortunate one, for he was arrested for a debt of £20,000, and put into the Fleet prison, where he was kept for nearly a year, till he was able to find bail. Some months after his release, being assured that the "Act of Indemnity" secured him against all the legal consequences of his political actions, he rashly returned to the Isle of Man. His advisers forgot that his offences were not against the Crown, but against the Lord of Man, who, in September, 1662, issued a mandate to his officers to proceed against him "for all his illegal actions and rebellions" in 1651, or before that year. He was thereupon imprisoned in Castle Rushen. At the trial which followed, CHRISTIAN refused to plead. This was a fatal mistake, because he thereby subjected himself to the same judgment as if he had pleaded guilty, or had been found guilty by a jury. In consequence of this, no evidence was taken on his behalf, so that he was virtually condemned without trial. His sentence was to be "hanged, drawn, and quartered," but this was commuted by an order of the deputy-governor that he be "shot to death." This was accordingly carried out on January the 2nd, 1663. An entry relating to his execution, in the Parish Register of Malew, states that "he died most penitently and most curragiously, made a good end, prayed earnestly, made an excellent speech, and next day was buried in the chancel of Kirk Malew."

According to his "dying speech," which, whether authentic or not, is eloquent and dignified in style, and contains nothing in-

---

[*] Dying Speech, *Manx Soc.*, Vol. XXVI., p. 35

consistent with any known facts, he protested against the charge
of treason brought against him by " a prompted and threatened
jury, a pretended Court of Justice, of which the greater part were
by no means qualified."* He appealed to those present to bear
witness how unjust the accusation against him was, and he de-
lared that " the rising of the people," in which he had engaged,
" did not at all, or in the least degree, intend the prejudice or
ruin of the Derby family."* During CHRISTIAN's imprisonment in
Castle Rushen, he had addressed a petition to the king and
Council, pleading that the proceedings taken against him by the
Earl of Derby were a violation of the Act of Indemnity, and pray-
ing that his case might be heard before them, but it did not reach
London till a week after his execution. In ignorance of this
event, orders were sent to Lord Derby to produce his prisoner.
ILLIAM DHONE's sons, George and Ewan, presented petitions for
redress, and, after some delay, the earl, the deemsters, and three
other members of "the pretended Court of Justice," were brought
before the King in Council, who decided that "the Act of General
Pardon and Indemnity did and ought to be understood to extend
to the Isle of Man."†

The Privy Council furthermore ordered that " intire restitu-
tion" be made of CHRISTIAN's estate, and that " to the end the
guilt of that bloud, which hath been unjustly spilt, may in some
sort be expiated" the deemsters "who decreed this violent death"
should remain prisoners in the King's Bench " to receive condign
punishment," while the others who had been summoned were discharged on giving security to appear when called upon.†

WILLIAM CHRISTIAN has been variously represented as a per-
jured traitor, or as the patriotic victim of a judicial murder, according to the sympathies of the writer. It is so difficult to judge
impartially of actions committed during a period of revolution,
and of which, moreover, we have but an imperfect record, that
the present writer has confined himself to laying the facts, as far
as he could ascertain them, before his readers. Whatever his
faults, CHRISTIAN undoubtedly suffered for the part he took in
endeavouring to protect his countrymen's laws and liberties. It
is this circumstance that has enlisted their sympathies in his
favour, while the plaintive ballad *Baase Illiam Dhone*, " Brown
William's Death," has invested his memory with the halo of a
martyr.

He is, as is well known, one of the characters in Sir Walter
Scott's " Peveril of the Peak," where the account given of him is
more remarkable for picturesqueness than historical accuracy.
Sir Walter's information about him was mainly obtained from his

---

* Dying Speech, *Manx Soc.*, Vol. XXVI., p. 40.
† *Ibid*, pp. 54-9.

younger brother, Thomas Scott, who resided in the island for some years at the beginning of the century.*

(Partly from the article in the *Dictionary of National Biography*, to which the writer contributed information.)

ROBERT HEYWOOD (b. 1633, d. 1690),

was "clerk of the green wax" for the County Palatine of Lancashire and was appointed Governor of the island in 1678. He is chiefly remembered for the interest he took in insular horse-racing. This sport was initiated by James, the 7th Earl of Derby, in 1628, when, with the view of encouraging his tenants to breed good horses, he presented a plate of the value of £5 to be run for by Manx horses on his birthday, the 28th of July. Every one wishing to compete had to enter his name with the clerk of the rolls, giving the name and colour of his horse or mare. The first race under these conditions was run at Langness in 1628, and it seems to have been continued annually until 1651. It was not run again till 1687, when Governor Heywood, "with the consent and approbation of the rest of the Lord's officers and 24 Keys"† renewed it under the same conditions as in 1628. He himself encouraged the sport in that year by entering "ane bay gelding, called by the name of Loggerhead,"‡ which "fairly won the race . . . at the first two heats,"‡ and he contributed a shilling "towards augmenting the plate for the next year.‡ His name is associated with some useful legislation, but, besides what has been stated, we know nothing of him, except that he was buried in the chapel at Castletown, and that his body was removed and interred in the same grave with his son Peter, in Kirk Malew, in 1699.

WILLIAM WATSON CHRISTIAN (b. 1799, d. 1893),

the youngest son of Thomas Christian, of Ballachurry, Andreas, a member of the House of Keys and Captain in the Royal Manx Fencibles, and Eunice Ann, eldest daughter and heiress of John James Murrey, of Ronaldsway, was born in Ramsey and educated at Whitehaven. He was called to the Manx Bar in 1820, and was a member of the House of Keys from 1829 to 1848. In this latter year he was appointed governor's secretary and Clerk to the Council, and he held these offices till 1851 when he became water-bailiff, with a seat in the Council. In 1852, the water-bailiff was appointed coroner for the holding of inquests for the whole island, and so he performed these duties, till they were

---

* See note p. 63.
† *Statutes*, Vol. I., pp. 140 and 142.
‡ *Manx Soc.*, Vol. XXI., pp. 186-7.

transferred to the high-bailiffs in 1866.   Between 1845 and 1867, he was captain of the parish of Andreas, and it may be noted as remarkable that he was the only captain of a parish in the present century who has had a lieutenant under him.   In 1858, he was made a magistrate, and, in addition to these various functions, he performed those of a member of the Highway Board for nearly thirty years.   He was, in fact, a most painstaking and useful official and an excellent lawyer.   He practically resigned all his public duties in 1867.   He had a most placid and kindly disposition, with the courtly manners of the old school, and he was distinguished by his great knowledge of insular affairs. These qualifications rendered him a charming and interesting companion to the very last, notwithstanding his great age.

WILLIAM BELL CHRISTIAN (b. 1815, d. 1886),

a son of Deemster John Christian, of Milntown, and Susannah Allen, was educated at Trinity College, Dublin, where he took his B.A. degree in 1840.   He was ordained in the same year and appointed Chaplain of St. John's, German.   In 1845, he became Vicar of Lezayre and held that living till 1861, when, except for a short time in 1865, he entirely gave up clerical work.   During his career in the Church he showed strong evangelical tendencies and was considered a powerful preacher.   He succeeded to Milntown in 1852, on the death of his father, and was made a magistrate in 1858.   In 1867, he was elected member for Ramsey in the House of Keys and continued to represent that town till he was made receiver-general in 1883.   He soon obtained an influential position in the House, being both a good speaker and a sound reasoner.   He was frequently selected as deputy-speaker. As receiver-general he was a decided success, being a capable administrator.   He was a man of distinguished appearance and polished and courtly manners.   It may be mentioned as remarkable that he was married four times, his last wife surviving him, and that he was one of the only two clergymen who have ever been members of the House of Keys.

RIDGWAY HARRISON (b. 1818, d. 1894),

son of Thomas Harrison, of Woodbourne, Douglas, and Alice Ridgway, served his apprenticeship with High-Bailiff Bluett and was admitted to the Manx Bar in 1840.   In 1856, he was elected a member of the House of Keys.   In 1864, he was appointed tithe agent;   in 1866, water-bailiff, or admiralty judge, with a seat in the Council, and, in 1868, seneschal.   In 1871, he was appointed receiver-general, or official head of the Harbour Board. This office, after the year 1872, when that board became subject to the Tynwald Court, also conferred a seat in the Council.   He continued to be receiver-general till 1883, when he was appointed crown-receiver, and he retired from the office of water-bailiff in 1885.* Among his numerous offices, the most important, as regards the island, was that of receiver-general, many large harbour works having been carried out during the time he held it. Chief among these were the Victoria and Battery Piers, in Douglas. He was also for upwards of 25 years a prominent member of the Highway Board, being chairman of that body during the greater part of the time.

RIDGWAY HARRISON will also be remembered as the first commander of the Douglas Rifle Corps, which post he held for ten years. He took a great interest in the building of St. Barnabas Church, Douglas, and was, for many years, superintendent of the Sunday School attached to that church.

He was a useful and reliable official, who did much good service for his country, and an amiable and cultured man.

JOHN FREDERICK GILL (b. 1842, d. 1899),

son of Joseph Gill, and Charlotte Augusta, daughter of the Rev. Thomas Stephen, vicar-general, was born at Marsala, in Sicily. Till he was ten years old he was educated at home. This was followed by about a year at school in Malta. He came to the Isle of Man at the age of 11, being placed under the care of his uncle, the Rev. William Gill, Vicar of Malew (see p. 36), and continued his education at King William's College. On leaving the College, he studied law with Sir James Gell, his second cousin, and, on being admitted to the Manx Bar, in 1864, he entered into partnership with him. Their firm, under the title of Gell and Gill, did a very large business. About 1882, this partnership was terminated, and he came to Douglas where he practised until his elevation to the Bench, as second deemster, in 1884. We will quote what Sir James Gell, who knew him intimately, said about him, both as advocate and judge: "I found him always, from the beginning of his study of the law, most painstaking, straightforward, and upright, with respect to whatever he had to do. He formed strong opinions on matters with which he was concerned, both professional and otherwise, and nothing would move him to swerve from what he considered to be right. Mere expediency never, I believe, influenced him. As a judge, he won the respect and admiration of the Bar, for the advancement of whose interest he was always a warm advocate, and I am sure it will be accorded to him by all that he acted judicially with the strictest impartiality. He had the sincere esteem of his colleagues on the Bench." He will, however, probably be best remembered by that invaluable

---

* By the Judicature Act of 1883, which abolished this office, it was provided that it was to be continued as long as he desired to hold it.

compilation, the revision of the Manx Statutes. Commencing in 1417, the six volumes containing them cover the legislation of the Isle of Man down to 1895. In these volumes, obsolete and repealed provisions are printed in a different type to those which are still in force. To enable this to be done, every single enactment had to be compared with previous enactments, a fact which is alone sufficient to show the immense research and labour involved. In his legislative capacity, he rendered the most valuable services, especially in connexion with committees of the Tynwald Court, of which he was frequently chairman. Both by temperament and judicial knowledge he was admirably suited for that position, the duties of which he performed in an unexceptionable manner. Deemster Gill's labours were, however, by no means confined to his judicial and legislative work. A thoroughly patriotic Manxman, everything that was for the good of his native land found in him an energetic supporter and sympathizer. As a young man, he was an enthusiastic volunteer, holding, for several years, the rank of lieutenant in the now defunct Castletown Rifle Corps. In charitable and philanthropic works, he was a well-known leader. We may especially notice his connexion with the Hospital, he having been a member of the committee of that institution for many years. He was an energetic president of the Isle of Man Natural History and Antiquarian Society, in the work of which he took a very keen interest, and a warm supporter of the Isle of Man Fine Arts and Industrial Guild, more particularly of the musical competitions promoted by it. And this leads to the statement that Deemster Gill will, perhaps, in the future, be even better remembered by his countrymen generally as the co-editor, with his brother, Mr. W. H. Gill, and Dr. Clague, of the volumes which contain their collection of "Manx National Music" than as the compiler of the standard Manx Statute Book. The value of this monumental collection will be more and more appreciated as time goes on. But for it the Manx people would have been deprived of a large portion of one of their most precious inheritances. In the social life of the island Deemster Gill, who was a man of handsome features, courtly presence, and genial, courteous, and dignified manner, took a leading part.

The Keys.

EWAN CHRISTIAN (b. 1644, d. 1712),

son of Robert Christian, of Lewaigue, is found, for the first time, as a member of the House of Keys, in 1673. In 1703, he, with Ewan Christian, of Milntown, and John Stevenson, of Balladoole, was appointed by the Keys to arrange with the Earl of Derby for the settlement of the dispute about the tenure of land, the agreement between them being embodied in the "Act of Settlement," which is called the Manx *Magna Charta*. In 1707, he was one of the delegates appointed to confer with the English Commissioners of Customs, and to ask them for the importation, duty free, of cattle, and of other products of the manufacture of the isle. Our knowledge of his character is mainly derived from his funeral sermon preached by Bishop Wilson, of whom he was a devoted friend. In it the bishop speaks of him as follows : "He is going to the grave with such a character among men and such a testimony of good works attending him that, when God thinks fit to call for any of us, the very best of us may wish his case to be ours. He lived to a good old age. . . . He did all the good he could for his country, for his family, for his friends, and for his neighbours ; in short, he has been a common benefactor to this poor place and his loss will be sooner felt than made up. . . . His understanding was stocked with abundance of useful knowledge, such as would surprise and edify those who knew him intimately."

JOHN STEVENSON, of Balladoole (b. circa 1655, d. 1737),

the eldest son of Major Richard Stevenson (see ch. vii), and Isabel, daughter of Deemster John Christian, of Milntown, is first heard of, in 1692, as the kindly patron of William Walker,* then a lad on his farm. Though probably a member of the House of Keys long before 1704, since he was then its speaker and one of the commissioners appointed to confer with the Earl of Derby with regard to the land question before the Act of Settlement was passed, his name does not appear in the Statute Book till that year. He was also a member of the Imperial Parliament, but it is not known what constituency he represented. In 1719, he was again asked by his colleagues in the Keys to go and see Lord Derby at Knowsley and to call his attention to various grievances in Church and State, which had, for the most part, arisen out of the arbitrary conduct of the governor and Council.

The earl declined to make any immediate reply, but he admitted, as regards some of the alleged grievances, that he saw " just cause of complaint," and he ordered the governor and officers to meet the Keys to confer about them. Nothing

* See pp. 21-22.

however, came of their interview, and consequently STEVENSON
was deputed to write to the earl appealing to him for justice.
He did so, with the result that he was called to account, tried as
a criminal and imprisoned, but was soon released.   In 1722, he
was, for the second time, imprisoned in Castle Rushen for assisting
Bishop Wilson to suppress the "Independent Whig," a book which
inculcated free-thinking principles.   In 1723, the grievances
referred to above being still unredressed, the Keys commissioned
him, with John Christian, Thomas Corlett, and Thomas Christian,
to apply to the King in Council, if they could not get redress from
Lord Derby.   They do not seem, however, to have done anything.
In 1727, JOHN STEVENSON was again in trouble, being accused of
saying that the "Boon men were hardly used by the governor in
weeding his corn,"* and of improper behaviour to the governor at
the mustering of the Arbory militia.   It seems, however, not to
have been possible to find sufficient evidence to convict him of any
serious misdemeanour, so he was discharged. After this we hear
nothing more of him, though he lived for ten years longer.   He
was styled "The Father of his Country" by Bishop Wilson, and
the writer of an account of him in Burke's Landed Gentry states
that he "devoted himself to the religious and civil welfare of his
country."†   Indeed, from all that we have been able to learn
about him, it is clear that Keble's verdict that he was "an
unflinching champion of popular rights and liberties,"‡ is a just
one.

GEORGE MOORE, Knight (b. 1709, d. 1787),

was the second son of Philip Moore, of "The Hills," Douglas, and
Margaret Bradshaw, and the owner of the estate of Ballamoore,
near Peel.   He was Speaker of the House of Keys, and their
leader in their efforts to obtain better terms for Manx commerce
after the Revestment.   It was largely due to his exertions that
the intention of annexing the island to Cumberland was not
carried out.   He received knighthood, in 1781, in recognition
of his services.

DANIEL CALLOW (b. 1751, d. 1790).

All we know of him is derived from the following inscription
in St. Mary's Chapel, Castletown : "Daniel Callow, Esq., H.K.,
who, in discouraging circumstances, cheerfully accepted a commission to attend the business of his country in the South of
England, where he died, zealously engaged in the duty of that
appointment, June 18th, 1790, aged 39.   As a grateful testimony
of their respect for his virtues, public spirit, and services, the
House of Keys, with others of his countrymen and friends, have
caused this monument to be erected."

---

* *Lib Scacc.*
† 8th edition. Vol. II., p. 1,922.
‡ Life of Bishop Wilson, p. 537.

JOHN CHRISTIAN CURWEN (b. 1756, d. 1828),

the eldest son of John Christian, of Ewanrigg and Milntown, and Jane, eldest daughter of Eldred Curwen, of Workington Hall, was educated at home till he went to Eton, and from thence he proceeded to Cambridge. But he did not complete his course there, leaving when he was 20, and marrying Margaret, daughter of John Taubman, in 1776. She died in 1778, leaving one son, John, afterwards deemster, and owner of Milntown and Ewanrigg. After his wife's death, he went abroad for four years, returning to marry his first cousin, Isabella Curwen, owner of Workington Hall, whose father had died in 1778. In 1784, JOHN CHRISTIAN filled the office of high-sheriff, and, in 1786, he was elected M.P. for Carlisle, defeating the Earl of Lonsdale. He embraced the Liberal, or rather the Whig, side in politics, and at once took a high position in Parliament. Being a student of the then new science of Political Economy, and, having a great knowledge of facts and a power of handling them effectually, he was soon looked upon as an efficient speaker. In 1791, he took the name of Curwen. In 1792, he signed a declaration addressed to the people of Great Britain in favour of freedom of election and of Parliamentary Reform, and it should be remembered that he was a consistent member of the small party who made a determined stand against the Tory autocracy under Pitt. Nor, notwithstanding his Parliamentary labours, did he forget his native island. He was a member of the House of Keys, and took a leading part in opposing the claims of the Duke of Atholl in that House, as well as in Parliament. He spoke at length in the debates in Parliament on this question, both in 1790 and 1805, and his masterly speech at the latter date, though not successful in its object, attracted great attention. In 1809, we find him introducing a Bill for the better securing the independence and purity of Parliament by preventing seats being obtained through corrupt practices; but, notwithstanding his able advocacy, it was rejected. It may be mentioned, also, that, in numerous debates, he continued to exhibit unwearied zeal in favour of peace and reduced taxation. Between 1812 and 1816, he was not in Parliament, but he renewed his connexion with it as member for Carlisle, in the latter year. His chief services at this time were in introducing a Bill to amend the law relating to tithes, which he failed to carry, though his main ideas became law some years later. He also endeavoured to have the duties on salt, soap, leather, &c., repealed. When Parliament was dissolved by the death of George the Third, in 1820, Curwen obtained the honour of being elected both for Carlisle and West Cumberland. He decided to sit for the latter, and, in returning thanks for his election, he remarked : " For 35 years I have had to contend against the whole aristocracy of Cumberland, and I have beaten them with the assistance of the people. For the fourteenth time I am about to receive the highest honour that can be bestowed upon an Englishman." In 1821, Curwen, who was regarded by the Whigs as the mouthpiece of the landed interest, made a very able speech on a motion for a committee of the House of Commons to inquire into the causes of agricultural distress, in which he urged a policy of economy and retrenchment. In the following month, he carried a Bill, the object of which was to exempt horses engaged in farming operations from duty, against the Government, and, in the following year, he succeeded in getting the salt tax removed. In 1824, he moved for papers relating to the Duke of Atholl's having expelled the Keys from the Court of General Gaol Delivery, and carried his motion by two votes. At this time, he admitted that he had changed his views about the Corn Laws, saying that he had come to the conclusion that a comparatively small fixed duty was preferable to the prohibitive duty in force. In 1825, he moved and carried the Roman Catholic Relief Bill. It was, however, rejected by the Lords. Long before this time, the greater number of his comrades, such as Burke, Grattan, Sheridan, and Romilly, who had fought with him against Pitt and the Tory party, had been claimed by death, and he had become advanced, not only by seniority, but by the superiority of his claims, to the first rank. Not long afterwards, his health began to fail, so that he could no longer take a prominent part in debate. He sat in Parliament, for the last time, in the autumn of 1828.

Let us now glance at his life's work out of Parliament, since he did much for his country in many other ways than as a legislator. As an agriculturalist, he conferred enormous benefits both upon Cumberland and the Isle of Man, not only by founding agricultural societies, but by his experiments, which tested the art of farming in all its branches, and he set a good example to his neighbours by his unwearying efforts to promote drainage and the reclamation and enclosure of waste lands. He wrote a valuable book on agriculture, entitled, "Hints on Agricultural Subjects, and on the best means of improving the condition of the Labouring Classes," which, among other items, contains chapters on agricultural works, the value of land, bargains, tithes, irrigation, choice of stock, &c. Many of his views are now looked upon as well established facts in husbandry, but, when he gave expression to them, they were novelties. In 1807, the "Society of Arts, Commerce, and Manufactures," in London, voted him their gold medal for various improvements in agriculture, and this was only one among many public recognitions made him by this and other societies for his discoveries. The reports of the Workington Agricultural Society, which had a branch in the Isle of Man, originated entirely with him, and they became the recognized exponents of what constituted good farming. In the following year, his Manx admirers presented him with a silver vase in grateful acknowledgment of his " strenuous and successful efforts in Parliament in defence of their country's rights and independence, and of the benefits the rising agriculture has received from his protection and example." As a country squire, his performance of the multifarious duties which pressed upon him was admirable. He instituted a Savings Bank, in the town of Workington, and " Friendly Societies" amongst his own and other workpeople. In many ways he strove to promote economy and thrift among the labouring classes. Invariably considerate and kind to the poor, he was wont, in times of dearth and high prices, to dispose of his farm produce among them at thirty per cent. below its sale price. He was at the expense of a local Sanitary Act—a thing scarcely dreamt of in that day—and he erected a pier at the mouth of the Derwent. In society, he was a great favourite, having an inexhaustible fund of humorous stories. He was master of the West Cumberland Hunt and an accomplished whip. As a man, he was distinguished by philanthropy, practical sagacity, great firmness of principle and good judicial sense. As a legislator, he was thoroughly independent and straightforward. He has filled a distinct niche in the history of the United Kingdom, and his native island regards him as one of her most distinguished sons. His name will remain in the records of the English Parliament, and in the agricultural archives of Great Britain and the United States of America, as a man of mark and a true benefactor to his species.

It may be mentioned that he was twice offered a Peerage, but declined it.*

EDWARD MOORE GAWNE, of Kentraugh (b. 1802, d. 1871),

son of Edward Gawne, of Mount Gawne, and Catherine Moore, of Pulrose, was born at Mount Gawne in the parish of Rushen. In 1829, he was selected as a member of the House of Keys, and in 1854, he became speaker of that body, having previously acted as deputy-speaker.† He retained this office till the dissolution of the non-elected House in 1867, when, in consideration of his distinguished services, he was offered knighthood, but declined that honour. He also declined to seek election in the new House of Keys, because he objected to the popular method of election, considering the old system had worked well. In politics, he was a strong Conservative, or, perhaps, a Tory of the old school is a better description. On his retirement from the Keys, he was presented with the antique speaker's chair belonging to the House.

He was an excellent landlord, being, indeed, an enthusiastic

---

* For full details see " The Worthies of Cumberland " by Henry Lonsdale, M.D., London.   George Routledge & Sons, 1867.
† His uncle, John Moore, of " The Hills," was then speaker.

agriculturist, having done much to improve the breed of stock by
the importation of pedigree sires.   In 1841, he was elected first
President of the Isle of Man Agricultural Society, which was
re-constituted in that year.   He had all the tastes of a country
gentleman, keeping his yacht and his kennels of beagles and
greyhounds.   He was remarkable, not only for the extreme
kindliness of his nature, for his unassuming manners, his geniality,
his unbounded hospitality and charity, but for his unaffected piety
and intense love of his native island.   No wonder, then, that
such a character was beloved and respected both by his fellow
members in the House and by all who knew him.   The *Manx Sun*
newspaper, in its obituary notice of him, remarks that " there are
not, we are sure, any living Manxmen who will not gratefully
acknowledge that they were proud of Mr. Gawne and that they
will ever affectionately cherish his memory."

WILLIAM CALLISTER (b. 1808, d. 1872),

was educated at the Liverpool Institute and afterwards at a
private school at Daresborough in Cheshire.*   On his return
home, he soon took an active part in his father's business, that of
a timber merchant, which he largely extended.   He was also,
after 1837, prominently associated with the movement for the
reform of the House of Keys, becoming its chief leader in the
north of the island.   Though nominated once or twice prior to
1847, as a member of that body, he refused to accept the position ;
but in that year, somewhat to the surprize of his friends, he
consented to do so.   It is probable that he came to the
conclusion that he could work more effectually from within
than from without, and so the result proved.   He almost
at once, owing to his great force of character and unusual
powers of speech, became one of the most influential members
of the Keys.   This was shown by his being commissioned,
together with the late George William Dumbell, in 1853,
to interview the Treasury with reference to the burning
question of the customs duties.   Their mission resulted in
obtaining some important financial advantages.   In recognition
of these services, they both received a handsome piece of silver
plate from the Keys.   Years later he formed one of the deputation
who went to London on the no less burning Port Erin question ;
and again, in 1860, he and the late William Farrant were deputed
to go to London to negotiate with the Woods and Forests
Commissioners about the commons lands, and succeeded in
obtaining more favourable terms than those first offered by the
commissioners. In 1851, he was appointed a magistrate ; in 1855,

---

* He had a remarkable faculty for figures, being able to add up three
columns of them at the same time.

chairman of the magistrates; and, in 1864, captain of the Parish of Bride. He was a member of the first Asylum Committee which was elected in 1863. In the popularly elected House of Keys he represented the sheading of Ayre, and continued to do so till his death. On the death of Edward Gawne, his friends desired to put him forward as their candidate for the Speakership of the House of Keys, but he declined the honour, and used his influence in favour of the late Sir John S. Goldie-Taubman. He was just as active in the new House as in the old, being especially vigorous in denouncing the financial settlement arrived at with the British Government in 1866, remarking, in the Tynwald Court, on one occasion: "It just comes to this, that we are to spend the money just as they (the British Government) tell us, and the idea that the representatives of the island will have the right to spend it is all moonshine." He was also made much use of in the executive work of the Tynwald Court, being a member of both the Harbour and Highway Board, and, for a long time, chairman of the latter board. Equally active in other ways, we find him a founder of the Isle of Man Banking Co., Ltd., and of a Savings Bank in Ramsey, and prime mover in starting the "Manx Fairy" steamer. He may truly be said to have been not only one of the most eloquent speakers that ever sat in the Manx Legislature, but one of the most valuable of Manx citizens.

WILLIAM FINE MOORE (b. 1814, d. 1895),

the youngest son of James Moore, of Cronkbourne, and Elizabeth Jeale, was educated at Imeson's School, in Douglas, but left at the early age of 14, to enter his father's business, which was that of a sail-cloth manufacturer. From his father's death, in 1846, till 1877, when he took his eldest son, Arthur William Moore, into partnership, he was the sole proprietor of this business, which he greatly improved and extended. Besides actively concerning himself in this way, he was connected with the management of other commercial undertakings in the island, such as the Isle of Man Banking Company, Limited, the Isle of Man Steam Packet Company, Limited, and the Isle of Man Electric Telegraph Company. He was also a large shareholder in insular mines, and took a keen interest in farming. Nor must we forget his services as a legislator and administrator. He entered the old House of Keys in 1857, being, at the same time, made a magistrate. He at once "lent his aid to the small party in the Keys which represented the cause of progress and popular control," and this was recognized by the people of Douglas in 1867, when they placed him at the head of the poll at the first popular election of that House. He had "a ready fund and force of speech," and was always an active and energetic member of the House, to which he continued to belong till ill-health led to his resignation in 1875. His chief legislative work was the in-

troduction of a Highway Bill which did away with the anomalies
and injustices perpetrated by the old Act.   Till 1867, he was a
member of the Board of Harbour Commissioners, and, both before
and after that date, he did much useful work on various Tynwald
Court Committees.   He was a staunch and enthusiastic Churchman, the erection of the new church at Braddan being largely due
to him, and a large and generous donor to insular charities.

ROBERT JOHN MOORE (b. 1816, d. 1884),

the only son of Robert Moore, of Peel, and Elizabeth Clark, was
admitted to the Manx Bar in 1838, and became High-Bailiff of
Peel in 1853.   Three years previously to this, he had been elected
as a member of the House of Keys, and, when the self-elected
House came to an end in 1867, he was chosen member for Peel in
the new House, and continued to represent the same constituency
till he retired, owing to ill-health, in 1881.   Both in his capacity
as Secretary to the House of Keys, and as an indefatigable worker
on boards and committees, he proved himself a most useful member
of the Legislature.   To the Harbour Board, in particular, his
services were very valuable.   For Peel, too, he did much useful
work, especially in the direction of promoting education, and of
forwarding the work for the preservation of the castle and
cathedral, in which he took very great interest.   Like Paul
Bridson, he had a remarkable knowledge of Manx families, and
a great love for the antiquities, history, laws, and customs of the
island.   He made a hobby of collecting Manx books and newspapers, a portion of his collection being now in the Free Library
at Douglas.
    A man of great amiability and geniality, he was greatly
esteemed and respected by all classes.   A stained glass window
has been erected to his memory in the new church at Peel.

JOHN FRISSELL CRELLIN (b. 1816, d. 1886),

the eldest son of John Christian Crellin, of Orrysdale,
and Catherine, only child of Robert Quayle, of West Hill,
Castletown, was educated at King William's College.   He
at first intended taking Holy Orders, but he abandoned
that idea, and studied medicine at St. Bartholomew's
Hospital, taking his diploma in due course, and becoming a member of the Royal College of Surgeons.   Shortly
afterwards, he was offered a Fellowship of that body, but declined it.   After his father's death, he settled at his property
of Orrysdale, and made use of his medical knowledge for
treating the poor in the neighbourhood gratuitously.   Elected
a member of the House of Keys in 1843, he continued to belong

to it till towards the end of 1874,* being one of its most useful, conscientious, and respected members. He acted for many years as deputy-speaker, and there is little doubt but that he might have succeeded Mr. Gawne as speaker, in 1867, if he had desired to do so. Archæology and numismatics were his favourite studies, and he attained distinction in both. Thus, we find him as one of the members of the committee appointed by Governor Loch, in 1876, to report on the antiquities of the island, and we know that he had an unrivalled knowledge of the various Manx coinages, and that his collection of them is unique. His assistance was, consequently, invaluable to Dr. Clay, with whom he collaborated in the production of Vol. XVIII. of the *Manx Society's* publications, which deals with Manx coins.

JOHN MOORE JEFFCOTT (b. 1817, d. 1892),

a son of Dr. Jeffcott, of County Kerry, and Catherine, daughter of the Rev. John Moore, Vicar of Braddan, completed his education at King William's College. He studied law at the Rolls Office, under John McHutchin, then clerk of the rolls. Called to the Manx Bar in 1839, he had, for a number of years, the largest legal practice in the south of the island, and earned the reputation of being a sound lawyer. In 1855, he became a member of the House of Keys, and he was returned to the reformed House, as member for Castletown, in 1867, continuing to represent that constituency till 1882, when he retired owing to failing health. He did very useful work in that capacity, also as a member of both the Harbour and Highway Boards. In 1866, he was appointed High-Bailiff of Castletown, a position which he held till his death with impartiality, benignity, and courtesy. But, although he was a competent public servant, his ability and energy also found an outlet in other directions. He painted with some skill, and was an enthusiastic naturalist, archæologist, and geologist.

WILLIAM FARRANT (b. 1826, d. 1891),

of Ballamoar, Jurby, the eldest son of William Farrant, of Ballamoar, and Susanna Eleanora Curphey, received his early education first in Ramsey, from the Rev. Archibald Holmes. Then, after studying privately in Douglas, he went to Magdalen College, Oxford. He was a good classical scholar, and both

---

* It may be mentioned that, in February 1872, he, as senior member of the Keys, attended the thanksgiving service in St. Paul's for the recovery of the Prince of Wales, together with Sir James Gell (then attorney-general) and the speaker (Sir J. S. Goldie-Taubman). They had the " three legs " painted on the panel of the carriage in which they drove to and from the service, and this, then almost unknown, symbol attracted considerable attention.

spoke and wrote French, German, and Italian with ease. Being in weak health after he left Oxford, he spent several years travelling, visiting, among other places, the Crimea, during the war with Russia. On his return to the island, in 1856, he was made Captain of the Parish of Jurby, and, in 1858, he became a Justice of the Peace, and a member of the House of Keys. He continued to be a member of the self-elected House till its dissolution. Its confidence in his ability was shown by his appointment, in 1860, as joint commissioner with the late William Callister, to negotiate with the Commissioners of Woods and Forests on their behalf. In 1874, he was elected as a member for Douglas, and, in 1883, he was returned for Glenfaba, continuing to represent this latter constituency till his death. An able, cultured, and eloquent man, he possessed considerable influence in the House of Keys, of which he was, for some years, the virtual leader. Conservative in his politics, his convictions were so strong that they often brought him into conflict with those who thought differently. But he always retained the admiration and respect of all, whether they differed from him or not. As an administrator, he did very good service, being a member of the Education and Harbour Boards. As a landlord, he did much to improve his estate, and, as an arboriculturist, he was an expert, succeeding in growing many rare trees and shrubs at Ballamoar. Conspicuous in every movement having the welfare of the Manx people for its object, he was highly esteemed generally, and his tenants and neighbours were greatly attached to him.

JOHN THOMAS CLUCAS (b. 1827, d. 1887),

was the only son of John Clucas, of Ballakilley, Rushen, and Margaret Gell, of Kenaa. The greater part of his early education was received from the Rev. William Corrin, Vicar of Rushen, from whom he went to Forrester's School, in Douglas, for six months, when he left, owing to ill-health. After studying farming for a few years, he was articled as law student at the Rolls Office with M. H. Quayle, the then clerk of the rolls. Observant, painstaking, and gifted with an excellent memory, he then gathered the intimate acquaintance with insular matters which was afterwards to be so useful to him and many others. Admitted to the Bar in 1856, he soon made his mark there. Since 1853, when his father died, he had superintended the farming of his estates, and, by 1862, he had acquired such a knowledge of Manx properties, that he was appointed a valuer under the Lunatic Asylum Act. In 1864, Governor Loch, with some difficulty, persuaded him to accept the offices of secretary to the governor and Clerk to the Council, and, in 1867, after the Isle of Man Customs Act was passed, he became Treasurer of the Isle of Man.

In 1873, probably as a result of overwork, his eyesight began to fail,* and so, in the following year, he resigned his offices, to the great loss of the insular community. This was, however, perhaps more than compensated for by his invaluable work in the House of Keys, where he represented Rushen Sheading from 1874 till his death. At various times a member of the Highway, Education, and Asylums Boards, and chairman of all three for a few years before his death, he did excellent service on them. But it is in connexion with the last in particular that he greatly distinguished himself, since it was mainly due to his exertions that the management of the Lunatic Asylum was placed on a more economical basis. In 1886, on the death of William Bell Christian, he was offered the post of receiver-general, but declined it. He was captain of the parish of Rushen, and a Justice of the Peace, a director of the Isle of Man Banking Company, Limited, and of the Isle of Man, Manx Northern, and Foxdale Railway Companies, being, indeed, one of the pioneers of railway enterprize in the Isle of Man.

EDWARD CURPHEY FARRANT (b. 1830, d. 1890),

the second son of William Farrant, of Ballamoar, Jurby, and Susannah Eleanora Curphey, of Ballakillingan, received his education at King William's College. On his father's death, in January, 1852, he was selected as a member of the House of Keys, at the early age of 21, being, as far as is known, the youngest member who ever sat in that House. But, notwithstanding his youth, his marked ability soon brought him to the front. Though one of the three members who voted against the measure dissolving the self-elected House of Keys, he allowed himself to be nominated for Ayre Sheading, at the first general election in 1867, when he was returned at the head of the poll. He was in the same position at the elections of 1875 and 1881, finally retiring, owing to failing health, in 1887, being then the oldest member of the House, having sat in it for 35 years, during the greater part of which period he had been one of its most prominent members. An excellent speaker, he was able to convey his meaning clearly and forcibly, and to season his, sometimes trenchant, utterances, with a keen and subtle wit. Though a strong opponent of many of the schemes, especially as regards harbour works, of Governor Loch, whom he thought wanted to expend more than the insular exchequer could afford, his opposition was always so courteous that it in no way interfered with the personal regard that the governor entertained for him. He was an active and enterprizing agriculturist, to whom the island owes much for the improved stock which he introduced, and a kind and generous friend to the poor, who, especially in the parish of Lezayre, of which he was captain, derived much benefit

---

* He became totally blind five years later.

from his efforts in aid of the voluntary system of Poor Relief. The Speaker of the House of Keys, in referring to his death, said : " I am sure we shall all agree and join in saying that he set up for himself a very high code of morality in public and private life, and he ever acted up to it. . . . In every way, socially and generally, his loss will be deeply felt."

JOHN SENHOUSE GOLDIE-TAUBMAN, Knight
(b. 1838, d. 1898),

the eldest son of John Taubman Goldie-Taubman, of the Nunnery, and Ellen, daughter of Humphrey Senhouse, of Netherhall, Cumberland, was educated at Eton, and, on leaving that school in 1856, he travelled extensively. In 1859, he was selected as a member of the self-elected House of Keys, and, in 1867, on being elected as one of the representatives of Douglas in the new popularly elected House, he was chosen as speaker. He continued both to represent Douglas and to hold the office of speaker till his death. It may be mentioned as remarkable that his father, grandfather, and great-grandfather were also speakers of the House of Keys. As a member of the House, he was thoroughly conscientious and straightforward, so that his constituents were fully justified in the confidence they continued to place in him. As speaker, it is difficult to write highly enough of him. Dignified in appearance and bearing, calm, impressive, and imperturbable in manner, always tactful, genial, and good-tempered, he was regarded with affection as well as respect. Well versed in the constitutional history of the island, and in the powers, prerogatives, and privileges of the House, as well as in parliamentary precedent and rules, he was thoroughly judicial, fair, and impartial. No wonder, then, that his decisions on points of order and procedure were never disputed. The qualities already referred to, combined with a remarkable capacity for rapidly and completely grasping details, rendered his services as administrator on several boards of the Tynwald Court, especially on the Asylums Board, of which he was chairman, most valuable. He was an admirable magistrate, and, as director of public companies, he also did much for his native island. The success of the Isle of Man Railway Company in particular, of which he was for many years chairman, is largely due to him. Manx Freemasonry, too, found a good friend in him, so that when, in 1886, he became the first Right Worshipful Grand Master of the newly-formed Provincial Grand Lodge of Freemasons, his appointment gave general satisfaction.

Though, as we have seen, he devoted a large portion of his life's work—and most valuable work it was—to this island, it was not till towards its close that this fact received any public recognition. In 1890, his fellow-legislators presented him with a carved oak chair as a mark of their respect for him, and, in 1897, he received the honour of knighthood.

CHAPTER IV.

Law and Medicine.

Law.

JOHN PARR (b. 1651, d. 1713),

the fourth son of Robert Parr, Rector of Ballaugh, began the study of law under Richard Tyldesley, comptroller and clerk of the rolls, in 1671. In 1679, he became a member of the House of Keys, and, in 1687, he was appointed episcopal registrar. His well-known abstract of Manx Customary Law appeared in 1690. In his dedication of it to Governor Heywood, he modestly states it to be " not a succinct module of the whole Laws and Constitution of this Isle, but as a tithe thereof, giving only an abridgment or compendium of such Laws and Acts as are of use." Others have, however, estimated the author and his work much more highly. Thus, James Clarke, attorney-general, writes of him, in 1817, as " that great and learned man Deemster PARR . . . whose work . . . abounds with great learning, and cannot be too closely studied by the members of the bar," and he remarks that its " style is clear and comprehensive," and that it " places the author very high as a writer on Jurisprudence." Sir James Gell pronounces it to be " the standard authority as to the common law." Unfortunately, it has never been printed. JOHN PARR was appointed deemster in 1693, an office which he held, with credit to himself and to the great advantage of his country, till his death. It is probable that his services were in request for the drafting of the Act of Settlement, but of this there is no proof. During his later years he lived at Parville, in Arbory, which was named after him.

JOHN COSNAHAN (b. 1754, d. 1819),

son of Hugh Cosnahan and Eleanor Finch,* was an advocate,
a member of the House of Keys, and High-Bailiff of Douglas.
In 1808, he was appointed water-bailiff, with a seat in the
Council.   In 1790, he, together with Norris Moore, afterwards
deemster, was sent to London by the Keys to oppose a Bill to
give the Duke of Atholl more compensation for the loss of
his sovereignty.   The petition, which they laid before
the House of Commons, closed with a prayer that they might
be heard by counsel at the bar of the House.   This was agreed
to, and JOHN COSNAHAN, who was a man of brilliant mind,
ready wit, and powerful elocution, acted as the counsel in
question.   His address was greatly applauded, and it con-
siderably affected the desired end, namely the withdrawal of
the Bill.   Not till a few months before his death did he receive
the appointment of deemster, an office which he would probably
have attained to at a much earlier date, but for the opposition
of the duke, who disliked him on account of his keen advocacy
for the popular side.

JOHN FRISSEL CRELLIN (b. 1764, d. 1816),

the only son of the Rev. John Crellin, Rector of Ballaugh and
vicar-general,† and Margaret, second daughter of John Frissel,
attorney-general, was a member of the House of Keys in 1793,
and High-Bailiff of Ramsey till 1796, when he was appointed
northern deemster.   In 1814, he became southern deemster
and began to build Beach House, Castletown, with the intention
of living there, but he died before its completion.   An
accomplished lawyer and an excellent judge, he also did good
service to his country as Commander of the Northern Battalion
of the Manx Volunteers.   At the disbanding of this corps after
the battle of Waterloo, his widow was presented with its colours
by the Duke of Atholl.   They are still to be seen at Orrysdale
in very good condition.   According to his obituary notice he
"held the situation of deemster . . . with the strictest regard
to justice, truth, and impartiality," and he was "regretted by
the Bar for his gentlemanly conduct and temperate language
and by the public for his patience, affability, and justice."†   He
was one of the wittiest of men, and many good stories of his
keen humour are still extant.

---

* Finch Road was named after an ancestor of hers.   His father, an M.H.K.,
was one of the commissioners appointed to try and modify the fiscal
arrangements made at the Revestment.
† *Manx Advertiser.*

THOMAS STOWELL (b. 1764, d. 1821),

was the second son of Thomas Stowell and Ann Brown.* In 1792, he published an alphabetical arrangement of "The Statutes and Ordinances of the Isle of Man," pointing out, in a brief preface, that "It may be deemed a matter of no small surprize that the Statute Laws, or Acts of Tynwald of the Isle of Man (except a few lately passed), have never heretofore been printed and published." In 1796, he was sworn in as acting attorney-general and, in 1804, he became clerk of the rolls. He built "Hampton Court" in the parish of Braddan and lived there. He was considered a very able lawyer. The *Manks Advertiser*, in an obituary notice of him, says: "The character of THOMAS STOWELL, late clerk of the rolls, is above enconium; and all attempts to emblazon his qualities are superfluous. To say that he was an honour and an ornament to his country, we give him not half his praise. He was not only a great but a good man. The people of this island did equal homage to his morals, as to his ability; and even his enemies (if he had any) could not deny him the character of an upright man and sincere Christian. At the same time that he embellished his public situations with more than ordinary talent, he threw a lustre on the sphere of private life by the practice of every Christian virtue."

JOHN McHUTCHIN (b. 1788, d. 1847),

son of Gilbert McHutchin, a Scotsman, and Miss Dawson, a Manxwoman, was born in Peel. He studied law with Thomas Stowell, clerk of the rolls, and his ability was so marked and his progress so rapid that Lieutenant-Governor Smelt appointed him his secretary before he had finished his student's career. His next appointment was that of High-Bailiff of Douglas, being made deemster in 1821, and clerk of the rolls in the following year. In 1844, he was a member of a commission which reported that Castle Rushen was not suitable for a jail. Though a very able lawyer, perhaps his greatest claim to distinction is the fact that during the long and bitter dispute between the Duke of Atholl and the Keys, he was the only person who held the entire confidence of both sides, so that his services as a mediator were very valuable.†

---

* Aunt of the Rev R. Brown (see p. 34).
† Information from Sir James Gell. We may note that it was in his office that Sir James received the early training which so greatly contributed to his profound knowledge of Manx law.

MARK HILDESLEY QUAYLE (b. 1804, d. 1879),

of Bridge House, Castletown, and Crogga, Santon, was the only
son of his father, of the same name, who was clerk of the rolls
from 1797 to 1804, his great-grandfather and grandfather, both
named John, having held the same office from 1736 to 1755, and
from 1755 to 1797, respectively.   Admitted to the Manx Bar
in 1825, he rapidly took a front rank in his profession.   From
1842 to 1847 he was a member of the House of Keys, proceeding
from thence to the Council as clerk of the rolls.   His appointment as magistrate dates from 1846, and, in 1873, he was elected
chairman of the insular magistrates.   He held Her Majesty's
Commission as deputy-governor on two occasions, i.e., in 1860,
on the resignation of Governor Hope, and, in 1863, on the death
of Governor Piggot.   He was distinguished, not only as a lawyer
and judge, but as an antiquarian and philanthropist.   It was
his scheme of voluntary poor relief for Castletown, which was
afterwards adopted by the other towns, that remained in opera-
tion for many years.   We extract the following remarks from his
obituary notice in the "Isle of Man Times":—"The island has
lost an able, painstaking, and upright judge, who had deservedly
won the respect and esteem of every class in the community.
Not only, however, as a judge will his name be honoured and
revered in the memory of Manxmen.   He was, besides, a kind
and genial man, one of Nature's gentlemen, whose grace and
urbanity of manner charmed every one who approached him
either on his own or on public business, while, as a politician
and member of the Council, his patriotism and independence
of all mere official influences were conspicuous, the votes he
gave on all public subjects discussed in Tynwald being the honest
and conscientious products of his own convictions."

JOHN CLOWES STEPHEN (b. 1806, d. 1880),

eldest son of the Rev. Thomas Stephen, vicar-general (see Ch. V.)
and Charlotte, daughter of the Rev. Daniel Gelling, Rector of
Ballaugh, was called to the Manx Bar in 1828, and, in 1855, he
was appointed northern deemster. He was a humorist as well as
a lawyer.   As a specimen of his witty sayings, we may quote
the following allusion to the leaders of his Bar : " . . . . is too
old and people are driven to . . . . by sheer necessity, but he
alas, like necessity, knows no law."   Deemster Drinkwater
speaking of him just after his death, said : " He was my colleague
for upwards of 25 years and one to whose honest advice I could
always refer in cases of difficulty. . . . The public have lost in
him a most honest and independent judge.   Every suitor who
went into his court knew that they would get an unbiassed
decision."   He was a true lover of his country, a wise counsellor

and legislator, and an able and upright judge. Many of his judgments will be remembered for their clearness and literary finish.

THOMAS CLUCAS (b. 1810, d. 1876),

a native of the Isle of Man, was, in 1856, appointed to the office of Jurat of Guernsey, i.e., a Judge of the Supreme Tribunal of that island, and, a little later in the same year, he was also appointed Judge of Alderney, in which island he resided.

RICHARD SHERWOOD (b. 1828, d. 1883),

born in Douglas, was articled, about 1843, to Samuel Harris, who was afterwards high-bailiff and vicar-general. As Mr. Harris, in addition to his practice, held the office of tithe agent, RICHARD SHERWOOD gained a practical knowledge of Manx properties which was afterwards exceedingly useful to him. After leaving Harris's office, he studied for a time with Deemster Stephen, but he then abandoned the law and took up farming. Though he became a successful farmer, the life soon palled upon him, and he therefore resumed his legal studies, seeking this time the office of L. W. Adamson, where he completed his articles. He was called to the Bar in 1857, and commenced practice in Ramsey. He soon, however, found there was not sufficient scope for his energy and ability at the north of the island and so he removed to Douglas, where he entered into partnership with A. N. Laughton, the present High-Bailiff of Peel. They speedily acquired an extensive practice, but SHERWOOD, being again, as it would seem, seized with a desire for change, went to Queensland. On the voyage out, he wrote his well-known treatise upon Manx Real Property, which under the title of " Manx Law Tenures," was published in 1899. It is universally accepted as the most authoritative exposition upon the subject. On arrival in Queensland, he found that there were difficulties in the way of his admission to the Colonial Bar, unless he served for a time in the Colony, and so he returned to the Isle of Man where he was at once retained, with A. W. Adams, in the important case of James Brown *versus* the House of Keys. He contested the constituency of Douglas, in the first election to the House of Keys, in 1867, but did not succeed in being elected. He was, however, returned for Glenfaba in 1869 and continued to represent that constituency till he was appointed deemster, in April, 1883. He soon became the acknowledged leader of the House, being, notwithstanding his extensive practice, indefatigable in his legislative labours. He was the introducer of female suffrage, and to him the Ballot Act, and various other legislative improvements, are mainly due.

As a lawyer he had few equals, and no superiors, at the Manx
Bar.   Between 1865 and 1883, he appeared in every important
suit, and gained some great successes, notably in three cases
against the Crown, all of which he won.   The most remarkable
of these was the Ballaharra Clay Case, in which he firmly established the right of Manx customary freeholders to the sand and
clay underlying their farms.   This had been disputed by the
Crown.   As an individual, he was generous and philanthropic,
being ever ready to assist the poor and needy, and he was remarkable for an indomitable will and iron determination, which
enabled him to overcome difficulties which would have daunted
any less able and persevering man.   His influence over the
Manx people and their confidence in him were extraordinary.
His sad death by his own hand, a few months after his elevation
to the Bench, was doubtless the result of temporary aberration,
induced by sleeplessness and mental depression.   (From the
" Isle of Man Times.")

ALURED DUMBELL, Knight (b. 1835, d. 1900),

second son of G. W. Dumbell (banker, member of the Bar and
of the House of Keys), and Miss Gibson, was educated at a
private school in Douglas. He then entered the firm of Harris
and Adams as a law student, afterwards serving a short period
of his articles with Mr James Spittall.   Admitted to the Bar
in 1858, he soon acquired a large and important practice at the
north of the island.   His appointments were — High-Bailiff of
Ramsey in 1873, second deemster in 1880, and clerk of the rolls
in 1883.   He was knighted in 1899, and, a short time before
his death, he acted as deputy-governor.   " There is no doubt,"
says " The Isle of Man Times," " That Sir Alured Dumbell was
a man of great ability, but the success which he achieved in the
legal profession was not so much due to the possession of any
very exceptional degree of forensic acumen, but to his ready
wit, his practical business-like instincts, and his uncommon
powers of penetration, combined with an integrity of purpose
that was never absent from anything in his public career."   In
the Legislature, though his work was largely confined to
criticism of others, he was, nevertheless, not only an influential,
but a very useful member, and, on its committees, in particular,
he did good service.   Apart from his legal and legislative work,
his chief interest was in agriculture, of which he had considerable
knowledge.   He was a prominent member of the insular
Agricultural Society, and, some years ago, took the leading part
in settling a dispute which arose between its northern and
southern members.   He is certainly one of the ablest men this
island has produced during the present century.

We may mention that a descendant, in the fifth
generation, of "Illiam Dhone's" grandson, William, who went
to Ireland, became a distinguished judge. This was the
RIGHT HONOURABLE JONATHAN WHITBY CHRISTIAN, P.C., who
was first Lord Justice of Appeal in Ireland. He lived at
Ravenswell, Bray, Co. Dublin,, and Merrion Square, Dublin.

Medicine.

SAMUEL CHRISTIAN NELSON (b. 1818, d. 1883),

son of the Rev. John Nelson, Rector of Bride, belonged to
an old Manx family which, for centuries, held landed property
in the parish of Rushen. In early life he was apprenticed to
his elder brother, Thomas, who, for many years, practised in
Douglas. He then studied in Dublin and London, taking the
diploma of the Royal College of Surgeons in 1845. For two
years after this he held the position of medical officer at
Chorlton-upon-Medlock, where he won golden opinions. From
thence he returned to the Isle of Man, and, after practising in
Castletown for a short time, he took up his residence in Douglas,
where he quickly gained and maintained the largest practice.
In 1862, he took his doctor's degree at St. Andrew's, and
in 1863 Govenor Loch appointed him "Physician to the
Household," a position which he held till his death. He was
for many years one of the surgeons of the Isle of Man Hospital,
and was medical officer to the Lunatic Asylum from its opening
until the appointment of a resident medical superintendent. He
was a noble and benevolent man, being especially distinguished
by the unpaid services he never grudged to the poor. His
sterling professional abilities and his thorough goodness made
him the object of love and respect among all classes.

CHARLES BLAND RADCLIFFE (b. 1822, d. 1889),

may fairly be claimed as a Manxman, as both his father and
mother were Manx, the former belonging to the well-known
family of Radcliffe, of Ballaradcliffe, in the parish of Andreas.
His father, Charles, a Wesleyan minister, happened to be
stationed at Brigg, in Lincolnshire, when Charles Bland, his
eldest son, was born.* The following account of him is taken
from the "Dictionary of National Biography."

---

* Two of his brothers were distinguished Wesleyan ministers and another
was an antiquarian.

Charles completed his education, begun at home, in the
Grammar School at Batley, near Leeds, and was subsequently
apprenticed to a general practitioner at Wortley. He finished his
medical training in Leeds, Paris, and London. In Paris he studied
under Claude Bernard. He graduated M.B. at the London
University in 1845, when he is said to have been the first student
from a provincial medical school who succeeded in obtaining a gold
medal. He graduated M.D. in 1851. He became a licentiate of the
Royal College of Physicians of London in 1848, and was elected a
Fellow in 1858. He filled the office of Gulstonian lecturer in 1860,
and of Croonian lecturer in 1873. He subsequently became a
councillor of the College of Physicians, and in 1875-6 he acted as
censor.

In 1853 he was appointed an assistant physician to the Westminster Hospital, where he succeeded to the office of full physician
in 1857, and he was elected to the consulting staff in 1873. He
lectured upon botany and *materia medica* in the medical school
attached to the hospital. In 1863 he was appointed physician to
the National Hospital for the Paralysed and Epileptic in Queen
Square, in succession to Dr Brown-Séquard, and it was in connection with this institution, and the diseases of the nervous
system which it was founded to relieve, that Radcliffe's name was
best known. He died very suddenly, and was buried in Highgate
Cemetery.

Charles Radcliffe, whose personal appearance was extremely
striking was a type of all that is best in a physician of the old
school, modified by a modern scientific training. His mind was
essentially metaphysical with a strong bias towards novel theories.
He was one of the earliest investigators in this country of the
electrical physiology of muscle and nerve, but he was too much
occupied with abstract theories to do much by way of experiment.
He was, as Dr Burdon-Sanderson points out, essentially a vitalist,
but with this difference—that in his doctrine electricity took the
place of the vital principle. Theological speculation also interested
him, and he read with almost equal zest the works of Plato,
Aquinas, and Maurice.

JOHN NETTEN RADCLIFFE (b. 1826, d. 1884),

epidemiologist, son of Charles Radcliffe, and younger brother of
Dr. Charles Bland Radcliffe, was born in Yorkshire, in 1826,
and received his early medical training at the Leeds School of
Medicine. Shortly after obtaining his diploma, he went to the
Crimea, as a surgeon attached to the head quarters of Omar
Pasha, and remained there till the close of the war. He re-
ceived for his services the order of the Medjidie, as well as the
Turkish and English medals, with a clasp for Sebastopol. On
returning home, he became medical superintendent of the
Hospital for the Paralysed and Epileptic in Queen's Square,
London.

In 1865, he was selected to prepare a special report on the
appearance of cholera abroad, and, in 1866, he was busily engaged in investigating the outbreak in East London, which he
traced to the infected supply of the East London Water Com-

pany. This report appeared as a Blue Book in 1867, and gained RADCLIFFE a wide reputation. He was elected a member of the Epidemiological Society in 1850, was its honorary secretary 1862-71, and president 1875-7. In 1869, he was appointed to the second of the two public health inspectorships then created by the Privy Council, and, on the formation of the local government board in 1871, he was made assistant medical officer. Owing to ill-health, he resigned this post in 1883.

Not only an expert in the distribution of oriental diseases, RADCLIFFE was an authority on all questions pertaining to public health. Of remarkably simple and straightforward nature, he was a most cautious worker, but where rapidity was essential, he showed himself equal to the situation.* (Dictionary of National Biography.)

Ibᴇrbalists, "ᖴairᴦ" Doctors, and Bonesetters.

A few Manxmen and Manxwomen have attained considerable skill in the practice of surgery and in the use of herbal remedies, these being occasionally accompanied by "charms," both for curing diseases and for counteracting the spells of fairies, sorcerers, and witches. The powers thus possesed were supposed to be hereditary, and were handed down in the same family for generations, it being said to be necessary, in order to preserve them intact, to pass them on from a man to a woman, and then, in the next generation, from a woman to a man, and so on. The best known family of herbalists and fairy doctors is that of TEARE, of Ballawhane, in Andreas, and, of bone-setters, that of CLUCAS, of the Strang, in Braddan. The most famous of the TEARE family is described by Train, in his "History of the Isle of Man," as follows :—

The seer is a little man, far advanced into the vale of life; in appearance he was healthy and active; he wore a low-crown slouched hat, evidently too large for his head, with a broad brim; his coat, of an old-fashioned make, with his vest and breeches, were all of *loaghtyn* wool, which had never undergone any process of dyeing; his shoes, also, were of a colour not to be distinguished from his stockings, which were likewise of *loaghtyn* wool.† He is said to have been the most powerful of all these practitioners, and, when their prescriptions had failed in producing the desired effect, he was applied to. The messenger that was despatched to him on

---

* The same preliminary remarks apply equally in this case as in that of C. B. Radcliffe.
† Vol. II., pp. 161-2.

such occasions was neither to eat nor to drink by the way, nor even to tell any person his mission. The recovery was supposed to be perceptible from the time the case was stated to him.

Marvellous tales are told about the cures performed by him.*

The first of the CLUCASES of whom we hear anything was WILLIAM (b. 1782, d. 1832). An obituary notice of him declares that his "services as a bone setter, &c., which he has practised for so many years with great success, will long be remembered by the inhabitants of this island." The same profession was carried on by his son and grandson. It is remarkable that women as well as men seem to have attained distinction as bone setters. One of these, MRS. RADCLIFFE, of Ballacrebbin, Andreas, (b. 1771, d. 1862), was spoken of as "the celebrated bone-setter of the north," who was "deeply regretted by the poor, to whom she rendered innumerable services." Another was widow MYLECRAINE, of Douglas (b. 1781, d. 1858).

---

* Folklore of the Isle of Man, p. 79.

CHAPTER V.

𝔏iterature.

With the exception of "Tom Brown,"* Manxmen have not attained any eminence in literature ; some of those whose names follow being, at the most, of only secondary rank in this respect, while others may be described as merely having literary tastes.

The Revs. PHILIP MOORE, JAMES WILKS, HUGH STOWELL, JOHN EDWARD HARRISON, and ROBERT BROWN, whose biographies have been given in Chapter I., must be considered as being among the leading names under this category also.

PETER JOHN HEYWOOD (b. 1739, d. 1790),

great-grandson of Governor Robert Heywood, was the last of his family who held the Nunnery estate, which he sold to John Taubman, of the Bowling Green, Castletown. Though he was deemster, he is chiefly worthy of remembrance as being one of the few Manxmen, in the 18th century, who took any interest in the literature of his native country. For it is to him that we owe the preservation of *Fin as Oshin*, probably the oldest Manx ballad in existence.† He sent a copy of it to Professor Thorkelin, of Copenhagen, by whom it was deposited in the British Museum. "I must own," he writes, "I was much surprised and delighted with the discovery and similarity of the subject to some of Ossian's poems."

---

* We do not refer to living men.
† *The Manx Note Book*, Vol. II., pp. 80-2.

JOHN KELLY (b. 1750, d. 1809),

only son of William Kelly, farmer and cooper, and Alice Kewley, was born on his father's property of Algare, in Baldwin. He received his early education under the Rev. Philip Moore, of whom, since he displayed a remarkable aptitude for learning generally and especially for his native tongue, he was a favourite pupil. He was thus marked out as a suitable person for taking an important part in the work of translating the Holy Scriptures into Manx. It would appear that he entered, at the age of sixteen, in collaboration with the Rev. Philip Moore, on the arduous work of revising, correcting, and preparing the second volume of the Old Testament (from Job to the end, including part of the Apocrypha) for the press. KELLY also transcribed the third volume, containing the New Testament, and corrected the proofs for the press of the whole of the Old Testament. When making a voyage from Douglas to Whitehaven for this purpose, with the MS. of the Bible from Deuteronomy to Job, he was shipwrecked, but managed to save the MS. by holding it above water for five hours, till he was rescued from the sinking ship. At this time also he began "to collect and form the rules"* of a Manx Grammar, being, as he says, without any printed or written documents to help him, except the Gospel of St. Matthew which was published by Bishop Wilson in 1748. This grammar was finished in 1780, but was not published till 1804.† Judged by the critical standard of the present day, it is wanting in many particulars, but it is, nevertheless, a praiseworthy and useful publication. To return to the Bible—the translation of the Old Testament was practically complete in 1772, and Kelly, having received a well-earned gratuity from the S.P.C.K. for his work, was thereby enabled to fulfil his long wished-for scheme of entering a University; and so, in October of that year, we find him at St. John's College, Cambridge. Of his University career we know nothing, except that he took his B.A. degree in 1775. In 1776, he was ordained deacon and appointed to the charge of the episcopal church in the town of Ayre. In 1779, he became tutor to the Marquis of Huntley, afterwards the last Duke of Gordon. During the period between 1779 and 1790, he accomplished the greater part of his *magnum opus*, the Triglot Dictionary of the Gaelic languages of Scotland, Ireland, and Man, with an English translation. The printing of this book was begun in 1807, and had proceeded as far as the letter *L*, when a fire broke out and destroyed the whole impression except one or two copies.‡ The

* Preface to MS. of grammar.
† It was re-published by the *Manx Society* in 1869.
‡ One of these, with the remainder of the MS., is in the possession of the *Manx Society*.

Manx-English part of it was reprinted, with emendations* and with an English-Manx part,† by the *Manx Society*, in 1866. The same criticism may be applied to this publication as to the grammar. In 1791, JOHN KELLY was appointed Vicar of Ardleigh, near Colchester. He took his LL.D. degree at Cambridge in 1799, and became Rector of Copford, near Ardleigh, in 1800, being, at the same time, placed on the Commission of the Peace for the county of Essex. Of Dr. KELLY's later years but little is known. He appears to have been a man of some mark in Essex and to have been generally respected as an earnest and liberal-minded divine. He married, in 1784, Louisa, eldest daughter of Peter Dollond, and granddaughter of the famous John Dollond, F.R.S., the inventor of the achromatic telescope, by whom he had an only son, Gordon William, afterwards Recorder of Colchester. It was Gordon William Kelly who gave the " Manx Prize " which is still competed for at King William's College.

HESTER (NESSY) HEYWOOD (b. 1768, d. 1793),

was a daughter of Deemster Peter Heywood and Elizabeth Spedding, and sister of Captain Peter Heywood. Her literary compositions both in prose and verse are all connected with the terrible period of her brother's trial for his alleged share in the mutiny of the " Bounty " (see Chapter VII.). The news of the result of this trial did not reach the island till a week after the sentence of the court, when Nessy at once hastened to England to endeavour to secure a reprieve. The following charming letter, which was written just before her brother's arrival in England, will serve as a specimen of her style :—

Fervent Assurance of Love and Confidence.

Isle of Man, June 2nd, 1792.

In a situation of mind only rendered supportable by the long and painful state of misery and suspense we have suffered on his account, how shall I address my dear fondly beloved brother? How describe the anguish we have felt at the idea of this long and painful separation, rendered still more distressing by the terrible circumstances attending it? Oh ! my ever dearest boy, when I look back to that dreadful moment which brought us the fatal intelligence that you had remained in the Bounty after Mr Bligh had quitted her, and were looked upon by him as a mutineer ! When I contrast that day of horror with my present hopes of again beholding you, such as my most sanguine wishes could expect, I know not which is the most predominant sensation, pity, compassion, and terror for your sufferings, or joy and satisfaction at the prospect of their being so near a termination, and of once more embracing the dearest object

---

* These were by the Revs. Hugh Stowell, Howard, and Fitzsimmons in 1811, and by the Rev. W. Gill in 1869.
† By Messrs J. Clarke and I. Moseley.

of our affections. I will not ask you, my beloved brother, whether
you are innocent of the dreadful crime of mutiny; if the transactions of that day were as Mr Bligh has represented them, such is
my conviction of your worth and honour, that I will, without
hesitation, stake my life on your innocence. If, on the contrary,
you were concerned in such a conspiracy against your commander,
I shall be as firmly persuaded that his conduct was the occasion of it;
but alas! could any occasion justify so atrocious an attempt to destroy
a number of our fellow-creatures? No, my ever dearest brother,
nothing but conviction from your own mouth can possibly persuade
me that you would commit an action in the smallest degree incon-
sistent with honour and duty; and the circumstance of your having
swam off to the Pandora, on her arrival at Otaheite (which filled us
with joy to which no words can do justice) is sufficient to convince
all who know you, that you certainly stayed behind either by force,
or from views of preservation

How strange does it seem to me that I am now engaged in the
delightful task of writing to you! Alas! my beloved brother, two
years ago I never expected again to enjoy such a felicity; and even
yet I am in the most painful uncertainty whether you
are alive. Gracious God! grant that we may be at length
blessed by your return; but alas! the Pandora's people have
been long expected, and are not even yet arrived. Should
any accident have happened, after all the miseries you
have already suffered, the poor gleam of hope with
which we have been lately indulged, will render our situation ten
times more insupportable than if time inured us to your loss. I
send this to the care of Mr Hayward of Hackney, father to the
young gentleman you so often mention in your letters while you
were on board the Bounty, and who went out as third lieutenant of
the Pandora, a circumstance which gave us infinite satisfaction, as
you would, on entering the Pandora, meet your old friend. On
discovering Mr. Hayward's residence, I wrote to him, as I hoped he
could give me some information respecting the time of your arrival,
and, in return, he sent me a most friendly letter, and has promised
this shall be given to you when you reach England, as I well know
how great must be your anxiety to hear of us, and how much
satisfaction it will give you to have a letter immediately on your
return. Let me conjure you, my dearest Peter, to write to us the
very first moment. Do not lose a post; 'tis of no consequence how
short your letter may be, if it only informs us you are well. I need
not tell you that you are the first and dearest object of our
affections; think, then, my adored boy, of the anxiety we must feel
on your account; for my own part, I can know no real happiness
or joy independent of you, and if any misfortune should now
deprive us of you, my hopes of felicity are fled for ever.

We are at present making all possible interest with every friend
and connection we have, to insure you a sufficient support and
protection at your approaching trial; for a trial you must
unavoidably undergo, in order to convince the world of that
innocence which those who know you will not for a moment doubt;
but alas! while circumstances are against you, the generality of
mankind will judge severely. Bligh's representations to the
Admiralty are, I am told, very unfavourable, and hitherto the tide
of public opinion has been in his favour. My mamma is at present
well, considering the distress she has suffered since you left us; for,

my dearest brother, we have experienced a complicated scene of misery from a variety of causes ; which, however, when compared with the sorrow we felt on your account, was trifling and insignificant ; that misfortune made all others light, and to see you once more returned and safely restored to us will be the sum of all earthly happiness.

Farewell, my most beloved brother ! God grant this may soon be put into your hands. Perhaps at this moment you are arrived in England, and I may soon have the dear delight of again beholding you. My mamma, brothers, and sisters join with me in every sentiment of love and tenderness. Write to us immediately, my ever-loved Peter, and may the Almighty preserve you until you bless with your presence your fondly affectionate family, and particularly your unalterable faithful friend and sister,

NESSY HEYWOOD.*

Her constitution sank under the violent emotions it had undergone at the time of her brother's trial, and she died at Hastings within a year of his liberation. A contemporary writer remarks that " if the tenderest love, the most generous self-devotion, and the liveliest sense of honour and virtue, be some of the noblest endowments of human nature, we shall not hesitate to class Nessy Heywood among eminent persons. She appeals for distinction neither to the understanding nor the fancy, but to the heart."†

JOHN STOWELL‡ (b. 1762, d. 1799),

the eldest son of Thomas Stowell and Ann Brown, an advocate and public notary, and on the staff of the "Manks Mercury and Briscoe's Douglas Advertiser," the first Manx newspaper,§ is chiefly known by his clever satirical poems. From two of them entitled "A Sallad for the Young Ladies and Gentlemen of Douglas, Raised by Tom the Gardener," and "The Retrospect," we will give some quotations, to show his style of writing. His other satires are : (1) "A Literary Quixote ; or, The Beauties of Townley Versified." In this he makes fun of the journal (chiefly concerned with the vagaries of Manx weather) of a valetudinarian Englishman who lived in the island for a short time at the end of the last century ; (2) "A Switch for Tom the Gardener ; or, The Sallad dressed and the Lamb roasted." Here the objects of his derision are the young ladies of Douglas.‖ He also wrote the following poems, which are not satirical :—" On the Death of the much-esteemed Mrs Callow ;" "On the Death of Miss M. Bacon ;" " An Elegiac Invocation of the Muses occasioned by the Death of

---

* This letter is extracted from " The British Letter Writers from the 18th Century to the Present Time" (lent by Mr J. J. Creer).
† Willimott.
‡ Thomas Stowell, C.R., was his brother.
§ It was first published in 1792.
‖ He also wrote a satire against the Earl of Lonsdale, but this is in no way connected with the Isle of Man.

D

the amiable Miss Nessy Heywood ;" and "An Address to the
Duchess of Atholl." All Stowell's poems were published anony-
mously in small pamphlets or broadsides which are now extremely
scarce. In the "Sallad" he eulogises the good old times "ere
Manxmen understood what noble was, and what plebeian blood,"
and he then proceeds to satirize the modern ways and fashions of
young ladies :

> The Packet's come, I'll lay my life upon it ;
> I know by Laura's strange new-fashioned bonnet.
> Her clothes are all exactly in the *ton* ;
> Could no one show her how to put them on ?
> Manks born, Manks bred, Manks made, Manks fed, Manks taught,
> She's Manks in everything but what she ought.
> Pray what is that ? In modesty and sense ;
> Virtues, alas ! too long departed hence.
> Daphne would fain disown from whence she sprung,
> Although the herring scales are on her tongue.

He then draws the following picture of the state of Douglas :

> O Luxury ! whom Eastern kings revere,
> Dost thou maintain a little empire here ?
> Could not whole kingdoms thy desires allay,
> But must poor simple Douglas be thy prey ?
> Ah ! see what desolation thou hast spread,
> Young Industry is sick and Virtue dead :
> While Pride and Pomp so absolute are grown,
> That friendless Modesty's kicked out of town.

He then diverges from his main subject with a reference to the
Duke of Atholl's well-known practice of employing "foreigners"
rather than Manxmen :

> Alas ! I see the case is but too plain,
> A Native here may seek for bread in vain.
> Had'st thou been Welsh, Scotch, Irish, French, or Dutch,
> The very name would recommend thee much.
> Yon swindler just arrived, not worth a groat,
> Gets credit here and wears a costly coat.

Fortunately all Manx men and women are not condemned by
him, as he writes :

> There still are virgins, lovely, fair, and good ;
> Some worthy youths. . . .

In the "Retrospect" he reviews the "memorable events of
Mona" in 1790. The chief of them was the introduction of a Bill
into the House of Commons on behalf of the Duke of Atholl to
enable him to get further compensation for the loss of his sovereign
rights :

> Alas ! what language or what poet's quill
> Can tell how Mona dreaded Atholl's *Bill* ?
> No timid dove so much the eagle feared,
> Nor partridge when the gunner's notes she heard.
> 'Twas confidently whispered by the wise,
> He fully meant to pick out Mona's eyes.

The debate in the House of Keys on the subject is satirized as follows :

> · · Senators are Senators though Manks,
> As well as Pitt and Fox with all their pranks.
>
> . . . . . .
>
> How that his country's precious rights were sold,
> He tore his wig,——he let his oxen go.——
> " O Yee !"* he cried, " what shall poor Mannin do !"
> Then posted on, ten times as mad as Paul,
> Nor stopt till he had reached the Council Hall ;
> Where in a gloomy sadly pompous state,
> The Great, the Grand, August Assembly sate.
> Our hero made his motion to the House,
> Thrice scratched his head,—the third time seized a l—se ;
> Nor smuggled him, as common people do,
> But held the culprit up to public view,
> And in the presence of the Twenty-four,
> Put him to death :—Could Cato have done more ?
> " Thus ev'ry tyrant should be serv'd," he said,
> " Who dares to trample on a Manksman's head."

He describes the result of the agitation :

> Now glares the town,—a frightful aspect wears,—
> A civil broil the peaceful neighbour fears :—
> Nor fears in vain,—so high the ferment rose—
> " To what ?—to shooting or to vulgar blows ?"
> Far worse—" What then ? to gibbets or to swords ?"
> More grievous far,—to FORMIDABLE WORDS."

And, finally, being evidently a strong partisan of the duke's, he concludes :

> And you, ye mimick patriots of the day,
> With love of country gilding love of sway ;—
> Trust me, your futile selfish schemes must fail,
> Strong is the truth and Atholl will prevail.

---

* God.

BASIL QUAYLE,

of the Creggans farm, near Castletown (b. 1765, d. 1816), a
younger brother of George Quayle (see Chap. VIII.) was an excellent,
and scientific, farmer. In 1794, he drew up a pamphlet* "for the
consideration of the Board of Agriculture and Internal Improvements" in London, in which he gave a "general view of the
agriculture of the Isle of Man, with observations on the means
of its improvement." In this, among other matters, he dwells on
the desirability of commuting the tithe for a money payment.
The pamphlet was not printed for sale, but was circulated among
Manx farmers, with a view to obtaining their suggestions† about
improvements.† When they had done so, the pamphlets were to
be forwarded to the Board of Agriculture.

THOMAS QUAYLE

wrote a book‡ with the same title as Basil Quayle's pamphlet,
which was published, in 1812, by the Board of Agriculture.
In this, after giving an account of the island, he describes
the state of the Manx landed estates, the buildings upon
them, the mode of their occupation, the live stock, &c. He
discusses the obstacles to the improvement of agriculture in the
island and the best methods of removing these obstacles. The
book is a valuable one, and contains evidence of a scientific knowledge of agriculture much above what was usual in his day. In
his "preface" he expresses his obligations, among others, to Mr.
Basil Quayle, "the former reporter of the board."

Among other Manxmen and Manxwomen who have dabbled in
literature may be mentioned THOMAS CHRISTIAN, Vicar of Marown
from 1750 to 1799, who translated selections from "Paradise
Lost" into Manx, which were published in a pamphlet in 1796,
and reprinted by the Manx Society in Vol. XX. of their
publications. It is generally considered a very good translation.
JOSEPH BRIDSON wrote, in 1760, a Manx poem entitled *Coontey
Ghiare Jeh Ellan Vannin*, "A Short Account of the Isle of Man,"
which is terribly dull and prosaic.§
    JAMES CRETNEY (b. 1767, d. 1851), translated Parnell's
"Hermit" and other poems into Manx. He was considered an
excellent Manx scholar.

---

* In 40 pages, *quarto.* It was published by the Board of Agriculture.
   † The letterpress was in *octavo* size for this purpose, so leaving a large margin
for the MSS. notes.
   ‡ "General View of the Agriculture of the Isle of Man, with observations on
the means of its Improvement. Drawn up for the consideration of the Board of
Agriculture and internal Improvements." (193 pp octavo.)
   § *Manx Ballads* (Moore), pp. 20-8.

THOMAS STEPHEN (b. *circa* 1770, d. 1841), Vicar of Patrick and vicar-general, was the author of a "Poetical Guide to the Isle of Man," published in 1832, also of a rhapsody in Manx entitled *O ! cre ta Gloyr ?** "Oh ! What is Glory ?" which is considered one of the best pieces of verse in the Manx language.

JOHN CANNELL, Vicar of Conchan from 1798 to 1810, wrote *Arrane y Skeddan*, "Song of the herring."† Among other Manx poets, not in a lower rank to those already mentioned, are LEWIN, generally known as "Fiddler Green," who wrote *Inneenyn Eirinee,* "Farmers' Daughters."‡ JOHN MOORE, the author of *Marrinys yn Tiger*, "The Voyage of the Tiger."§ QUAYLE VESSIE, *i.e.*, Quayle the son of Bessie, the author of the "Loss of the Herring Fleet,"‖ and WILLAM SAYLE, who wrote the temperance dialogue called *Illiam as Isabel*, "William and Isabel."

The only Manxwoman who wrote verse in her native tongue of whom there is any account, is WIDOW TEAR, the authoress of the lament, entitled *Illiam Walker as Robin Tear*, on her two sons thus named.** This dates from about 1740 ; of similar date are the carols written in Manx by the REV. HENRY ALLEN, Vicar of Maughold (see p. 45).

Among minor Manx writers of English verse at the end of the eighteenth century are ROBERT CALLISTER and MARGARET CRELLIN. The former lived in Liverpool, and published a volume of poems there in 1785. One of these is an invitation from him as captain of the north division of Manx archers in Liverpool to Captain Harrison of the south division. The fact that there were to be fifty men on each side shows that the number of Manxmen then residing in Liverpool must have been considerable. The proposed meeting place was at Bank Hall. The latter was a daughter of the Rev. John Crellin, Vicar of Michael from 1771 to 1799, and sister of Deemster Crellin. She composed a poem on the Herring Fishery, which was published by Feltham in his account of the Isle of Man in 1798.††

ARCHIBALD CREGEEN (b. 1774, d. 1841),

third son of William Cregeen and Mary Fairclough, was born at Colby, where his father practised the trade of cooper. From Archibald's infancy he spoke Manx, which was then more commonly spoken than English. Nothing is known of his early

---

* *Manx Ballads*, p. 195.
† *Ibid* p. 170.
‡ ,, p. 190.
§ ,, p. 158, and see Chap. VIII.
‖ ,, p. 150.
** ,, pp. xxviii. and 203.
†† *Manx Soc.*, Vol. VI., pp. 83-7.

education, but, from the fact of his having selected the trade
of marble mason, it is evident that he must have been able to
read, write, and spell English. During the term of his apprenticeship, he spent his leisure in studying the scanty literature in Manx,
which mainly consisted of the Bible and Prayer-book, and some
MS. carols and ballads, and he then began to critically examine
the structure and idiomatic characteristics of the Manx language.
After his marriage, in 1798, he built a cottage near his father's,
which he occupied all the rest of his life. In 1813, he was
appointed Coroner of Rushen Sheading. It must be remembered
that this office was then a more important one than it is now,
seeing that the coroners had at that time to hold inquests. In
1818, he began to prepare a vocabulary of the Manx language for
publication. No such work had as yet appeared, for Dr. Kelly's
Manx and English Dictionary, though in MS., was not published
till 1866. He had not access to this MS., nor is it much to be
regretted that this should have been the case, since, if he had
been able to avail himself of it, it is probable that much of the
originality by which his own work is marked would have been
wanting. He had, however, the Manx Grammar by the same
author, which was issued from the press in 1804, and he also
received much assistance from the Revs. Hugh Stowell, Thomas
Howard, John Nelson, and, more especially, John Harrison, then
Vicar of Jurby, with whom he stayed for three months for this
purpose. John Harrison was thoroughly conversant with the
language, and it seems probable that the preface of the dictionary
and a portion of the introduction to it were written by him. For
twenty years he worked slowly but sedulously at his book (which
was not published till 1838),* in the intervals of rest from his
more active employment. Considering his imperfect education,
it is a very praiseworthy piece of work and, in many respects,
superior to Kelly's dictionary. Its prominent features are the
indication of the radical initials of words and the number of Manx
proverbs to be found in its pages. Some of the introductory
remarks on the linguistic peculiarities of Manx have been
borrowed from Dr Kelly's grammar, but others, which are
original, denote an accurate knowledge of the idiomatic
characteristics of the language. CREGEEN was a man of middle
stature and heavily made. His forehead was broad, his eyes
dark-brown, and his eye-brows dark and bushy. He always wore
a low-crowned, broad-brimmed hat, like a quaker's. He spoke
but little and that very slowly, except when the conversation
related to topics connected with his native tongue or the manners
and customs of the Manx peasantry. "I reverence," says George
Borrow of Cregeen, "the very ground upon which that man

---

* The date, 1835, on the title page seems to be an error.

trod, because he was one of the greatest natural Celtic scholars who had ever lived." (An abstract of an account by the late J. M. Jeffcott.)

THOMAS CALLISTER

wrote, in 1815, a book which, according to his own very voluminous description contains " An accurate, interesting, and particularly entertaining description of that lucrative branch of business, the herrring fishery of the Isle of Man, which affords employment for more than three months every year to above five thousand poor people, to a number of coopers all the year round, and to a variety of other crafts periodically. Of the superior quality of the red herrings manufactured in Douglas, as that of the pickled herrings, in a comparative point of view with all such as are caught and cured elsewhere. Of the various curious modes of preparing these monarchs of the finny tribe, throughout the Island in their fresh state, for their immediate consumption, and also the several amusing ways of making use of pickled herrings. A particular and very pleasing account of the flourishing town of Douglas, which has been long considered the emporium of the island with regard to commerce ; comprising its present state, its commodious quay and harbour, its new streets, its ·many genteel houses built in the modern taste in many of the old streets, the several places of public worship, the grand new public library, the famous new charity school, the large new poor house, etc. Like-wise a list of the several packets and constant traders, and a correct abstract of the British Act of Parliament passed in July, 1814, repealing the old harbour dues of the Island and substituting new ones in lieu thereof, on the fishing boats and·on all British and foreign vessels not only entering its harbours, but even anchoring in its bays ; also the duties payable on every kind of merchandise imported into the Island. To all which is added a very curious, descriptive, entertaining, and picturesque view of the much admired seats and estates of the nobility and gentry in the vicinity of the town. Humbly inscribed to his Excellency the most noble John, Duke of Atholl, Governor-in-Chief and Captain-General of the Island." (All the details, of which the foregoing is the summary, are given in 30 pages *octavo !*)

GEORGE HORSELEY WOOD (b. 1794, d. 1874),

a son of General Wood, and grandson of John Wood, Governor of the Isle of Man from 1761 to 1777, was educated at the Cathedral College, Hereford, and went into the army, joining the 20th Regiment, then in the Peninsula. He afterwards went to India, and then, about the year 1818, to St. Helena, where his regiment guarded Napoleon till his death. It is evident from his poem relating to St. Helena—which he re-visited in 1826— and to the emperor's death that he regarded Napoleon with the greatest affection and veneration,* not unmixed with dread :—

> Oft have I gazed on this wondrous man,
> But aye with a strange emotion undefined,
> Akin to fearful dread and wonderment,
> As if oppress'd by some mysterious power.

In 1821, on the return of the regiment from St. Helena, he left the army and went to his native island.† He occupied the rest of his long life in writing poems, *critiques* on metaphysical subjects, mainly on the opinions of Bishop Berkeley, of whom he was a fervent admirer, and in the exercise of his considerable musical and elocutionary talents. Some of his poems were published in 1827, and a more complete edition, with the *critiques* referred to, was issued in 1853. Of the poems it will suffice to say that, though many of them are melodious, they are not sufficiently striking to stand out from many similar volumes of forgotten verse, and of the *critiques*, that they do not betoken the profound philosophy of which he believed himself the possessor. Lieut. Wood was, nevertheless, a genius, though an erratic one, and his wide knowledge was evident, though his fantastic and dogmatic opinions frequently caused him to be regarded with ridicule instead of respect. "With him," writes T. E. Brown, "to believe, or even to see intensely, a truth was to be possessed as if with some veritable demon of conviction, assertion, propagandism. By dint of force and a dialectic method sufficiently unscrupulous, though by him regarded as perfectly honest, by the wildest gesticulation, by paradox, by terror, he would reduce an opponent to silence."‡ Besides metaphysics, he had two other favourite pursuits—music and public reading. He had taken lessons on the contra-bass from Dragonetti, and this instrument, as well as the violin, he played very well. His reading was very remarkable, and never to be forgotten, owing to what Mr Brown calls "a trick of snorting," which had an indescribable effect. It is, in fact, quite impossible to adequately portray him to anyone who did not know him. (Partly from "Manx Recollections," by Katherine A. Forrest.)

---

* In 1852, he visited Napoleon III. at the Elyseé Palace, and presented him with an original portrait of his uncle, drawn by an artist at St. Helena as he lay in death. In return he received a beautiful diamond and emerald ornament.

† As there has been some doubt as to whether Lieutenant Wood was a Manx-man, let us remind our readers that in the introduction to his poems, and in the poems themselves he several times claims the Isle of Man as his birthplace, for instance, in a poem to "Mona : Land of the generous and free, blest isle of my nativity."

‡ In "Manx Recollections," by Katherine Forrest.

MRS. KERRUISH.

In 1832, a book was published* entitled "Christianity considered of as founded in the nature, reality, and necessity, or eternal fitness of things ; the original constitution of existing beings ; the actual and necessary correspondence of existing objects." Its author was "Mrs. Kerruish," who, writing from Castletown, makes the following statement in her preface :—

The author of the following pages, though conscious of their many defects, ventures to dedicate them, as the first efforts of a female pen, to true Christians of all denominations, trusting that when her views do not meet those of the divinely enlightened reader, they may yet be treated with that lenity, forbearance, and candid scriptural investigation, which is all that a Christian should desire ; and their defects may be overlooked in consideration of the object that pervades the whole, namely, the exaltation of the Redeemer, and the consequent glory of the redeemed.

The writer, who treats her subject at some length,† shows that she has studied the Bible and various writers on religious subjects with much zeal and care. She declares that it was not her design "to trace the progress of the divine life further than respects that grace, to the immediate enjoyment of which the believing soul is called at justification." Any one who reads her efforts will be more struck by her piety than by her clearness of expression. Diligent enquiries have failed to discover what Mrs. Kerruish's maiden name was, or where and when she was born or died.

JOHN QUIRK (b. 1800, d. 1885),

was probably the last remaining specimen of the kind of men who composed the Manx carols. With only the rudiments of education and but little knowledge beyond their immediate surroundings,—John Quirk, indeed, had only once been in Douglas, and that when he was eighteen, and only once in Peel, when not much older—they combined an intimate knowledge of the Bible with a vivid imagination and a tinge, at least, of the poetic faculty. John Quirk's carols, though he had a good knowledge of Manx, were almost entirely in English. He strayed occasionally, too, into secular poetry, having written an amusing account, in Manx, of the Port Erin breakwater and its untimely fate, and having composed the versified paraphrases of most of the Manx ballads which appeared in the two volumes of the *Manx Miscellanies*, published by the Manx Society. He lived in a lonely house at Carn-e-Greie in Glen Rushen, with a comparatively young wife and several young children. The writer had the pleasure of

---

* London. Hamilton, Adams & Co.. Paternoster Row.
† The book contains 518 pages, *crown octavo*.

visiting him in his extreme old age, and when he told him of his
love for all things Manx and of his desire to hear him read some of
his carols, his face at once lit up, as he took down his MSS. from
the "latt" and complied with the request. Generally speaking,
they were of much the same character as those published in the
Manx Carol Book ; but the following passage of one, in which the
blind leaders of the blind are compared to frogs, is so striking
and so interesting, as showing what the writer might have accomplished if greater educational advantages had been obtainable by
him, that we quote it :—

> Some said that frogs could sweetly sing,
> That they were music for a king,
> That every court in church and state
> Should of their melody partake.
> Vast multitudes, both high and low,
> Took this for granted to be so,
> And numerous thousands charmed to sleep,
> Pursued the frogs into the deep.
> Still thousands cried and followed on,
> That these to Paradise were gone.
> Through thick and thin, curraghs and bogs,
> They hailed the music of the frogs,
> And when their songs old-fashioned grew,
> The frogs proposéd something new.

ESTHER NELSON (b. *circa* 1805, d. *circa* 1845),

daughter of the Rev. John Nelson, Rector of Bride, wrote a book
of miscellaneous poems, published in 1839, entitled "Island
Minstrelsy," some of which illustrate the traditions and legends
of the Isle of Man. Her two best known poems are "The
Carrasdhoo Men," a legend connected with the parish of Jurby
and the Curragh, and "The Island Penitent," which is founded
on a tradition that the Calf of Man was, in the reign of Elizabeth,
occupied by a man who went there as a penance for having killed
a woman in a fit of jealousy.* The Rev. T. E. Brown writes
of her :—

We should not forget that true woman of genius. Hester Nelson.
Often I think of her, and her early doom ; and Bride seems to me a
shrine of splendid promise and aspirations unfulfilled, save in God.
  . . . My father thought very highly of her poems. Some he
thought worthy of Milton. And that was all breathed in and bred
from your Bride hills, and the long stretches of the Ayre.†

---

* It may be mentioned that Miss Elizabeth Cookson and Mrs. E. S. Craven
Green, who wrote poems about the Isle of Man, were not Manx by birth.
† "Letters of T. E. Brown." Vol. I., pp. 110-11.

PAUL BRIDSON (b. 1809, d. 1876),

of Virginia, in the parish of Braddan, entered the office of Messrs. Key & Matthews, solicitors, at Bolton, when he was 16 years old, but soon abandoned legal studies and came to reside in the island. He was distinguished by his great amiability of character and his intimate knowlege of the genealogies and histories of Manx families. For many years honorary secretary to the Isle of Man Hospital in Douglas, he did much for the welfare of that institution, in which he took a very great interest. He also served in the same capacity for the Manx Society for the Publication of National Documents, from its foundation in 1858 until his death. His only contribution to literature, which was published in a small pamphlet, was an account of a London hospital, where he spent some weeks in 1860.

BELLANNE STOWELL (b. 1814, d. 1889),

a daughter of William Stowell, and a sister of William Hendry Stowell (see p. 51), for many years conducted a school at Ballabeg in the parish of Arbory, together with her sister, and she afterwards had a school in Douglas. She was greatly loved and respected by her old pupils, and, indeed, by all who knew her. "Manxland," a novel, with an introductory sketch about Manx home missions,* and "Nellie Brennan," a biography of a pious Irishwoman, who devoted herself to nursing the sick at the time of the cholera in Douglas, in 1832, were written by her.

HUGH SHIMMIN (b. 1820, d. 1879),

was born in Castletown, and went, when a child, with his parents, to Liverpool, where they apprenticed him to a stationer and book-binder. When he arrived at early manhood, an excellent opportunity arose of buying this bookbinding business, but, since he had not saved any money, he, to his great mortification, could not do so. On telling this to his wife, he was amazed to find that she had saved, without his knowledge, quite enough money to buy the business. He then bought it, and, though his habits were fitful, he never failed to prosper, being both skilful and hardworking. Meanwhile, he developed a considerable literary talent, which was exhibited in such writings as "Rambles in the Lake District," contributed under the pseudonym of "Harry Hardnot ;" also in some articles called "Liverpool Life." These last made a great sensation, and led to some reforms. Eventually, with some three or four others, he founded the "Porcupine," and, while his colleagues attended to the amusing side of the paper, he developed it into a unique social power which he used with tremendous effect

---

* Chiefly relating to the Isle of Man Diocesan Association, founded in 1839 It was published in 1863.

in revolutionizing the condition of Liverpool. "I never," writes
Sir Edward Russell, referring to him and a few friends of his,
"knew a small combination of men who did such great things."
Shimmin was famed for humorous mystifications.* One of his
oddest traits was that he never objected to make himself out as
bad as he could possibly be ; and he enjoyed the impression made
upon others by this, as much as anyone else would have enjoyed
producing a good impression. Another trait was a marvellous
power of telling incredible tales ; and in this he had extraordinary
luck, for it frequently happened, when he had told something
which everyone assumed to be a fiction, that something transpired
to show that that particular statement was literally true. Then
he turned on the assembled company and made the most of his
triumph, his inference from it being that he obviously ought never
to be doubted again, whatever he said. A humorous, but scarcely
a witty, man, he had a keen enjoyment of wit in others. His
moral courage was very great. As a proof of this we may mention
his exposure of the ship-scuttling practices of a large firm of ship-
owners. To him, more than to any other single person, may be
attributed the sanitary reforms in Liverpool, and the improvement
in the treatment of the neglected children in that city. He
constantly urged the necessity of supporting the Children's
Infirmary and the Seamen's Orphan Institution in the pages of the
"Porcupine ;" and in the inauguration and management of this
last great work he took a very earnest and conspicuous share.

(Information from Sir Edward Russell and Captain Edward
Stubbs, R.N., Secretary of the Liverpool Seamen's Orphan
Institution).

THOMAS EDWARD BROWN (b. 1830, d. 1897),

the third son of the Rev. Robert Brown (see p. 34) and Dorothy
Thompson, and younger brother of Hugh Stowell Brown (see
p. 53) was born in New Bond Street, Douglas.† He received his

---

* An excellent instance of this is given by Sir Edward Russell in his interesting book, "That Reminds Me."
† As it has been frequently stated that "Tom Brown" was Manx by birth only,
we append a note on his family. Mrs Williamson, his sister, writes: "My
father (the Rev. R. Brown) was certainly Manx, and both his parents were born
in the Island. His father (T. E. B.'s grandfather), Captain Robert Brown,
married Jane Drumgold, who belonged to a family which originally came from
the North of Ireland, but had been for a long time settled in Douglas. It was
from them that Drumgold Street took its name. Captain R. Brown's mother is
said to have been a Stowell of Ballastole, Maughold, and his sister, Ann,
married Thomas Stowell of Ballastole, and was mother of the Rev. Hugh
Stowell, Thomas Stowell, c.r., John Stowell, and Joseph Stowell." . . . .
T. E. Brown himself. in writing about his father in the *Ramsey Church
Magazine*, says: "The name (Brown) is not Manx, but the family belonged to
an old Manx stock, the Cosnahans. A cousin of Mr. Brown's, Lieutenant
Cosnahan, took part in the engagement between the Shannon and Chesapeake :
another cousin, Major Bacon, of Seafield, was at the Battle of Waterloo."

early education partly from the parish schoolmaster of Braddan, but, as he himself says, mainly from his father. To him, no doubt, he owed much of his marvellous instinct for style. For education of another kind, he, many years afterwards, owned his indebtedness to a humbler source, his Scottish servant, "Old John."

> You were not of our kin nor of our race,
> Old John : nor of our church, nor of our speech :
> Yet what of strength, or truth, or tender grace
> I owe, 'twas you that taught me—born to teach
> All nobleness. . . . .

Doubtless, too, it was mainly at this time that he stored his receptive and retentive memory with many of the quaint stories depicting the characteristics of his fellow-countrymen which he afterwards reproduced so inimitably in his poems. When he was fifteen he went to King William's College, then under the head-mastership of Dr. Dixon, a deeply religious and earnest-minded man of the evangelical school of thought. There he greatly distinguished himself. In 1847, he won the second prize for a poem,* and, on leaving, he took with him an "exhibition" to Oxford.

Through the influence of Bishop Shirley, he was admitted, in October, 1849, to a servitorship at Christ Church College by Dean Gaisford, and he went into residence in the following January. At first he read too hard, till, in his own words, he found his brain "almost on fire." He thereupon wisely took more leisure and exercise. In November of the same year, he was elected to a "Boulter Scholarship," which placed him in a more comfortable position pecuniarily, and so, characteristically, his first thought was what he could do for his mother and sisters. "It is my intention," he says, "still to practise the most rigid economy, . . . and in this way I do not despair of yet enjoying that greatest perhaps of earthly blessings, the ability to administer to the wants of those who, near and dear to me, are still in a condition bordering on penury."† In May, 1851, he was head of the list in his College examination, and he gained a further exhibition. Can one wonder that the earnest and self-denying young man thought the time had come when he might be justified in taking a little relaxation ? "Indeed," he writes, "you must not think that I am becoming 'fast' when I tell you that I not infrequently go on the river. Rowing is a very favourite exercise of mine and does me good." In May, 1853, he announces

---

* The first prize was gained by F. W. Farrar, now Dean of Canterbury.
† The letters quoted between 1849 and 1853 are all addressed to the late Archdeacon Moore.

his first class *in literis humanioribus*, or " classical finals" :   " I
must not be vain ; and yet the examination and its results have
been altogether so exciting that I cannot help feeling a little
triumphant." In the following December, he gained a first class
in the School of Law and Modern History :   " I am the only first ;
and thus am entitled to the honour of being the first double first,
as I was among the first ' firsts ' under the new system.   .   .   .
Am I justified in recognising the guidance of Providence in these
successes ? This last one absolutely places me in advance of the
whole University ; for the tutors themselves have said that I
occupy the same place relatively to the new system that Sir Robert
Peel did to the old." Of his social life at Oxford, his letters give
but scant glimpses. Indeed it would seem that he, who was afterwards such a cheery, social soul, the best of good fellows, was so
absorbed in his books, so circumscribed by poverty, and so out of
sympathy with his colleagues, as to have but little time or
inclination for society.   "I must say," he writes, "I feel very
lonely in Oxford.   I seem to have no sympathy with the men
around me." Many of them were imbued with the principles of
the Tractarian party, which he evidently viewed with the greatest
detestation :   "Their absurdities when beheld in all their hated
profusion are to me very sickening." Now that he had taken his
degree, the question of his future career naturally arose.   He was
swayed in two directions.   His Oxford friends urged him to remain
at the University, declaring that his "attainments were
altogether beyond the requirements of the Isle of Man,"
but he, feeling, very properly, that his exhibition from
King William's College laid an obligation upon him to offer himself
for the service of the Church in the island, felt bound to do so.
Moreover, he did not desire a university life.   Even in his first
year at Oxford, he writes : "It is not my wish to lounge about the
college and fatten on a fellowship all my days.   I am always
trying to look upon a college life as a medium not an end," and, at
the time he took his degree, "There is an influence exercised
by the life of an Oxford tutor which I cannot help perceiving.   I
feel it even now working in myself, and I shrink from its baneful
consequences.   It is a disposition to avoid and shirk all ministerial
labour, to degenerate into mere cultivators of the intellectual
field, abandoning the moral." He, however, decided to try for a
fellowship at Oriel, then the highest academic honour at Oxford,
and he obtained it in the following year.

Soon after this, having refused an offer from Gladstone of
political work, he went to King William's College as vice-principal,
remaining there for eight years.   In 1856, he was ordained by the
Bishop of Oxford, Wilberforce, but did not do any parochial work
till 1884, when he was priested by the Bishop of Gloucester and
Bristol, and licensed to the curacy of St. Barnabas, Bristol, which

he held for three years.   In 1863, he accepted the headmastership
of the Crypt School at Gloucester.   In the following year, he was
appointed second master of Clifton College, where he was to spend
nearly thirty years of his life.   One who knew him well writes of
his work there as follows :   " It is impossible to convey to those
who did not know him what was his effect on the school.   His
form appreciated his splendid teaching and his eye for genius of
all kinds.   His house was passionately loyal.   The school over-
flowed with delight in his Sunday evening addresses."*   And yet
it would seem that he was glad to leave, since, by his own con-
fession, teaching had never been congenial to him : —

> I'm here at Clifton, grinding at the mill
> My feet for thrice nine barren years have trod,
> But there are rocks and waves at Scarlett still ;
> And gorse runs riot in Glen Chass—thank God !

He repaired to his beloved island, residing at Ramsey, where,
during the last five years of his life he spent most of his time,
(when not engaged in reviewing for the " Times " and other newspapers, in writing articles for magazines and giving his inimitable
lectures† on various subjects), in revelling in the beauties of nature,
in visiting his old friends, and in helping the clergy in their work.
The most remarkable incident during this calm and peaceful
period was his refusal of the Archdeaconry of Man, which, on
the resignation of Dr. Hughes-Games in 1894, had been offered to
him by Mr. Asquith ; his reasons for doing so are characteristic
of the man : —

I must be free . . . . free to do what I like, say what I like,
write what I like, within the limits prescribed for me by my own
sense of what is seemly and fitting.   Literature is my calling.
To hold up the mirror to my countrymen comes natural to me ;
and in the open field of invention I am not without hopes of giving
them pleasure.‡

And in another letter :   " Every man should follow the bent of his
nature in art and letters, always provided that he does not offend
against the rules of morality and good taste."§

This leads to a brief summary of his literary work.   Nearly all
his poems were written during his residence at Clifton.   " Betsy
Lee," which he began soon after he went there, was first printed
in the " Isle of Man Times," not appearing in book form till 1873 ‖
This poem, with " Captain Tom and Captain Hugh,"** " The

---

* Account in the London *Times*.
† His powers as a lecturer were said, by one who heard his Clifton lectures
only, to have excelled those of " the most brilliant lecturer from Faraday
downwards." *(Ibid.)*
‡ Letter to the writer.
§ *Ibid.*
‖ Published by Macmillan & Co.
** " Captain Tom and Captain Hugh " had previously appeared in the *Isle
of Man Times*.

Christmas Rose," and Tommy Big Eyes," all in the Manx dialect,*
was re-published under the title of " Fo'c's'le Yarns " in 1881.   In
1887 followed " The Doctor and other Poems,"† and, in 1893,
" Old John and other Poems," only a few of which were in
dialect.‡   A complete collection of his poems was issued by
Messrs. Macmillan in 1900.

After he settled in the Isle of Man he did not write much
poetry, but was a not infrequent contributor of short prose stories
and articles in "Macmillan's Magazine," "The National Observer,"
"The New Review," and the Manx newspapers and magazines,
particularly " The Isle of Man Times," " The Isle of Man
Examiner," " The Ramsey Courier," and " The Ramsey Church
Magazine."   His last important prose composition was the able
preface which he contributed to the book of " Manx Ballads,"
edited by the writer, and published in 1896.

Brilliant and interesting as much of his prose writings are,
especially those in which he dealt with such subjects as " Manx
Character" and " Old Manx Parsons," none of them are equal
as literature to his letters.   Others besides the recipients will
now be able to read some few of these letters in the collection
published by Mr. Sidney T. Irwin,§ which also contains an
interesting and sympathetic memoir of their writer.   Most of
Tom Brown's letters cannot, for excellent reasons, be published
for many years to come, and many of them, notably those to Mr.
Hall Caine, were not placed at Mr. Irwin's disposal, but those
that have been published suffice to justify his claim that " the
man who wrote them was rarely gifted."   It is, however, by his
verse that he will be chiefly remembered, and especially by his
verse in dialect.   To portray his countrymen was his chief aim :—

> Dear countrymen, whate'er is left to us
> Of ancient heritage—
> Of manners, speech, of humours, polity,
> The limited horizon of our stage—
> Old love, hope, fear,
> All this I fain would fix upon the page ;
> That so the coming age,
> Lost in the empire's mass,
> Yet haply longing for their fathers, here
> May see, as in a glass,
> What they held dear—
> May say, " 'Twas thus and thus
> They lived," and as the time-flood onward rolls
> Secure an anchor for their Keltic souls.

---

* *i.e.*, The dialect of English spoken in the Isle of Man.
† Published by Swan, Sonnenschein & Co.
‡ Some of these these first appeared in *Plain Talk*, a periodical of his brother
Hugh's church in Liverpool.
§ Letters of Thomas Edward Brown, author of "Fo'c'sle Yarns."   Edited
with an Introductory Memoir by Sidney T. Irwin. (Westminster: Archibald
Constable & Co., Limited, 1900.   2 vols.)

and again :—

>   . . . to my own people do I sing
> And use the old familiar speech,
> Happy, if I shall reach
> Their inmost consciousness.

But, exquisite as is his dialect verse, we think that such poems as "Bella Gorry," "Mary Quayle," "Aber Stations," and "Clevedon Verses," which are not in dialect, are as fine as any he has written. "Most of his poems smack of the sea, and some deal directly with it. As stories the poems are full of interest, while, as represented by the poet, with a rare vividness of diction and style, and an overmastering dramatic power, they are of their kind unequalled."* "Foremost among the characteristics of his verse is an extraordinary power of presentation, of character and incidents alike. He also reveals an immense capacity for feeling, both in his treatment of nature† and his analysis of human emotion. . . . The unspoiled lusciousness of nature and of simple human lives breathes in his every line. . . . Sometimes the feeling is robust and vigorous, even rude. At others it is calm, soft, tranquil. But it is always deep. . . . His pages teem with passion. The hidden springs of human joy and sorrow were unsealed to him : nothing was alien from his . . . . far-reaching humanity."‡ Another salient point is "his extraordinary force of expression, his gift of instant and persuasive speech."§ He possessed an admirable raciness, a peculiar, irresistible flavour, which leaves a taste in the mouth. . . . Humorous often, often serious, these strong utterances burst into sight like shooting stars, and, like shooting stars, bring trails of glory. They have a quality which is indefinable—which, too, is their own." Again, observe that his "phrases are expressions of fact. He was the closest observer of things, the craftiest expert in human character and life ;" and no one could "question his knowledge at first hand of what he was writing about." In brief, then, it may be confidently stated that his poems show him to have been gifted with humour, pathos, knowledge, and sympathy, with "an abounding humanity, a unique capacity for presentation, a singular genius in style." It was his "to perfect, if not to invent, a certain genre, and to fit to local uses a genius which was big enough and comprehensive enough to take in the whole English race."‖ "To

---

* Quoted, by permission of the publisher, from an able article on "T. E. Brown," in the December (1897) number of *The New Review*, by Wm. Storr.
† "There was something so intense in his love of nature that I have felt it as some strange deep secret that he knew or knew of and was trying to penetrate." (*The Cliftonian*, Dec., 1897.)
‡ Storr.
§ *Ibid.*
‖ *Ibid.*

the claim of genius," says Mr. Canton, "no one who knows Mr.
Brown's work will demur. In the essential qualities of the
genuine poet he is not lacking ; and in spiritual vision, in the
tenderness which springs out of a large humanity, in genial
humour and gaiety, there are few poets of our century, there are
no living poets, who have been equally gifted. There is a big
burly naturalness, a heartiness, a contempt of trick and artifice,
a broad sanity and placidity observable in all his work. These
mask the finer, the more delicate and evanescent characteristics,
like a hardy serviceable husk ;"* and, finally, a recent writer in the
" Quarterly Review " says :—

Mr Brown depicts for us a region that has never been depicted
before ; he shows us men and women different from any men or
women that poet or novelist has hitherto shown—but men and
women real, full of life, natural in spite of many peculiarities and
oddities, strong in spite of many weaknesses. Such pictures of life
are worth preserving ; and the poet himself, in his personal feeling,
has also phases that have never before been rendered in verse ;
sudden turns, opening out in a few words unexpected vistas.
Individuality stamps the lyrics in these volumes as well as in the
narrative poems ; and this (provided it be a worthy individuality) is
the surest guarantee of permanence.

But the man himself—great classical and English scholar,
historian, preacher, and musician, as well as poet—with his
geniality, his force, his intellectual sincerity, was greater than
his work.

Let us quote Dr. Percival, now Bishop of Hereford, who first
brought him to Clifton :—

I have never known anyone at all like him. His whole nature—
head and heart, intellect, imagination, emotion—was cast in a
larger and more richly varied mould than that of ordinary men ;
and I have often felt that if his great gifts and powers had only
been fused just a little differently he would have been one of the
greatest lights in the literature of our day. To compare Brown
with even the average run of the distinguished men who are all
around us is like trying to compare the Bay of Naples with an
English bay or Scotch loch. We can find plenty of beauty in the
familiar northern scenes : but we miss the pent-up forces, the
volcanic outbursts, the tropic glow, and all the surprisingly manifold and tender and sweet-scented outpourings of soul and sunshine,
so spontaneous, so inexhaustibly rich, and with the great heart of
fire burning and palpitating underneath all the time.†

And another friend describes him as follows :—

Strong, almost rugged, loveable, a poet of many-sided, deep-
streaming human nature, full of faith in God, independent of, but
never scorning nor neglecting, the accessories of religion, flooding

---

* *The Bookman*, May 1897.
† *Oxford Magazine*, November 3rd, 1897.

all life with light and truth and generous sympathies, one in whose presence meanness and shame were impossible—such is the picture which his strong individuality has impressed on all who knew him.*

His individuality has been so aptly and deftly portrayed by Mr W. E. Henley in the following charming quatrain, that this brief sketch could not close more appropriately than by giving it† :—

> He looked half parson and half-skipper : a quaint
> Beautiful blend, with blue eyes good to see
> And old-world whiskers. You found him cynic, saint,
> Salt, humorist, Christian, poet ; with a free
> Far-glancing luminous utterance ; and a heart
> Large as St. Francis's : withal a brain
> Stored with experience, letters, fancy, art,
> And scored with runes of human joy and pain.
> Till six and sixty years he used his gift,
> His gift unparalleled, of laughter and tears,
> And left the world a high-piled, golden drift
> Of verse : to grow more golden with the years,
> Till the Great Silence fell upon his ways,
> Brake into song, and he that had Love hath Praise.

TRANSLATORS OF THE BIBLE INTO MANX.

No account of literary Manxmen would be complete without mention of those who translated the Bible, Prayer-book, and other religious books into Manx : The Rev. WILLIAM MYLREA, archdeacon and Rector of Andreas, in collaboration with the Rev. ROBERT RADCLIFF, vicar-general and Vicar of Patrick, translated Genesis. The Rev. HENRY CORLETT, Vicar of German (see Chapter I.) translated Exodus. Leviticus was translated by the Rev. NICHOLAS CHRISTIAN, Vicar of Rushen ; Numbers, by the Rev. WILLIAM CREBBIN, Vicar of Jurby ; Deuteronomy by the Rev. JOHN MOORE, Vicar of Arbory and vicar-general ; Joshua, by the Rev. JAMES WILKS, Vicar of Kirk Michael (see Chapter I.) ; Judges and Ruth, by the Rev. ROBERT QUAYLE, Curate, and afterwards Vicar, of Braddan ; 1 Samuel, by the Rev. SAMUEL GELL, Vicar of Lonan ; 2 Samuel, by the Rev. JOSEPH COSNAHAN, Vicar of Kirk Braddan ; 1 Kings, by the Rev. THOMAS QUAYLE, Vicar of Conchan ; 2 Kings, by the Rev. JOHN CHRISTIAN, Vicar of Marown ; 1 Chronicles, by the Rev. DANIEL GELLING, Vicar of Malew ; 2 Chronicles and part of the Psalms, by the Rev. JOHN GILL, Vicar of Lezayre ; Ezra and Nehemiah, by the Rev. THOMAS CUBBON, Vicar of Santon ; Esther, by the Rev. JOHN CRELLIN, Chaplain of Ramsey (who was afterwards vicar-general and Vicar of Michael) ; Job, by the Rev. THOMAS CORLETT, Curate of Bride, and afterwards Vicar of Lezayre ; Psalms, by the Rev. JOHN GILL and the Rev.

---

* From the London *Times*.
† By permission of the author. It was published in the December number of "The New Review."

PHILIP MOORE; Proverbs, by the Rev. W. J. WOODS, Vicar of
Maughold, afterwards Vicar of Braddan; Ecclesiastes, by the Rev.
CHARLES CREBBIN, then Curate of Douglas, afterwards Vicar of
Santon; Song of Solomon, by Rev. WILLIAM CLUCAS, Curate of Kirk
Marown (who was afterwards Vicar of Malew and then Vicar of
Bride) It is not known who translated Isaiah, Jeremiah, and
Lamentations, but it was probably the Rev. PHILIP MOORE.
Ezekiel was translated by the Rev. NICHOLAS CHRISTIAN;
Daniel, by the Rev. PHILIP MOORE; the Minor Prophets by the
Rev. W. FITZSIMMONS, a Manxman, and minister of the Episcopal
Chapel at Edinburgh.   The Gospels and Acts, according to the
Rev. William Crebbin, were translated by Dr. WILLIAM WALKER;
the Epistles and Revelation, by the Rev. JAMES WILKS. The
whole was revised by the Rev. PHILIP MOORE, with the
assistance of the Revs. JAMES WILKS, MATTHIAS CURGHEY, and
JOHN KELLY (see page 94).   The Prayer-book is said to have
been partly translated by Dr. WALKER, but we learn from the
minutes of the Convocation held in 1761 that it had then been
recently translated by the Revs. R. RADCLIFFE, MATTHIAS
CURGHEY, PAUL CREBBIN, JAMES WILKS, JOHN CHRISTIAN,
WILLIAM MYLREA, PHILIP MOORE, NICHOLAS CHRISTIAN, and
WILLIAM CREBBIN.

Lewis's Catechism was translated by the Rev. HENRY CORLETT,
and the Christian Monitor by the Rev. PAUL CREBBIN.*   In
1778, DANIEL COWLEY, of Kirk Michael, translated an explanation of the Church Catechism, and, in the same year, he
published some of Wesley's Hymns in Manx, which had been
translated by him.   He had been educated by Bishop
Hildesley, who apprenticed him to a printer.   In 1799,
a larger number of Wesley's Hymns and some of Watts's, translated into Manx by GEORGE KILLEY (b. 1763, d. 1842), parish
clerk and schoolmaster of Conchan, were published in the first
edition of the "Book of Hymns," or *Lioar dy Hymnyn*.   He is
said to have been very ready at impromptu rhymes, and the
following story is quoted to show it :

An old man called Hugh, who could neither read nor write,
asked KILLEY to write something in his new Bible, so he promptly
sat down and wrote in Manx and English ;

> Lesh Hugh yn Lioar shoh, sleih my chree,
> As shen-y-fa nagh geid shiu ee ;
> Son ga nagh vod e scrieu ny lhaih,
> T'an Lioar eunys echey ny-yei.
>
> This Book, good friends, belongs to Hugh,
> Steal it not then whate'er you do ;
> For tho' he cannot read or write,
> To have this Book is his delight.

---

* Memoirs of Bishop Hildesley, pp. 252-6.

George Borrow, who visited his (Killey's) daughter when he was in the Isle of Man, remarked that the hymn-book had been translated by him in a manner which showed that he "possessed powers of versification of the very highest order."* GEORGE KILLEY was a Wesleyan Methodist. (See also WILLIAM KENNISH, pp. 118-121.)

---

* "Life, Writings, and Correspondence" (Knapp), 1899, Vol. II., p. 130.

CHAPTER VI.

Science.

There are only a few Manxmen who have attained distinction in scientific pursuits, but the fact that the brothers EDWARD and DAVID FORBES attained almost the first rank as scientists makes up for the absence of a number of less distinguished names. It is as practical mechanists and engineers, that Manxmen have gained their chief successes. Among these may be mentioned ROBERT CASEMENT, engineer of the "Great Laxey" mine, who designed the huge wheel there; AMBROSE LACE, who is said to have made the model of the famous racing yacht "America," and JAMES AUGUSTUS CALEY (d. 1885), C.E., F.G.S., brother of Precentor Caley (see p. 40), who accomplished much valuable engineering work, chiefly in Ceylon. But the most interesting and remarkable of all is

WILLIAM KENNISH (b. 1799, d. 1862),

who was a poet, and an inventor, as well as a practical engineer. We have placed his name under the heading of "Science," as he was certainly more distinguished as an engineer and an inventor than as a poet, though he is best known to his countrymen, on this side of the Atlantic, in the latter capacity. Born in the parish of Maughold, "close by the foot of the bridge of Cornay," or the Corrany Bridge, as we now call it, he was, in his own words, "a *Mannanagh dooie*"—a true Manxman. His father was a small farmer, and his early years were spent partly in following the plough and partly in learning the trade of a ship carpenter at Ramsey. It was not till his twenty-second year that he entered the Royal Navy, doing so, it is said, because he had been jilted. At that time he could scarcely speak any English, and was unable either to read or write. So great, however, was his natural ability and his technical knowledge of his trade that, in the short period of seven years, he rose to the position of master-carpenter of the whole British fleet in the Mediterranean. During this time he acquired not only the rudiments of education, but a considerable knowledge of science, as was soon to be shown by his contributions to it.

In 1829, when on board H.M.S. "Hussar," on the North American station, he invented "a method for concentrating the fire of a broadside of a ship of war,"* for which he received the thanks of the Admiralty and the *Isis* gold medal of the *Society of Arts and Commerce.* An account of this was published in a pamphlet, together with a description of two of his other inventions, viz. : "A method for Floating Guns on shore by means of Water Tanks," and "A Fuse intended to burst the shell on striking the object without reference to distance." He also sent the *Society* communications respecting "an artificial horizon ; a pneumatic sounding instrument ; a method of drowning the magazine of a ship of war ; an hydraulic ventilator ; discontinuing the use of black paint on ships ; a hydrostatic diving machine," &c. In 1832, the committee appointed by the Admiralty to report upon naval inventions, recommended his pamphlet as a text book for use in the navy. "It was at this time," says his son, "that steam was seriously thought of as a propelling power in the navy, and the fertility of Mr. Kennish's inventive mind is proved by the fact that he devised several marine steam engines and submitted them to the consideration of the Lords of the Admiralty. He also urged the adoption of the screw propeller, one of which he also designed, and submitted a model of."† Another invention of his, a pneumatic tube. which he suggested to the Admiralty for the transport of letters in 1845, was not accepted then, but a similar tube "is now used for the conveyance of mails to the General Post Office in London."† About 1840, KENNISH retired from the navy and settled at Ballasalla, where, "to while away the tedium occasioned by the abandonment of his scientific pursuits,"* he took to composing poetry. This poetry is, as its author remarks in his preface, distinctly "rude," but it portrays many of the most characteristic Manx customs and superstitions with truth and vigour.

---

* Preface to poems.
† Paper by his son. This was read before several learned societies in America (published in the *Mona's Herald* of Sept. 14, 1890). Our readers are referred to it for further particulars.

In 1845, he became a schoolmaster, announcing his intention of
doing so as follows: "William Kennish, R.N., author of the
'Method for concentrating the Fire of a ship's Broadside,' and of
other mathematical and mechanical inventions now in use in the
British Navy, also of 'Mona's Isle and other Poems,' begs to
inform his countrymen of the southside of the island that he has
taken charge of the Parochial School at Ballasalla, where he
intends teaching." The list of subjects which he proposed to
teach was a truly ambitious one, and yet, at the same time, he was
able to make a survey of the Manx coast for the British Government, together with a plan for a harbour of refuge.* To form
this harbour, he proposed to join the mainland and the Calf by
way of the Thousla and Kitterland islets, and to throw out a
breakwater from the Calf towards Spanish Head. In 1849, he
emigrated to America in search of a larger field for the exercise of
his talents, and he seems to have speedily obtained congenial
employment in exploring the auriferous tracts in New Grenada.
When there, he was attracted by the problem of a canal across the
isthmus. Into the story of his repeated journeys we cannot enter
here, and it must suffice to say that they were accomplished at
terrible risk to his life, and with the greatest gallantry and skill.
His final survey, in 1855, was highly approved by the United
States Government, and he then submitted, both to it and various
scientific bodies, a scheme for a canal which was to join the
Atlantic and Pacific Oceans by channels and a tunnel in connexion
with the rivers Atrato and Truando. In this remarkable scheme
he designed the canal without locks. "He was the first to
assert," says his son, "that the oceans were upon a level. . . .
Up to this time no canal had been projected without locks—it was
an entirely new thought; but to accomplish it he had to make one
of the boldest suggestions in the history of civil engineering,
namely, to cut a tunnel through the dividing ridge, of sufficient
capacity to admit of the largest vessel passing through without
interruption." That his scheme was considered a practicable one
was shown by the fact that at the De Lesseps banquet in New
York, in 1880, a public tribute was paid to WILLIAM KENNISH as an
"able engineer," and the discoverer of "the first and only feasible
route without locks, gates, or dams, for a ship canal, two hundred
feet wide, and thirty feet deep, including a tunnel three miles long
through the Cordilleras."† The length of this canal was estimated
at 130 miles, and its cost at one hundred and thirty million
dollars. Who can say that it will not be the Manxman's scheme
which may ultimately be adopted? This scheme was duly set forth

---

See the Paper by his son.
G. F. Nesbitt & Co., New York. Publishers.

by him in a pamphlet entitled, "The Practicability and Importance of a Ship Canal to connect the Atlantic and Pacific Oceans."*

Nor did his mechanical inventions cease, since he sent an "hydraulic and hydrostatic engine" to the international exhibition at London in 1862.* Both of these inventions were afterwards patented and manufactured by a Wakefield firm.

With the exception of KENNISH, Manxmen have not been specially notable as inventors. The first invention by a Manxman that we hear of is is one by

JAMES KEWLEY,

who, in 1817, obtained "a patent for regulating the temperature by opening and closing flues, doors or windows, without personal attention."† This, if it could have been practically applied, would have been most useful, but, as no more has been heard of it, we fear that it could not.

GEORGE QUAYLE (see Chapter IX.) was also the originator of several mechanical inventions.

There have been at least three Manxmen who have been distinguished by their ability for mathematical and astronomical studies. The first of these is PHILIP GARRETT, to whom we have already referred (see p. 49), the second is ROBERT CORTEEN, and the third, JOHN GOLDSMITH.

ROBERT CORTEEN (b. 1791, d. 1853),

was a remarkably clever and versatile man. Born in Maughold, his boyhood was spent as a clerk in an advocate's office at Ramsey. He then went to Douglas, where he became an assistant to Messrs. Gelling, who were iron merchants. While in their employ he erected a small gas plant and supplied St. Matthew's Church, as well as several business establishments, with gas, which had not, till then, been used in the island. He was also the first to start an iron foundry, and, for melting iron there, he applied two puncheons fitting into each other like a gasholder, instead of a blast. On leaving Messrs Gelling, he surveyed Douglas for the purpose of laying down gas and water in its streets, and he was the engineer who constructed the earliest gas-works in that town.

---

* These machines were brought over to England by his son-in-law, Mr. C. S. Dawson, who has approved of the above sketch. We are glad to learn that Mr. Dawson proposes issuing a new and largely increased edition of Kennish's poems.

† "Annals of the Isle of Man," in Fargher's Directory.

We next find him in quite a different capacity, viz., as a teacher
of mathematics and navigation.   Many of our most skilful
navigators, notably Captain Brown (brother of the Rev. T. E.
Brown), Captain Joughin, commodore of Brocklebank's line;
and Captains Gell and Corlett, of the Isle of Man Steam Packet
Company, were taught by him.   This indefatigable man then went
to England, where he acted as one of the surveyors for the
Lancashire and Yorkshire Railway, at the time when the fever
for railway construction was at its height.   During the last seven
years of his life he was secretary and manager of the Douglas Gas
Company.   For many years he made calculations for Jefferson's
and other almanacs, which, like those of his successor, William
Goldsmith, were remarkable for their accuracy.   He was the first
to publish a complete list of the lighthouses round the British
coast, with their bearings, nature of their lights, &c., and, notwithstanding his multifarious occupations, he found time to
acquire a knowledge of Hebrew and Greek.   (Information from
Mr. Henry Corteen, his son.)

JOHN GOLDSMITH (b. 1803, d. 1876),

who was chief clerk to Messrs. Quiggin & Co. in 1830.   From
thence he went into the service of the Isle of Man Steam Packet
Co., and, after he left this company, he was appointed secretary
and manager of the Douglas Gas Co.   He did good work as the
honorary secretary of the *Manx Society*, and he was also for many
years teacher and superintendent in the Primitive Methodist
Sunday School in Douglas.   But his chief claim to remembrance
is his wonderfully extensive and accurate knowledge of astronomy.
He was employed in calculating the tide tables in the widely
circulated "Jefferson's Almanac," the proprietor of which stated
that its success was largely due to their absolute reliableness.
George Borrow, who was in the Isle of Man in 1855, spoke of him
as "a very intelligent and amusing man."‡
   We think that the name of

THOMAS KEWISH,

blacksmith, of Ballaugh, is worthy of a place under this heading,
as the skill he showed in putting together the skeleton of the fossil
elk which was dug up near Ballaugh, in 1819, is very remarkable.
This elk is now in the museum at Edinburgh.

---

‡ Life, Writings, and Correspondence of George Borrow (Knapp), 1899.
Vol. II., p. 132.

EDWARD FORBES (b. 1815, d. 1854),

son of Edward Forbes, of Oakhill and Cronkbane, near Douglas, banker, and Jane, eldest daughter and heiress of William Teare, of Corvalla and Ballabeg, Ballaugh, was born at Douglas, where he received his early education. He very early displayed marked and widespread tastes for natural history, literature, and drawing. When at school he was described as tall and thin, with limbs loosely hung, and wearing his hair very long. His schoolbooks were covered with caricatures and grotesque figures, which so impressed his parents with his artistic talent that they sent him to London to study art at the age of sixteen. However, since he was refused admittance to the Royal Academy School, and had not been found sufficiently promising by his teacher, Mr. Sass, FORBES entered Edinburgh University, in 1831, as a medical student. While in London, he wrote a paper "On Some Manx Traditions," which was published in the *Mirror* newspaper in 1831. In his first year at Edinburgh, he attended Knox's lectures on anatomy and Graham's on botany, and became a devoted student of natural history. At this early period his powers of generalization were as noticeable as his perfect familiarity with natural objects and his varied experimental studies. His peculiar vein of humour showed itself in sketches of the most grotesque kind and in equally broad comic verses. During the vacation of 1832 he investigated the natural history of the Isle of Man. He returned to Edinburgh with a bias against medicine, and he was far more congenially employed in writing and drawing for the "University Maga," which he and a few other students brought out for some weeks. The death, in 1836, of his mother, who had particularly wished him to become a physician, left him free to resign medical studies.

Meanwhile his vacations had been utilized for much natural history work. In the summer of 1833 he went to Norway, sailing from the Isle of Man to Arendal in a brig. Both the voyage and the land trip were occupied with the keenest observation of natural history. The return journey was through Christiana and Copenhagen, and at these places FORBES made several botanical friends. In the summer of 1834, he dredged in the Irish Sea and continued to explore the natural history of the Isle of Man. In the summer of 1835, he visited France, Switzerland, and Germany, and was so much attracted by the Jardin des Plantes that he resolved to spend the winter of 1836-7 in Paris, studying at the Jardin. When there he attended the lectures of De Blainville and Geoffroy Saint-Hilaire, which impressed him with the necessity of studying the geographical distribution of animals. After this winter he travelled in the South of France and in Algeria, collecting many natural history specimens.

In 1837-8, FORBES was back in Edinburgh, working at natural history, and bringing out his little volume on "Manx Mollusca." In the summer of 1838, after a fruitful tour through Austria, during which he collected about three thousand plant specimens, FORBES attended the British Association at Newcastle, read before it a paper "On the Distribution of Terrestrial Pulmonifera in Europe," and was asked to prepare another on the distribution of pulmonary mollusca in the British Isles, which he presented at the succeeding meeting.

After studying the starfishes of the Irish Sea he published a paper on them. The winter of 1838-9 found him delivering a course of lectures before the Edinburgh Philosophical Association on "The Natural History of the Animals in the British Seas." At this period he describes himself as studying "with a view to the development of the laws of species, of the laws of their distribution, and of the connexion between the physical and mental development of creatures."

At the British Association meeting of 1839, held at Birmingham, FORBES obtained a grant for dredging researches in the British seas, with a view to illustrating the geographical distribution of marine animals, and he started the famous club of "Red Lions," named from the inn where the first dinner took place. Throughout his life FORBES's humorous songs, the subject of which was often taken from some branch of science, were among the most conspicuous after-dinner features. About this time he undertook to publish a "History of British Starfishes," many of which had been first observed by himself. This work was completed in 1841. In 1839-40 he lectured on natural history both at Cupar and St. Andrew's with great success, having much original material, and aiding his lectures by excellent chalk drawings. Towards the end of 1839, he founded a "University Club," under whose auspices an "Academic Annual" (the only one which appeared) was published, containing FORBES's paper "On the Association of Mollusca on the British coast, considered with reference to Pleistocene Geology," in which he established his notable division of the coast into four zones, and pointed out the effects on the *fauna* of subsidence and elevation. He gave a series of lectures at Liverpool in the spring of 1840, visited London, where he made the acquaintance of many leading men of science, and travelled and dredged extensively.

In 1841, he was appointed naturalist to H.M.S. Beacon, engaged in surveying work in the Levant. Gaining the interest of all on board in his studies, he made extensive collections of marine animals, and learned many facts of importance in the natural history of the Ægean Sea. He also studied the relations of animals and plants on the islands of the Archipelago. In the autumn FORBES dredged on the south and west coast of Asia Minor, and went on antiquarian and natural history excursions into the uplands of Lycia. In the spring of 1842, he made an extended journey in Lycia, discovering the ruins of Termessus, and exploring many other interesting sites. Besides making antiquarian discoveries, FORBES made collections of land and fresh water mollusca, and of plants, and ascertained the main features of the geology of Lycia.

During his absence he had been elected to the Professorship of Botany at King's College, but it was worth less than £100 a year. He consequently applied for the curatorship of the museum of the Geological Society at £150 a year, and was elected. The work of the new appointment absorbed nearly all his time, and necessitated the postponement of full publication of his researches in the Ægean ; but he presented a valuable "Report on the Mollusca and Radiata of the Ægean Sea" to the British Association in 1843, which raised his reputation greatly. His botanical lectures opened well, and became popular from their philosophical tone and practical illustrations, which were based on a wide knowledge of plants in their native habitats. He had frequent returns of intermittent fever, and his labour at the Geological Society was incessant. The want of a skilled palæontologist on the Geological Survey became evident in 1844, and at Mr. (now Sir A. C.) Ramsay's suggestion FORBES received the appointment in October. Meanwhile he delivered an important lecture before the Royal Institution on "The Light thrown on Geology by Submarine Researches," in which he expounded his discoveries about littoral zones, the character of deposits formed at various depths in the ocean, and the migration of mollusca. The Government now granted £500 towards the publication of his Ægean researches, which unfortunately he never had time to complete for the press. The Fullerian professorship was then offered to him but he declined it. The success with which his fertile mind was still grappling with important zoological questions is shown by his ingenious paper "On the Morphology of the Reproductive System of the Sertularian Zoophyte, and its Analogy with the Reproductive System of the Flowering Plant."

His work in connexion with the Geological Survey, which was not only to discriminate, describe, name, and arrange the fossils collected by the survey, but also to visit the districts where the surveyors were working and examine the rocks with the fossils in them, gave a new and important development to FORBES'S ideas. Relieved by his improved income, he now became a Fellow of the Geological Society in 1844, and of the Royal Society in 1845, and, in the same year, he was elected a member of the Athenæum Club by special vote, on the strong recommendation of Professor Owen. It was at this time that he gave a course of lectures at the Royal Institution on "The Natural History and Geological Distribution of Fossil Marine Animals," and he contributed a remarkable paper on the geographical distribution of local plants, at the meeting of the British Association. After the meeting, he

went on a dredging expedition from the Shetlands round the west
coast of Scotland, and found many new *medusæ* and several living
molluscs which had previously only been known in a fossil
state. Wearied by routine work at the survey, and by the attempt
to complete his book on Lycia, he had a severe illness in the
winter of 1845-6, but, in the spring of 1846, he gave a course of
lectures at the London Institution on "The Geographical and
Geological Distribution of Organised Beings." The King's College
lectures on botany followed immediately, but FORBES was able to
finish his important paper "On the Connection between the
Distribution of the existing Fauna and Flora of the British Isles
and the Geological Changes which have affected their Area,"
published in the first volume of the memoirs of the Geological
Survey, and to complete his "Lycia," which appeared in the
autumn and became a standard work. Early in 1847, a
remark of FORBES's led to the formation of the Palæontographical
Society, which has done so much for British palæontology. In a
lecture at the Royal Institution in May on " The Natural History
Features of the North Atlantic," FORBES referred to the bearing
of scientific research on deep sea fisheries, and censured the
Government and the public for their neglect of the subject, which has
only lately received much attention. He continued his preparation
for his great work on the "History of British Mollusca " (in
onjunction with Mr Sylvanus Hanley) which appeared in four
volumes (1848-52). It was a work of vast research, for which
many summer dredging excursions and visits to the museums of
well-known collectors were made. During the autumn of this year,
as throughout his remaining years in London, geological excursions
were made on survey work. Of FORBES on these excursions Mr.
(afterwards Sir A. C.) Ramsay writes : "There never was a more
delightful companion. It was on such occasions that his inner life
best revealed itself ; his knowledge was so varied, his conversation
often so brilliant and instructive." The winter of 1849-50 found
him busy with the arrangement of the new geological museum of
the Survey at Jermyn Street, but literary and lecturing work
absorbed most of his time. In the summer a dredging expedition
among the Western Hebrides added many species to the British
fauna and many valuable facts to geology. In the spring of 1850,
he gave twelve lectures at the Royal Institution on the
"Geographical Distribution of Organised Beings." The Jermyn
Street museum was opened by Prince Albert in May, 1851, and
during the summer a scheme for establishing a school of mines was
matured. FORBES was appointed lecturer on natural history as
applied to geology and the arts. We may note that at this time
he wrote a delightful article on "Shellfish, their Ways and
Works " for the first number of the new series of the " Westminster
Review " (January, 1852). During the winter of 1852-3 he worked
out important new views on the classification of the tertiary

formations, which he did not live to complete in memoir form, but they were published by his colleagues in 1857. In 1853, he was elected President of the Geological Society, an office never before held by so young a man, and, in 1854, he became Professor of Geology at Edinburgh.

He entered on his work there with an eager zeal which proved far too exhausting for his strength. Crowded audiences stimulated the lecturer's powers to the highest degree. He set vigorously to work to remodel the museum, and geological excursions with large numbers of students filled up each week. Early in August he returned to London to complete unfinished work, but illness overtook him. He was, however, present at the Liverpool meeting of the British Association, and presided over the Geological section. His last writing was a review of Murchison's "Siluria," which appeared in the "Quarterly Review" of October, 1854. He lectured through the first week of the winter session in manifest ill-health, but in the second week had to desist, owing to disease of the kidneys, of which he died. He was buried in the Dean Cemetery, Edinburgh.

FORBES lived an unusually full life, occupied in promoting science and arousing enthusiasm and awakening intelligence in others. To almost every department of biology he rendered much service, especially by connecting various branches together and illustrating one by the other. He played an important part in elevating palæontology to a high position in practical geology, and in elucidating ancient British zoology. He had a remarkable talent for discovering the relations of detached phenomena to the general scheme of nature and making broad generalizations; and he looked on the world not as mere piece of mechanism, but as a visible manifestation of the ideas of God. Many who knew him testified that "the old mourned him as a son, the young as a brother." An eminent naturalist, writing in the "Literary Gazette," of the 25th of November, 1854, said : "Rare as was the genius of Edward Forbes, his character was rarer still. . . A thorough spirit of charity seemed to hide from him all but the good and worthy points in his fellow-men. Worked to death, his time and knowledge were at the disposal of all comers ; and though his published works have been comparatively few, his ideas have been as the grain of mustard-seed in the parable." FORBES's love of social life, and his vigorous and genial humour are apparent throughout his career. His humorous verses have not been collected, but several of them have been published. One on the "Red Tape Worm" contains the following lines :—

> In Downing Street the tape worms thrive ;
> In Somerset House they are all alive ;
> And slimy tracks mark where they crawl
> In and out along Whitehall.

When I'm dead and yield my ghost,
Mark not my grave by a governnent post,
Let mild earth worms with me play,
But keep vile tape worms far away.

And if I deserve to rise
To a good place in Paradise,
May my soul good angels guide,
And keep it from the official side !

A marble bust, now in the vestibule of the Government Buildings, and a tablet in St. George's Church, have been erected to FORBES's memory by his countrymen.

An impartial estimate of what FORBES actually did will not enable us to place his name quite in the first rank of naturalists, as his published works are rather suggestive than demonstrative. But it must be remembered that he passed away ere reaching his prime, and he must be tried, not merely by what in his short life-time he did himself, but by the ideas which, scattered by him broadcast over the world, have sprung up and are bearing fruit in many lands.   He did more, perhaps, than any other man of his day to spread abroad a love for natural history ; more, undoubtedly, than any one of his contemporaries, to indicate how natural history and geology must be woven together.   The name of EDWARD FORBES will go down to posterity inseparably linked with the history of palæontology, as one of the greatest naturalists that ever strove to bring his knowledge of the living world to elucidate the physical and organic changes in the past history of the world.   He attained this high eminence not as a solitary worker.   In nothing was his career more marked than in the power he possessed of interesting others in his field of labour. His broad philosophical spirit enabled him to appreciate the researches of the chemist and the physicist, and in return he drew their sympathy with him into his own domain.   In bearing down all jealousy and envy among his fellow-naturalists, and enlisting their active co-operation in the common cause, he stood forth conspicuous among the scientific men of his time.   And this he accomplished not so much by the weight of his authority in matters of science, as by the influence of his manly, true-hearted nature.   His wit and humour too, which made him the life and soul of every circle in which he moved, were, doubtless, not without their effect in attracting many to him.   Our affections cling to character, and not to intellect, and rare as was the genius of EDWARD FORBES, his character was rarer still.   The petty vanities and heart-burnings, which are the besetting sins of men of science and of men of letters, had no hold upon his large and generous nature.   It was not his mental powers, great though these were, nor his vast knowledge of those branches of science which he made his especial study, that gained him the love and respect of all men, but a simple kindly heart that knew no selfishness, and embraced in its wide and generous sympathy all that was honourable and good.

(From the Dictionary of National Biography, and the Memoir of Edward Forbes by Dr. Wilson and Prof. Archibald Geikie; Edinburgh, 1861).

DAVID FORBES (b. 1828, d. 1876),

a younger brother of the naturalist, was first sent to school at Athol Academy, Douglas, and from thence went to Brentwood in Essex, whence he passed to Edinburgh University. He left Edinburgh when only 19, and then spent some months in Dr. Percy's metallurgical laboratory in Birmingham, being under 20 when he went to Norway, where he received the post of superintendent of the mining and metallurgical works at Espedal. In 1848—his last year in Norway—he received the personal thanks of the king for his services in arming 400 of his miners to aid the government against a threatened revolution. After this he entered into partnership with a firm of nickel smelters in Birmingham. In 1856, he was elected a Fellow of the Royal Society, and in the following year he went to America, on account of his firm, in search of the ores of nickel and cobalt. Between 1856 and 1860 he traversed the greater part of Bolivia and Peru, and embodied his observations on the minerals and rock-structure of those countries in a classical paper, which was printed in the "Quarterly Journal of the Geological Society" for 1860. Returning to South America, he traversed the mining districts of the Cordilleras, and increased the large collection of minerals he had already formed in Norway. From thence he went to the South Sea Islands for the purpose, more especially, of studying their volcanic phenomena. In 1866, he travelled in Europe and became foreign secretary to the Iron and Steel Institute. This distinguished scientist wrote no less than 58 papers on scientific subjects ; among these was one on "The Microscope in Geology," with reference to which it may be mentioned that he was one of the first to apply the microscope to the study of rocks. Igneous metamorphic phenomena occupied much of FORBES's attention, and at Espedal he experimented, on a large scale, on the action of heat on minerals and rocks. He wrote some important papers on this subject, also on chemical geology, to which he tried hard to direct the attention of British geologists. During his travels he had amassed a large fund of geological information, of which only a part was used in his published papers. He was a member of the Geological and Ethnological Societies, having been one of the secretaries of the former since 1871.

(From the Dictionary of National Biography).

E

Manx schoolmasters have usually been clergymen also, and so will be found in our first chapter.   Of the schoolmaster whose name follows, we know nothing except from his epitaph :—

Exuviæ Dom. Gul. Tear, Ludimagist, de Peel, sepultæ Julii vto, MDCCLVI., Anno ætatis lxxiv.
Epitaphii loco GULIELMI TEAR, authore scripso.

> Mors heu ! pœna quidem tamen est certissima vitæ
> Janua felicis, denique lœta piis.
> Me licet hic retinent pro tempora vincula mortis,
> Spes tamen in Christo non moritura manet.
> In Christi meritis Patrisque clementis amore
> Est humilis mea spes : hac moriorque fide.
> Tu Deus ipse meum cor scis secretaque cordis,
> Obscure cui non abdita quaque patent.
> Hic nihil optari dignum est ; heu ! omnia vana.
> Ergo beata veni, vanaque vita vade.

The translation of this, which follows, is by the Rev. John Quine :—

Remains of Sir (Bachelor) Will. Tear, Schoolmaster, of Peel, buried July 5th, 1756, in the 74th year of his age.
By way of epitaph of WILLIAM TEAR, an author having written.*
Death, alas ! the penalty indeed (of life) is nevertheless a most certain portal of a blessed life, and that a glad one to the good. Although the bonds of death retain me here temporarily, hope nevertheless in Christ, (a hope) that will not die, remaineth. In the merits of Christ and in the pitying Father's love is my humble hope : in this faith I die.   Thou God Thyself knowest my heart and the heart's secrets, to whom obscurity not hidden all things are open.   Here nothing worthy to be descried is ; alas ! all things are vain.   Therefore come blessed (life) and vain life go.

---

* Literally, " having been written."   Who was the author ?

CHAPTER VII.

Army, Navy, and Civil Service.

We are able to record the names of a greater number of "Worthies" under the first two headings than under any other. This is not, of course, because their careers as soldiers and sailors were more distinguished than those of Manxmen whose occupations lay in other fields, but simply because military and naval services are necessarily conspicuous, and therefore likely to be recorded. The number of Manxmen who served in the Army and Navy, particularly in the latter, between 1778 and 1815 is very large. This is referred to by a committee of the House of Keys, which was appointed in 1798 to take measures to prevent Manx fishermen from being "impressed." With this object, a letter was written to the Commissioners of the Admiralty, in which it is stated that "the island had done all in its power towards the general safety, and, poor as it is with a population of less than 28,000, without a port that can boast of a square-rigged vessel, has furnished above 3,000 seamen to the British service, and to the army in Fencibles and otherwise not less than 1,000."* After 1803, the numbers were still larger. According to Lord Teignmouth, who visited the island in 1829, "the Isle of Man has perhaps furnished a much larger number of able and excellent seamen to the public service, in proportion to its population, than any other individual district of the British empire."† Before the

dates mentioned the number of Manxmen in the Army and Navy
was, doubtless, much smaller.

The first Manx officer we hear of in the Royal Navy is
EDWARD CHRISTIAN (see p. 60). We may mention that
Hepworth Dixon, in "Her Majesty's Tower," refers to the fact
that THOMAS CHRISTIAN* (b. 1716, d. 1752), a grandson of *Illiam
Dhone's* son, Thomas, took out letters of marque and captured
several Spanish galleons. BRABAZON CHRISTIAN,* a son *Illiam
Dhone's* grandson, William, who had settled in Ireland after
selling Ronaldsway, was a captain in the Royal Navy. Captain
Brabazon's nephew, JONATHAN WHITBY CHRISTIAN,* was also a
captain in the Royal Navy and, afterwards, Controller-General of
the Irish Coastguard.

The first Manx officer we hear of in the British Army is
RICHARD STEVENSON (d. 1683), of Balladoole. His rank was that
of major, but of which regiment is unknown. He was deputy-
governor, presiding over a Tynwald Court on the 24th June, 1661,
in this capacity, and receiver-general.

His grandson, also RICHARD STEVENSON (b. 1716, d. 1785), son
of John Stevenson, of Balladoole, and Isabel Senhouse, of Netherhall, Cumberland, was a cornet of the Royal Horse Carbineers,
and A.D.C. to Richard Boyle, Viscount Shannon, his uncle by
marriage.

His brother, JOHN, was a colonel in the guards. He was owner
of Ashley Park, Walton-on-Thames, which he inherited from his
first cousin, the Countess of Middlesex.

Of about the same date were WILLAM QUAYLE (b. 1721, d.
1744), son of John Quayle, C.R., of Bridge House, and Elizabeth
Harrison, of Wyreside, Lancashire, who was a lieutenant in a
dragoon regiment ; and JOHN COSNAHAN, a major, who fought at the
Battle of Quebec in 1759. He afterwards married Lady Janet
Scott, daughter of the Duke of Buccleuch, but died without issue.

In the Navy, at a somewhat later date, was PETER FANNIN,
master of the "Adventure," one of the ships which accompanied
the famous Captain Cook in his first expedition. He retired in
1775, and set up a school in Douglas where he taught navigation.
In 1789, he published a map of the Isle of Man, which was highly
esteemed for the correct way in which it noted the anchorages.
It contained a plan of Douglas Harbour, and a view of the south
side of it taken from a house in which the Duke of Atholl then
resided.

---

* Manx by descent only.

ROBERT COTTIER,

who was one of the Cottiers of Narradale in Lezayre, went to sea at an early age. In 1777, he was second mate on H.M.S. frigate "Lowestoffe."* In the following year, he became first mate, and, in 1780, master of the same vessel by warrant from Sir Peter Parker, vice-admiral. During this period the "Lowestoffe" had been cruising in West Indian and American waters, England being then at war with America, and, since 1778, with France and Spain also. ROBERT COTTIER had taken part in the capture of several French West Indian islands and in the three indecisive actions fought by Rodney with Count de Guichen, in April and May, 1780, off Martinique. Besides these affairs, the "Lowestoffe," when he was on board of her, had a sharp fight with a French frigate, but, on seven other French frigates turning up, she made off. Shortly afterwards she captured a French frigate and brig, an American brig, and a Spanish sloop, in all cases after a determined fight. In February, 1782, Cottier was appointed to the command of H.M.S. frigate "Fox." During the whole of that year nothing more important happened than the capture of a French brig. Early in the following year he had a fight with a French frigate, a shot from which killed him. In the confusion which ensued the Frenchman escaped. (Information from Miss Graves.)

Contemporary with Robert Cottier was

HUGH CLOBERRY CHRISTIAN,† Knight
(b. 1747, d. 1798),

who was a son of the Captain Thomas Christian already referred to. Between 1779 and 1783, he took part in various actions in the West Indies, and, in 1796, he was appointed to the chief command there. Sir Ralph Abercromby, in his despatch of the 31st of May of that year, announcing the surrender of St. Lucia, wrote : "Rear-Admiral Sir Hugh Christian, and the Royal Navy, have never ceased to show the utmost alacrity in forwarding the public service. To their skill and unremitting labour the success which has attended his Majesty's arms is in a great measure due."‡ Early in 1798 he was commander-in-chief at the Cape of Good Hope, where he died suddenly in November of the same year, just before the patent of the peerage which had been conferred upon him arrived. It is interesting to note that, mindful of his Manx origin and descent from *Illiam Dhone*, he had selected the title of Lord Ronaldsway. The "Naval Chronicle," referring to

---

* Nelson was third lieutenant on this vessel from April, 1777, to the spring of 1778.
† Manx by descent only.
‡ *Naval Chronicle*, Vol. XXI., p. 187.

him, says : "His services . . . had been arduous and useful ; and by his death the country lost an attentive, able, and active officer."[*]

There are only two Manxmen who are recorded as being officers in the army between 1776 and 1783, viz., WILLIAM CUNNINGHAM and JOHN TAUBMAN. WILLIAM CUNNINGHAM (b. 1754, d. 1825) was colonel of the 50th Regiment. He retired in 1802, and became a member of the House of Keys.

JOHN TAUBMAN (b. 1746, d. 1822), son of John Taubman, S.H.K., and Esther, daughter of Deemster Nicholas Christian, was, in 1769, a cornet in the 3rd Regiment of Horse in the Irish Establishment, but he soon retired. He purchased the Nunnery from Deemster Peter Heywood. In 1793, he joined the Manx Fencibles, being made major. He was afterwards Speaker of the House of Keys.

During the next French War (1783-1802), the following Manxmen served as officers in the Royal Navy : THOMAS FARGHER, of Shenvalla (d. 1794), the gallant surgeon of H.M.S. "Bellerophon ;" JOHN FRISSELL, son of John Frissell and Elizabeth, daughter of Captain John Llewellyn, a lieutenant, who was wounded in the battle of the 1st of June, 1794. He afterwards married a French marchioness and settled in France. His brothers, Charles and William, were also in the Navy. PAUL CREBBIN[†] (lieutenant), and John Cowley (quarter-master), who served in the "Phœnix" frigate ; JOSEPH CURPHEY (b. 1766, d. 1826), who attained the rank of master, and served both before and after 1802, and HUGH GARRETT, master (b. 1777, d. 1833), who also served in both wars. During the later years of his life he lived on the island, and was one of the early workers in the temperance cause. The Rev. W. T. Radcliffe, who knew him well, told the writer that he was a man of high character, and that he had considerable powers as a preacher. He is described in the notice of his death as being "a faithful and zealous local preacher in the Wesleyan Methodist Connexion."

There were, doubtless, several Manxmen serving "before the mast" at this time, but we have heard of the names of three only : CHARLES CORLETT, JOHN CORKILL, and WILLIAM KEWLEY. KEWLEY (b. 1772, d. 1846), fought under Lord Howe in the battle of the 1st of June, 1794, and under Sir John Jarvis at Cape St. Vincent in 1797. He was with Lord Nelson, when he lost his arm at Teneriffe, and at the Battle of the Nile. He was also in the fleet which blockaded the French and Spanish fleets off Toulon and Cadiz. He served in the "Princess Royal," 74, and in the "Culloden," 74, and, when he sought his discharge from the latter ship, on peace being proclaimed in 1802, he was

---

[*] *Naval Chronicle*, Vol. XXI , p. 188.
[†] He had seen some Privateer service (see Chapter VIII.)

described as a "deserving, sober, and diligent seaman." He settled in Douglas, where he worked as a shoemaker, but, finally, being incapacitated by age and infirmity, he sought an asylum in the House of Industry. JOHN CORKILL, of Ballagorry-Moar, Maughold, was in the Royal Navy between 1792 and 1801, and CHARLES CORLETT (see p. 141.) served both during this and the following period.

In the Army there were JOHN JOSEPH BACON (b. 1770, d. 1805), son of John Joseph Bacon by his first wife, Jane Johnstone, who was a captain in the Fifth Veteran Battalion at Guernsey ; EDWARD GELLING (b. 1770, d. 1828), son of Edward Gelling of Castletown, a captain in the 59th Regiment (he also served after 1803) ; JOHN QUAYLE (b. 1762), son of John Quayle, C.R., of Bridge House, and Margaret, daughter of Sir George Moore of Ballamoore, a lieutenant in the Royal Artillery. He served in Flanders under the Duke of York, and he was also in the East and West Indies, having been present at the siege of Seringapatam, and various other important engagements ; and RICHARD TYLDESLEY (b. 1776, d. 1805), son of Richard Tyldesley, of The Friary, and Margaret Quayle, who was first in the Manx Fencibles and then a lieutenant in the 39th Regiment. He retired in 1802 and went to Guadaloupe, where he died. The careers of Captain QUILLIAM and Captain KELLY had begun at this time, but they belong, to a greater extent, to the period of 1803-15, to which we will now refer.

Let us take the Navy first.

JOHN QUILLIAM (b. 1771, d. 1829),

was the son of a farmer in the south of the island.* He first came into notice at the Battle of Camperdown in 1797, when he was made a lieutenant by Admiral Duncan. At the Battle of Copenhagen, in 1801, he was on a frigate of such light draught of water that she could get close under the batteries She was there subjected to such a tremendous fire that all QUILLIAM's superior officers were killed, so that he was left in command. At this juncture, Nelson came on board and enquired who was in charge of her, when a voice, that of QUILLIAM, ascended from the main deck, "I am," and, on the further question, "How are you getting on below?" the answer to the unknown inquisitor was "middlin'." This greatly amused Nelson, who so appreciated QUILLIAM's coolness, that he took an early opportunity of getting him on his own ship the "Victory," of which he was appointed first lieutenant. As the following extract from "James's Naval History of Great Britain" will show, he assisted in steering her into action at the Battle of Trafalgar :—

Just as she (the "Victory") had got about 500 yards of the larboard beam of the "Bucentaure," the "Victory's" mizzen-topmast

---

was shot away, about two-thirds up. A shot also struck and knocked to pieces the wheel; and the ship was obliged to be steered from the gun room, the first lieutenant (John Quilliam) and master (Thomas Atkinson) relieving each other at the duty.*

It seems somewhat curious that an officer of Quilliam's rank should have been engaged in steering, but some years ago a Manxman, a son of the late Rev. George Quirk, who was an engineer in the employ of the Trinity Board, discovered a reason for it from a document at Trinity House. It would appear that QUILLIAM had caused the damage which had been done to the steering gear "to be repaired according to a plan of his own, and then not feeling quite sure how this would act he took the tiller with his own hand."† After Trafalgar he was probably on shore for a time, since, in 1807, he was elected a member of the House of Keys, and, though he was at sea again in the following year, he did not resign his membership till 1810.

In 1808, he was commander in the "Spencer," Admiral Stopford's flag-ship, and, in the same year, according to a letter of Lieutenant Edward Christian's he was appointed captain of a vessel of 24 guns,‡ probably a sloop. In this letter Christian says that he is writing to him (Quilliam) "in favour of the son of Lady Napier, who is a midshipman under his command," and that he would also take the opportunity of mentioning his cousin, Evan Christian (see p. 140) to him.§ In 1812, he was in command of the "Crescent" and continued to serve in her till after the conclusion of the war in 1815. He then retired to his native island, living at the "White House," Kirk Michael. He was re-elected a member of House of Keys in 1817, and took a conspicuous part in the enquiry made by the Tynwald Court into the condition of the herring fishery in 1827. He died in 1829, being buried in Kirk Arbory Churchyard, where the following inscription may be read on his tombstone :—

Sacred to the memory of John Quilliam, Esq., Captain in the Royal Navy. In his early service he was appointed by Adml. Lord Duncan to act as lieutenant at the Battle of Camperdown; after the victory was achieved, this appointment was confirmed. His gallantry and professional skill at the Battle of Copenhagen attracted the notice of Lord Nelson, who subsequently sought for his services on board his own ship, and as his lordship's first lieut. he steered the Victory into action at the Battle of Trafalgar. By the example of Duncan and Nelson he learned to conquer. By his own merit he rose to command : above all this he was an honest man, the noblest work of God. After many years of honourable and distinguished professional service, he retired to this land of his

---

* Vol. III., p. 398. Edition of 1886.
† Letter from Mr W. A. Stevenson, J.P., a connexion of Quilliam's, in the *Tourist*, of December, 1898.
‡ The name of the vessel is illegible.
§ "The Letters of Lieutenant Edward Christian," p. 30. (Published by S. K. Broadbent & Co., Limited, Douglas, 1898.)

affectionate solicitude and birth, where in his public station as a member of the House of Keys, and in private life, he was in arduous times the uncompromising defender of the rights and privileges of his countrymen, and the zealous and able supporter of every measure tending to promote the welfare and the best interests of his country. He departed this life on the 10th October, 1829, in the 59th year of his age. This monument is erected by Margaret C. Quilliam to the memory of her beloved husband.

From the newspaper notice of his death we learn that he was a "benevolent friend . . . a sensible, social, pleasing companion," and "a kind and good master," also that "he was highly esteemed and much respected by all." Of

WILLIAM KELLY (b. 1771, d. 1823)

comparatively little is known. Appointed to the "Haarlem," in 1799, he became lieutenant of the "Illustrious" in 1804.* He was present at the capture of Cape Town in 1806, and received a silver cup for his bravery on that occasion.† He afterwards took part in the unfortunate expedition to Buenos Ayres. In 1814, he was in command of the brig "Insolent," which was sent on a recruiting expedition to the Isle of Man in that year. He retired in 1817, when he was named by the Keys as one of the candidates for admission to their body. He was not, however, selected by the governor till 1821.

PETER HEYWOOD (b. 1772, d. 1831)

was the third son of Deemster Peter Heywood (see p. 93.) and Elizabeth, daughter of James Spedding, of Whitehaven. He entered the Royal Navy in 1786, and made his first voyage as midshipman in the "Bounty," commanded by Captain Bligh, in the following year. The "Bounty" was bound for the South Sea Islands to make scientific observations. Captain Bligh was a great martinet, and there was, consequently, much discontent among the crew. On arrival at the Friendly Islands this feeling culminated in open mutiny, which was headed by FLETCHER CHRISTIAN, the "master's mate" (also a Manxman and one of the Christians of Milntown). The mutineers put Captain Bligh, together with 19 of the crew who remained faithful to him, on board a launch. They suffered the most extraordinary dangers and privations, but ultimately reached England. As soon as the English Government heard

---

* The commissions to these ships are in the possession of Mr. G. Preston.

† This, together with his cocked hat, were given by him to his housekeeper, Eleanor Kewish (Mr. Preston's grandmother), who afterwards married Thomas William Corlett, of Brough-jiarg, Ballaugh. They are now in the possession of her eldest son, Mr. Thomas Corlett, of Liverpool. Miss Preston, Mr. Preston's sister, has Captain Kelly's gold snuff-box.

of the mutiny it sent out the "Pandora" frigate, which, in
March, 1791, arrived at Otaheite, where HEYWOOD and thirteen
others were found. On the way home the "Pandora was wrecked,
and some of the crew and of the prisoners were drowned The
remainder, among whom was HEYWOOD, arrived in England in
June, 1792. HEYWOOD was at once brought to trial, and, though he
stated that he had been confined below while the mutiny was going
on, and did not learn what had happened till after Captain Bligh
had been cut adrift, he was found guilty, not of mutiny, but of
not having endeavoured to suppress it. He was recommended to
His Majesty's mercy, and in due course received a free pardon.
On the express recommendation of Lord Hood, who had presided
at his court-martial, he was permitted to re-enter the navy, going
on board the "Bellerophon." He took part in several actions
against the French, and, in 1797, Earl Spencer, who had attentively
considered the evidence given at HEYWOOD's trial, wrote to his
captain, Sir Thomas Pasley, to say there was nothing in it to stand
in the way of his promotion, "more especially when the gallantry
and propriety of his conduct in his subsequent service are taken
into consideration."

He became a post-captain in 1803 ; and, after a career of
important and responsible service, including two diplomatic
missions to South America, he was, in 1813, appointed to the
command of the "Montagu," of 74 guns, in which he served in
the North Sea and afterwards in the Mediterranean under Lord
Exmouth. He returned to England in 1816, when the "Montagu"
was paid off. He was greatly beloved by his officers and crew, by
one of whom the following lines were written at that time :—

> Farewell to thee, Heywood ! a truer one never
> Hath exercised rule o'er the sons of the sea ;
> The seamen who served thee would see for ever,
> Who sway'd, but ne'er fettered, the hearts of the brave.

In this same year he married, and, as he was in a weak state of
health, having never really recovered from his sufferings after the
mutiny, he declined a commodore's command in the Canadian lakes
which was offered to him by Lord Melville in 1818. From this
period he lived in London in complete seclusion. This excellent
officer and man had a well-proportioned figure, and was rather
above the middle height. His features were regular and good,
and indicative of a calm, observant, and reflecting mind. He was
cheerful in demeanour, and was a lively and versatile conver-
sationalist. "We do not hesitate," says Marshall in his "Naval
Biography," "to say that his king and country never had a more
faithful servant, nor the naval service a more worthy and
respectable member." (From the Memoir by Edward Taggart
London, 1832.)

HOOD HANWAY CHRISTIAN* (b. 1784, d. 1849),

son of Sir Hugh Cloberry Christian and Ann Leigh, was made a commander in the Navy at the very early age of sixteen for the gallant way in which he commanded a division of boats at the siege of Genoa. In 1809 he took part in the ill-fated Walcheren expedition, after which he saw no active service. In 1838 he became rear-admiral.

PHILIP COSNAHAN (d. 1819),

son of Deemster John Cosnahan and Catherine Finch,† was a midshipman on board H.M.S. "Shannon" when she fought her celebrated action with the American frigate "Chesapeake," and was specially mentioned in Captain Broke's report.‡ It is to him that Mr Fitchett, in his recently-published "Deeds that Won the Empire," referred when he wrote : "Another middy tried to attack the Chesapeake's mizzen top from the starboard mainyard arm, but, being hindered by the foot of the topsail, stretched himself out on the mainyard and from that post shot three of the enemy in succession."§

He did not reach a higher grade than that of lieutenant, as he was drowned when quite young in the Isle of Man sailing packet "Lord Hill," with the rest of the passengers and the whole of the crew, on the 16th of January, 1819. It is remarkable that he owed his death to his great agility, for the "Lord Hill" was actually some yards away from the Red Pier in Douglas, having begun the voyage, when he leaped on board.

He had two elder brothers in the Navy—HUGH (captain) and MICHAEL FINCH (commander). Hugh died in 1822, in Wales. His obituary notice describes him as being "a gentleman whose amiability of manner and unwarping integrity had gained him in every relation of life the sincere attachment of all who knew him." The latter died in 1885, at the great age of 95, in the Isle of Thanet, being buried in St. Peter's Churchyard there. There were also two TOBINS, nephews of Sir John Tobin (see Chapter VIII.) in the Navy. One, EDWARD, a lieutenant, the youngest son of Patrick Tobin, died when only twenty, in 1811, and the other, JOHN CÆSAR, a midshipman, third son of Major Tobin of Middle and

---

* Manx by descent only.
† Finch Road in Douglas was named after her father.
‡ "Shannon," Halifax, June 6. . . . It is impossible to particularize every brilliant deed performed by my officers and men . . . but I must mention, when the ships' yards were locked together, that Mr. Cosnahan who commanded in our maintop, finding himself screened from the enemy by the foot of the topsail, laid out on the mainyard to fire upon them and shot three men.
§ p. 133.

Ann Moore of Pulrose, was drowned at Demerara in 1812, aged eighteen. He had been serving on board the sloop "Bridget," Captain Vernon, which beat off an American privateer of seventeen guns. In this action his captain reported him as having behaved with great skill and gallantry.

There were also EDWARD GELLING, master (b. 1785, d. 1848), ROBERT KELLY, commander, THOMAS CRAINE*, commander (b. 1776, d. 1851), RICHARD CLARKE, lieutenant, son of Captain Edward Clarke* (b. 1788, d. 1823), THOMAS FREER, lieutenant (b. 1791, d. 1851). After the war Thomas Freer went into the merchant service, and, in 1851, was in command of the P. and O. steamer "Oriental," on board of which he died ; and EVAN CHRISTIAN, midshipman, son of Vicar-General Christian and Ann Kelly of Peel, and cousin of Lieutenant Edward Christian (see p. 143), who was first on board the "Barfleur" and then on the "Brunswick"† when she was at the bombardment of Copenhagen in 1807.

CHARLES CREBBIN, son of the Rev. Charles Crebbin, Vicar of Santon, was a major in the Marines. He, like Philip Cosnahan, was drowned in the "Lord Hill."

A number of Manxmen also served in the Navy before the mast. Of these, the seven following are known to have fought at Trafalgar : —

JOHN COWELL (b. 1786, d. 1863),

son of a northside farmer, was carried off by a press-gang from Douglas and became one of the crew of the "Temeraire," on board which ship he lost his right arm by a cannon-shot which struck him just as he was in the act of ramming home a cannon charge. On his return home, duly pensioned, he became a student, acquiring a knowledge not only of navigation and the Manx language, but of science and the classics. Notwithstanding his physical disability he was invited to enter the ministry of the Wesleyan Methodist Church, but he preferred the profession of a schoolmaster. He was also a land surveyor, and conducted a survey of the island for the English Government. As a lay preacher he was both able and eloquent. For many years he was parish clerk of Bride, thus uniting, like many of the early Wesleyans, service in the Church of England with fidelity to his own denomination. On one occasion his zeal in holding religious meetings brought him into collision with the archdeacon, who complained to the bishop. The latter, who thereupon summoned

---

* See Chapter VIII.
† This vessel had been Admiral Hood's flagship in 1778, when Prince William, afterwards King William IV., was a midshipman on her.

him to Bishop's Court, on finding that he was well versed in the old English divines, and was able to give reasons for his faith and to make it clear to others, sent him away with his blessing, telling him to continue his good work. During the epidemic of cholera at Dalby, he distinguished himself by his tender care of the sufferers whom others shunned. We may mention that he was a brother-in-law of William Kennish, (see p. 118), that several of his grandsons are now in the Wesleyan ministry, and one, Mr. J. T. Cowell, is a Justice of the Peace and a member for Douglas in the House of Keys. Endowed with real genius, JOHN COWELL was also a man of the highest character, and he has left an honourable name behind him.

CHARLES CORLETT (b. 1771, d. 1862) was present at the battle of the Nile in 1798, at Copenhagen in 1801, and at Trafalgar in 1805. He was also at the siege of Rangoon, and took part in several cutting-out expeditions. During the whole of his career, though he was several times taken prisoner and several times made his escape from prison, he only received one wound. He latterly resided with his son at Rock Ferry. He was interred at Bebington with naval honours, being accompanied to the grave by about 60 of the crew of H.M.S. "Majestic." (See also p. 135.)

JOHN LACE, of the Kerroodhoo, Kirk Bride, was on board the "Victory," where he lost his right arm. In fact he believed that the shot which mortally wounded Nelson, first passed through his (Lace's) arm. After leaving the Navy he was a pilot off Ramsey, and lost his life in Ramsey Bay when endeavouring to board a vessel to pilot her to Douglas.

JOHN COWLE, of Kirk Bride, was quartermaster of the "Victory." THOMAS CURPHEY (b. 1778, d. 1854) was boatswain in the "Britannia."

WILLIAM KELLY (b. 1787, d. 1866) was in the "Royal Sovereign." He entered the Navy in 1803, and continued to serve till 1819, when he retired on a pension.

THOMAS CANNELL, of Kirk German (b. 1783, d. 1864), was in the "Conqueror."

JOHN CRELLIN (b. 1791, d. 1855), born at Port St. Mary, was apprenticed when a lad to the owners of the brig "Sally," of Whitehaven. He was impressed into the Royal Navy and served on the "Bellerophon," Captain Maitland, being on that vessel when Napoleon came on board of her and surrendered. After the war he returned to the island and followed the avocation of a fisherman.

Another "man of war's man" at this time was PHILIP TEARE, of Ballaugh, who made use of his experience by drilling the northside people who took part in the potato riots in 1825, and he marched at their head against Bishop's Court.

JAMES GALE served on the "Apollo" frigate till he was discharged on becoming blind. We know from a subscription list dated 1811 that there were 25 Manx sailors prisoners in France in that year.

In the Army at this period, and probably also in the previous war, as regards the first three names, there were : CALCOTT HEYWOOD (b. 1766, d. 1852), a son of Robert Heywood, water-bailiff, and Margaret, daughter of Richard Joiner, who was a captain in the Manx Fencibles in 1794. In 1810, he was chosen as a member of the House of Keys, but refused to serve. The House then petitioned Lieut.-Governor Smelt to "take the proper and necessary steps according to Law and Custom in that case provided"* to make him do so. Instead of yielding he joined the 9th Regiment and went to the Peninsular War. Retiring in 1815, with the rank of captain, he was again elected a member of the House of Keys, and seems to have accepted his fate without further protest.

JOHN TAUBMAN (d. 1812), son of John Taubman, Speaker of the House of Keys, and Dorothy Christian of Milntown, was in command of the 66th Regiment and then of the 101st. After he retired from the Army he was commandant of the South Manx Volunteers, and he became a member of the House of Keys.

THOMAS CORLETT, of Loughan-e-Yeigh, Lezayre, was, after the war, made barrack-master of King's Mews Barracks in London.

THOMAS WATTLEWORTH (b. 1785), son of Thomas Wattleworth and Catherine Kelly, was a lieutenant in the 26th Regiment, and fought at Martinique and Guadaloupe in the West Indies. His brother, JAMES KELLY WATTLEWORTH (b. 1787, d. 1812), was an adjutant in the Dragoon Guards. He was killed by a fall from his horse at Brighton. They were sons of Thomas Wattleworth and Christian Kelly, of Peel.

JOHN CHRISTIAN CRELLIN (b. 1788, d. 1842),

the only son of Deemster Crellin and Charlotte, only daughter of Thomas Christian, of Ballachurry, Andreas, obtained a commission as lieutenant in the Sixth Dragoon Guards (Carabineers), for which regiment he raised twenty-four troopers from the Isle of Man. Shortly afterwards he exchanged into the 4th, "King's Own," but, owing to ill-health, he was soon obliged to resign without seeing any active service. He returned to the island in 1816, and was, in 1817, elected a member of the House of Keys, to which he continued to belong for 25 years. He was Chairman of the Highway Board for a long time, and, in this connexion, it may be mentioned that he was the means of substituting granite for wood as the substance of the roadside drinking troughs throughout the island. He was a

* Keys' Journals.

keen horticulturist, being the introducer, among other things, of the red flowering currant tree to the island.

EDWARD CHRISTIAN (b. *circa* 1780), probably a son of Edward Christian, of Lewaigue, and Catherine Allen, of Ballavarry, and certainly a nephew of Vicar-General Christian, was a lieutenant in the 43rd Regiment, which formed part of the army intended to oppose Napoleon's threatened invasion. He fought at Copenhagen in 1807, and at Corunna, but it is not known whether he went through the Peninsular War with his regiment or not. A number of letters written by him to his uncle, which have been published by Messrs. S. K. Broadbent & Co., throw a very interesting light on the history of the time.

NICHOLAS CHRISTIAN (b. 1790, d. 1814), son of the Rev. John Christian, Vicar of Arbory, was a lieutenant in the 47th Regiment. He joined it in India, where it had gone after the Battle of Maida, and died there.

THOMAS MOORE, youngest son of Deemster Thomas Moore, of the Abbey, and Margaret Moore, of the Hills, was a captain in the 59th Regiment. He fought in the Peninsular War.

GEORGE HORSLEY WOOD (b. 1794, d. 1874), served as lieutenant in the 20th Foot in the Peninsula and in India, and was one of the body-guard of the Emperor Napoleon at St. Helena (see p. 103).

CÆSAR BACON (b. 1791, d. 1876),

son of John Joseph Bacon and his second wife, Anne, daughter of the Rev. J. Cosnahan, of Ballakilley, now Seafield, was an ensign in the 23rd Light Dragoons when he fought at Quatre-Bras and Waterloo. At the latter battle he was slightly wounded in two places. He afterwards rose to the rank of major, and, retiring from active service in 1818, he went to the island. He was shortly afterwards elected a member of the House of Keys, and was appointed captain of the parish of Santon and a justice of the peace. He was a considerable landowner, and by the introduction of improved methods he did much for the improvement of agriculture in the island. At the time of his death, a contemporary newspaper spoke of him as "a native of this island of whom Manxmen might be justly proud ; a man of strict integrity and honour ; a gentleman of the old school, whose kindly manners and hospitality will be missed among a large circle."

There were a number of Manxmen in the ranks at this time, but, except their names, we know nothing of them. COLONEL MARK WILKS and SIR MARK CUBBON were also in the army at this period, but their chief claim to distinction arises from their services as civil servants (see pp. 154-159).

THOMAS COSTEAN.

We have now to refer to the extraordinary story of THOMAS COSTEAN, COSTAIN, or CASTINE, of the parish of Lonan, who is said to have been identical with the famous General Custine. It can, however, be proved beyond doubt that this was not so,* but it is possible, and indeed probable, that there was a Manx Costain who served in the French army, and attained high rank.

Let us give the account of him in the "Biographical Anecdotes of the Founders of the French Republic,"† quoted by Train :—

Thomas Custine, one of the most conspicuous chiefs of the French Republic, was born at Ballaneille, in the parish of Lonan. . . When a youth he enlisted in a British "regiment of the line" called the "King's Own," in which he rose to the rank of sergeant. Having returned, after a few years' absence, to his native isle, on leave from his regiment, he married a young woman named Helen Colace (Quilleash), with whom he had been acquainted previous to his departure ; but, indulging too freely with his former companions in the dissipation which then prevailed in the island, he outstayed his pass so long that he was about to be apprehended as a deserter, when he escaped on board a smuggling lugger to Dunkirk. He then entered into the French service, and, it is said, served some time in America.‡

The account of him up to this time is all probable enough, but, after it, COSTEAN is identified with the famous revolutionary general who was beheaded in 1793. It would seem that the Manx-French COSTEAN had a son, also Thomas, who, according to Train, was a servant in the Isle of Man. He afterwards enlisted in the Manx Fencibles, and, in 1837, was a merchant in the village of Auchencairn, in Galloway. It is said that he, understanding that his father died possessed of some property in France, applied to Prince Talleyrand in the hope of regaining it. But, on the prince making enquiries, it was found "if General Custine had really been possessed of property at the time of his death, all trace of it was lost amid the confusion into which France was thrown subsequent to the year 1793."§ Here again it would seem that the comparatively obscure Manx-French COSTEAN had been confused by Talleyrand with the Austrian-French Custine. The probabilities of the case are, then, that there was actually a THOMAS COSTEAN, whose name would easily become Custine in France, who served in the French army, probably attaining the rank of general, and that he married Helen Quilleash, which is not an uncommon name in the parish of Lonan. There is no

---

* "Count Adam Philippe de Custine . . . almost a German, born of a high family at Metz." (Lamartine, "History of the Girondists." Vol. II., p. 371.)
† London, 1798. Vol. II., p. 303.
‡ History of the Isle of Man. Vol. II., p. 349.
§ *Ibid,* p. 350.

reason to doubt the account of THOMAS COSTEAN the younger, and it may be mentioned that there are only two Thomas Costeans recorded in the parish register in the 18th century. One of these was baptized on the 2nd of November, 1746, and his son of the same name was baptized on the 28th of September, 1777.

The following distinguished Manx sailors and soldiers are of later date.

BALDWIN WAKE WALKER, K.C.B., Baronet (b. 1802, d. 1876),

son of John Walker of Whitehaven and Frances, daughter of Captain Drury Wake, of the 17th Dragoons, and niece of Sir William Wake, eighth baronet, was born at Port-e-Vullen, near Ramsey. He entered the Navy in 1812, was made a lieutenant in 1820, and served for two years on the Jamaica station, then for three years on the coast of South America and the west coast of Africa. In 1827, he went out to the Mediterranean in the "Rattlesnake," and, in 1828, was first lieutenant of the "Etna" at the reduction of Kastro, in the Morea. For this service he received the crosses of the Legion of Honour and of the Redeemer of Greece. He continued in the Mediterranean, serving in the "Asia," "Britannia," and "Barham," and was made commander in 1834. In that rank he served in the "Vanguard," in the Mediterranean, between 1836 and 1838. By permission of the Admiralty he then accepted a command in the Turkish Navy, in which he was known as Walker Bey, and afterwards as Yavir Pasha. In July, 1840, the Capitan Pasha took the fleet to Alexandria and delivered it over to Mehemet Ali, who then refused to part with it Walker summoned the Turkish Captains to a council of war, and proposed to them to land in the night, surround the palace, carry off Mehemet Ali, and send him to Constantinople. This would probably have been done had not Mehemet Ali in the meantime consented to let the ships go. Walker afterwards commanded the Turkish squadron at the reduction of Acre, for which service he was nominated a K.C.B. in 1841 ; he also received from the allied sovereigns the second class of the Iron Crown of Austria, of St. Anne of Russia, and of the Red Eagle of Prussia. Returning to England in 1845, he commanded the "Queen," as flag-captain to Sir John West at Devonport, and, in 1846-7, the "Constance" frigate in the Pacific. From 1848 to 1860, he was surveyor of the Navy; he was made a baronet in 1856, a rear-admiral in 1858, and in 1861 he was appointed commander-in-chief at the Cape of Good Hope, whence he returned home in 1864. He became vice-admiral in 1865, and admiral in 1870. He died at his residence at Diss in Norfolk.

(From The Dictionary of National Biography.)

ALEXANDER TAUBMAN-GOLDIE, R.N.
(b. 1811, d. 1893),

the third son of General Goldie and Isabella Christian Taubman,
entered the Navy as a first-class volunteer in 1824. His first ship
was the "Brazen," of 26 guns, in which he assisted in the capture
of a number of armed slavers and in the liberation of nearly a
thousand slaves. In 1826, he joined the "Ganges," of 84 guns,
and served in her at the time of the mutiny among the German
and Irish mercenaries at Rio Janeiro, where a landing party from
the British squadron was instrumental in subduing the revolt.
His next vessel was the "St. Vincent" in 1829, and in the same
year he joined the "Druid," of 46 guns. He was made a lieutenant in 1831, and, as such, joined, first, the "Volage," of 28
guns, and, second, the "Andromache," of 26 guns, in the
Mediterranean. In 1839, he was promoted to be commander of
the sloop "Blossom," and from 1841 to 1856 he was an inspecting
officer of coastguards. He retired with the rank of captain in the
latter year, and from thenceforward he lived in his native island,
where he was appointed a magistrate in 1851, and in that capacity
did much useful service. He was generally respected and
esteemed for his many excellent qualities.

THOMAS LEIGH GOLDIE (b. 1807, d. 1854),

was the second son of General Goldie and Isabella Christian
Taubman, of the Nunnery, where he was born. Till 1825, when
he joined the 66th Regiment, he lived in the island. After
attaining the rank of major in that regiment, he acted as military
and private secretary to Sir John Colborne, afterwards Lord
Seaton. He saw no active service till 1839, when he went with
his regiment to Canada to assist in quelling the disturbances there.
For the ability and zeal he displayed at that time he was promoted
to the colonelcy of the 57th Regiment. His next service was in
the Crimea, where he commanded a brigade, at the head of which
he fell fighting at the Battle of Inkermann on the 5th November,
1854. He was interred at Cathcart's Hill, near Sebastopol, where
there is a monument to his memory. A large monument in the
Nunnery Grounds, and a tablet in Malew Church, with the same
object, were erected by public subscription. On the tablet are
the following words:—"After repeated charges at the head of
his Brigade of the 4th Division [he] . . fell mortally wounded
and a few hours after departed this life." Lord Raglan,
in the despatch announcing the result of the Battle of
Inkermann, speaks of him as "an officer of considerable
promise," who "gave great satisfaction to all whom he
has served;" and the "Manx Sun," in an obituary notice, states

that "he was remarkable alike for the strict performance of his own duties to the minutest item, and for his equally strict enforcement of the duties of those under him, but that without the needless severity of the martinet," and that "this in no way diminished his personal popularity, which was very great."

ALEXANDER J. J. MACDONALD (b. 1829, d. 1889),

son of Captain Ronald Macdonald, a brother of the Chief of Glencoe, and Maria, daughter of Dr. Thomas, of Ballacosnahan, and Ann Cosnahan, was born in Douglas, and was educated, for the most part, at Forrester's school in that town. He entered the 95th Regiment in 1847, and went to Varna and the Crimea in 1854. He was present at the Battle of Alma, where he received a slight contusion, a bullet having struck his breastplate, in which it remained embedded. At Inkermann he was adjutant of his regiment, and was very severely wounded, being struck on the knee by a bullet and knocked off his horse. When lying on the ground he got no less than twenty bayonet wounds, which, marvellous to relate, did not kill him. He went home invalided, and, being retired, as colonel, upon half pay, he was appointed fort major at Edinburgh Castle. On succeeding to the estate of Balla-cosnahan, after the death of Miss Anne Thomas, he gave up this appointment and went to live in London, where he remained till his death. (Information from Col. Anderson, receiver-general.)

The other Manx army officers in the Crimea were :—

JOHN TAUBMAN QUAYLE, whose epitaph in St. Mary's Church, Castletown, gives the following account of him :—

In memory of John Edward Taubman Quayle, eldest son of John Quayle, Esq., of Castletown, brevet major and senior captain of the 33rd, Duke of Wellington's Regiment, who died at Surat on the 29th of May, 1859, aged 35 years, from the effects of a sunstroke received whilst in command of a field force sent against the mutineers. He served in the W. Indies and N. America, and was at the Battle of Alma and the Siege of Sebastopol, where he was shot through the body, for which service he received the Cross of the Legion of Honour, the Crimean medal and clasps, and the Turkish Order of the Medjide ;

ROBERT C. CUNNINGHAM, captain in the 42nd Highlanders, who was at the Battle of Alma. He was invalided home in August, 1855, but died in September of low fever at Malta ;

EDWARD GAWNE (b. 1836, d. 1869), who was the eldest son of the Speaker of the House of Keys. He served as lieutenant in the 79th Regiment, but, not being in good health, he was granted leave of absence after a short stay in the Crimea. He died at

Pulrose, Braddan; WILLIAM DALRYMPLE THOMPSON, captain in
the 17th Regiment. He, like Major Quayle, received the Legion
of Honour; and

JOHN JOSEPH BACON, captain in the 95th Regiment.

In the Navy there were LIEUTENANT, now ADMIRAL, PARSONS,
son of the then government chaplain, brother of Mrs Crellin, of
Orrysdale, who was in the naval brigade; and LIEUTENANT LEWIS
GENESTE—the late Captain Geneste—who did good service during
this war in the "Herring" gunboat, which was stationed in the
Baltic. LIEUTENANT PARSONS also received the Legion of Honour.
He and Messrs. Quayle, Thompson, and Lewis Geneste were
educated at King William's College.

There were several Manxmen who served in the ranks during
this war.

There seems to have been only one Manxman serving as an
officer in the Indian Mutiny, namely, MAXIMILIAN GODWIN
GENESTE, brother of Lewis Geneste, who was a lieutenant in
the Bengal Engineers. He took ill during the operations before
Delhi, and died in the Isle of Wight in 1858.

In the ranks there were, among others, COLOUR-SERGEANT
BURROWS, who served in the 53rd Regiment during the Sikh
campaign, as well as in the Mutiny. He was at the relief of
Lucknow. After the war, when he became drill instructor to the
Cumberland volunteers, he was presented by the War Office with
£10 and a medal "for long and faithful service and good conduct."

There were also ROBERT and JOSEPH CREER, sons of Thomas
Creer, commonly called "Tom Juty." his wife's name being Judith.

JAMES SPEDDING QUAYLE (b. 1843, d. 1882), of Bridge House,
Castletown, was a captain in the Royal Artillery, and served with
distinction in the Abyssinian campaign, for which he received
a medal.

It is said that about one hundred Manxmen have been engaged
in the recent war in South Africa, and we have reason to be
proud of the conduct of all of them, from COLONEL GAWNE
to little BUGLER DUNNE, who was presented to Queen Victoria
and received a bugle from her in recognition of his gallantry at
the Battle of Colenso.

Of these we know that COLONEL GAWNE and COLOUR-SERGEANT
WALLACE have been killed, but we fear that others of whom we
have not heard may have died also.

JOHN MOORE GAWNE (b. 1854, d. 1900),

the youngest son of Edward Moore and Emily Maria Gawne (see
Ch. I. and Ch. IX.) was educated at Lieutenant Shaw's school in
Douglas, at Cheltenham College, and at Sandhurst. He served in

the Zulu War of 1878, and in the South African War since June last. At the end of September he was appointed district commissioner and general commander of forces at Vryheid, in the Transvaal, "on account of his tact and impartiality in dealing with the Boers." His command was attacked on several occasions by the Boers, who were invariably repulsed with heavy loss. It was during the last of these attacks, on the 11th December, that Colonel Gawne, who had been complimented by General Hildyard on his "able and prompt measures," was mortally wounded. He died on the following day. According to a brother officer, who knew him well, he "was a most zealous and active officer. All through his military career his profession came first with him. He stood alone, and asked favours from none. He saw his duty in front of him, and did it truly and well. His juniors went to him for advice and help, and did not go in vain, and his seniors knew they had in him one they could trust, and whose advice would always be what was right. He was loved by officers, n.c.o.'s., and men, and he has left a blank, not only in the regiment, but in the hearts of his friends, that can never be filled."

William Wallace, colour-sergeant (b. 1870, d. 1900), eldest son of John Wallace, master of Ballagawne School, Lonan, was born in Ballaugh. He joined the Seaforth Highlanders in 1892. His promotion was rapid, he being made colour-sergeant in 1897. He served through the Chitral expedition with great credit. In South Africa he fought bravely at Belmont and Graspan, and he was under heavy fire at Magersfontein, finally meeting with his death at Paardeburg. The writer of his obituary notice speaks of him as being "a fine specimen of a soldier and a man."

The Fencibles.

Towards the end of the eighteenth century "Fencible" regiments, which belonged, it must be remembered, to the regular army, but with service only within the British Islands, were formed in Man, as elsewhere. The first regiment of "Royal Manx Fencibles," as it was called, which numbered 333 of all ranks, was formed in 1780. It was disbanded in 1783, after the Peace of Versailles, and was re-embodied in 1793. In 1795, a second regiment of five companies, numbering about 360 men in all, was formed, and five more companies were added in 1797. This force, of about 700 men, served during the Rebellion in Ireland, while the first regiment was kept in the island. Both regiments were disbanded in 1802. On the renewal of the war, a single regiment of 800 men was formed. This

regiment was disbanded in 1810. Its members were more remarkable for the breadth of their shoulders than their height, which
averaged 5 feet 7½ inches, since they are said to have covered
more ground than any other regiment in the British Army. They
were, no doubt, a very fine body of men. Some of their officers
have already been mentioned under other headings, and we
give here the names of all the others about whom we have
been able to obtain any information. The following were
majors :* WILLIAM CUNNINGHAM, probably a son of Col. William
Cunningham.† He was an M.H.K.; CÆSAR TOBIN (b. 1770, d.
1841). He was the proprietor of Middle in Braddan, and brother
of Sir John Tobin. He was an M.H.K. from 1819 till his death.

The following were captains : THOMAS CHRISTIAN, probably the
father of William Watson Christian, and proprietor of Ballachurry,
Andreas. He was an M.H.K. in 1797 ; JOHN CHRISTIAN, the eldest
son of John Christian of Pooildhooie and Catherine Callow of
Ballaglass ;‡ WILLIAM BACON, probably an uncle of John Joseph
and Cæsar Bacon ; PHILIP MOORE (b. 1769), a son of Deemster
Thomas Moore of the Abbey and Margaret Moore of the Hills ;
RICHARD HARRISON (b. 1774), probably an ancestor of the late
Ridgway Harrison ; JOHN FRISSELL (b. 1737, d. 1793), an M.H.K.
from 1758 till his death. He was also High-Bailiff of Ramsey,
father of John, Charles, and William, who were in the Royal
Navy (see p. 134) and son of Attorney-General Frissell and
Margery, daughter of Deemster Nicholas Christian of Ballastole ;
JAMES QUIRK probably belonged to the Parville family and was
an M.H.K. in 1797. He was afterwards attorney-general ;
DANIEL F. WILSON was one of the Farm Hill family. He was
an M.H.K. in 1824.

The following were lieutenants : CHARLES MOORE, brother of
the Philip Moore already mentioned ; RICHARD QUIRK, probably
James Quirk's son. He was afterwards receiver-general ; EDWARD
QUAYLE (b. 1761), a son of John Quayle, C.R., and Margaret
Moore, daughter of Sir George Moore of Ballamoore. He was an
M.H.K. in 1813 ; MARK HILDESLEY QUAYLE, his brother (b. 1770,
d. 1804), became clerk-of-the-rolls in 1797 ; ROBERT FARRANT
(b. 1753, d. 1820), High-Bailiff of Peel, became the proprietor of
Ballamoar, Jurby, through his marriage with the heiress, Miss
Christian. He was an M.H.K. in 1813 ; NORRIS MOORE (d. 1818),
afterwards deemster ; WILLIAM QUILLIN, probably a son of the
attorney-general of that name. He was an M.H.K. in 1797;
MARK COSNAHAN (b. 1773), son of Hugh Cosnahan and Eleanor
Finch ; PHILIP THOMAS MOORE (b. 1772) ; JOHN LAMOTHE

---

* We give the highest rank to which they attained in each case.
† See p. 134.
‡ She afterwards married Thomas Howard (see p. 32).

(b. 1764, d. 1808), the eldest son of Dominique Lamothe and Susanna, daughter of Henry Corrin of Castletown. The history of Dominique Lamothe, the French progenitor of a Manx family which has done good service to the island, is interesting enough to deserve a few lines. He was the son of Sieur Armand Lamothe of Bayonne, in the Basses Pyrenees, and Marguerite Perez. In 1760, he went as surgeon on board the privateer brig "St. Lawrence," of 10 guns. She captured several English vessels, the crews of which rose and took possession of her, bringing her into Douglas. Dominique, with the rest of the French crew, was imprisoned in Castle Rushen, but was released on parole. When H.M.S. "Delight" came to take off the prisoners, he, "having gone on an exploring expedition into the island,"* was not to be found, and so the "Delight" sailed without him. He was then re-imprisoned, but it it said that his medical skill proved so success-ful in the case of the governor's wife that he was released, and as, after the conclusion of peace in 1763, he remained in the island of his own free will, he continued the practice of his profession there ; RICHARD and ROBERT GELLING, probably sons of Edward Gelling of Castletown and Isabella Moore of Pulrose. This family is now, we believe, represented by Mr H. E. Gelling, advocate, Castletown ; HENRY WHITESIDE, an ancestor of Mr. Robert Whiteside, now residing in Douglas.

The following were ensigns : FREDERICK LAMOTHE, John's brother (b. 1773, d. 1838), was both ensign and "surgeon's mate." He was afterwards an M.R.C.S., and practised in Ramsey for 35 years. He was the late high-bailiff's grandfather ; EDWIN HOLWELL HEYWOOD, a brother of Captain Peter Heywood ; ROBERT BANKS (b. 1779, d. 1818), proprietor of Howstrake, Onchan. He was an M.H.K. in 1808 ; JOHN MOORE (b. 1778, d. 1854), a son of Robert Moore of Pulrose, and Eleanor Gelling. He married Eunice Teresa Caterina Oates, neé Moore, heiress of the Hills' property in 1808. He was a member of the House of Keys from 1819 to 1854, being speaker from 1852 to 1854 ; JOHN BRIDSON probably belonged to the Ballavarvane family ; DANIEL MYLREA, probably a son of Archdeacon Daniel Mylrea ; JAMES TOBIN (b. 1790, d. 1818), a son of Major Cæsar Tobin and Ann Moore ; THOMAS MOORE, son of Charles Moore, of Billown, and Jane Clucas, of Maryvoar. He was afterwards an M.H.K. The present proprietor of Billown is his grandson ; JOHN LLEWELLYN, probably a son of Captain John Llewellyn, already mentioned.† He was an M.H.K. in 1813 ; WILLIAM GENESTE, a member of a well-known family which settled in Douglas early in the eighteenth century. He was probably an ancestor of the two Genestes who

---

* From an account by the late J. C. Lamothe.
† See p. 134.

served in the Crimean War ; PHILIP OATES CHRISTIAN, a son of
Captain John Christian* and Catherine Oates.   He died at
Omagh in 1801.

There were also the following officers, with Manx names, whom
we have not been able to identify : Lieutenants HENRY MOORE,
R. CLAGUE, WILLIAM KEWLEY, WILLIAM BREW ; Ensigns JOHN
CLAGUE, ROBERT CHRISTIAN, THOMAS CLUCAS, WILLIAM CUBBON,†
WILLIAM CALLOW,† JAMES GARRETT, and PHILIP CALEY.

The Militia.

Every Manxman was, and is, bound to give free military
service. Early in the sixteenth century we find the militia
divided into twenty-two companies, under their captains,
lieutenants, and ensigns. Of these companies, one came from
each of the seventeen parishes, except Lezayre, which had
two, and one from each of the towns.‡   Their only
appearance on active service, as far as is known, was in
1651, when, under the command of Receiver WILLIAM CHRISTIAN
(*Illiam Dhone*), they rose against the Countess of Derby and
captured all the forts, except Rushen and Peel. Their chief
leaders, in addition to William Christian, were WILLIAM CHRISTIAN
of Knockrushen, EWAN CURGHEY of Ballakillingan, SAMSBURY
RADCLIFFE of Gourden, and JOHN CÆSAR of Ballahick, of whom
we will give brief notices.§

WILLIAM CHRISTIAN, of Knockrushen, near Castletown,
was a younger brother of Captain Edward Christian (see
p. 60). We know that this was so from some interesting
evidence given in the records, in 1716, in reference to the
property of Ballakilley, in Maughold, a part of which was then
in the hands of the descendants of one of Edward's and William's
sisters. This evidence is to the effect that "Vicar Christian"
(of Maughold) "had three sons. His eldest was a clergyman
called young vicar, his second son Edward, who for some time
was Governor of this Island, and after Receiver and Major Generall,
his third son was William marryed to the heiress of Knock-
rushen."|| Like his namesake, William held for a time the office
of receiver. The first reference to his name in the records is in
1642, when the inhabitants of Castletown petitioned the governor

---

   * See p. 150.
   † A William Cubbon and a William Callow were "M.H.Ks." in 1797.
   ‡ For full details about the Manx Militia and Fencibles see "The military
organisation of the Isle of Man," in *Yn Lioar Manninagh.* Vol. II., pp. 141-53.
   § We assume that they were the chief leaders, since, except William Christian
of Knockrushen, who died either at the end of 1651, or early in 1652, they were
the only Manxmen who had their estates seized and confiscated in 1662 on
account of the rising in 1651.
   || *Lib. Scaccar.*

to prevent him from making any more use of his "kill," as it "hath been twise fired in one yeare to the hazard of the utter overthrowe of the whole towne."* In July, 1644, he was confined in Castle Rushen on suspicion of having incited the people to revolt against the earl, and having given them the "dangerous oath and covenant."† When there, he was accused of treason because he was supposed to have said, "A petition [for his release] will do noe more good than a straw ; but if the Captain and Comptroller weare taken and kept at Bishopp's Court, he might then gett released."* This was referred to the Tynwald Court, which stated that "if it can be lawfully proved that there was an intention to put in practice the taking of the Captaine and detaining him by force against his will, in such a case we are all of opinion that it is Treason by the Lawe of the Island."* He was acquitted of this charge, but was detained in prison some months longer. In 1651, he was one of the chief of those who were consulted about the rising. He seems to have been a member of the House of Keys, since at a meeting of that body in 1652, it is recorded that he had recently died.

EWAN CURGHEY, son of John Curghey, of Ballakillingan,‡ was *Illiam Dhone's* brother-in-law, having married his youngest sister, Margaret. He was a member of the House of Keys, and Captain of the Parish of Lezayre, and took a very active part in the rising of 1651. At this time, his father, then described as "old John Curghie," was captain of the parish, but his son acted for him. After raising the parish, his first exploit was the capture of the fort at Ramsey, and, the next day, of the "loyall fourt" near Ballachurry, in Andreas, where he took Major Thomas Stanley prisoner. From thence he went to Ronaldsway. He then seems to have been present at the siege of Peel Castle under Captain Samsbury Radcliffe, and he was one of those deputed to arrange terms on behalf of the islanders with Colonel Duckenfield.

SAMSBURY RADCLIFFE, also a member of the House of Keys, was owner of the estate of Gourden, in Patrick. He was in command not only of his parish company, but of all the northern companies who laid siege to Peel Castle. The castle was actually taken by them, but they were afterwards driven out again. In 1657, he got into trouble for "defaming the Governor and Deemster."*

JOHN CÆSAR, of Ballahick, Malew, a member of a once well-known insular family, now extinct in the male line, was lieutenant of the parish company of Malew, and seems to have

---

* *Lib. Scaccar.*
† *Manx Soc.*, Vol. III., p. 35.
‡ For full particulars about his family see the *Manx Note Book*, No. 7.

been engaged in the vain attempt to take Castle Rushen. He was one of the delegates who met Colonel Duckenfield. He was a member of the House of Keys till 1654, and then, till 1660, attorney-general. We have only one more glimpse of JOHN CÆSAR, and that is in connexion with his wife, Jane, who, in 1659, was acquitted of a charge of witchcraft, but was, nevertheless, ordered "to declare her innocence" in church. On the reading of this order, "Mr. Jo: Cæsar (and his said wife beinge in their own seate in the Chancle) said to his wife, 'Can't you say that you renounce the Divell?' which she accordingly did."* JOHN CÆSAR'S property, as well as that of Ewan Curghey and Samsbury Radcliffe, was restored by order in Council in 1663.

Civil Service.

There have also been some distinguished Manxmen in the Civil Service of the Crown:

JOHN MURREY (d. 1770),

a son of John Murrey and Susannah Patten, a first cousin of Bishop Wilson's wife and grandson of John Murrey of "Murrey's Pence" (see Chapter IX.), was born in Douglas. He went to England when quite young, and became a member of the English Bar. During the reign of George the First, he was appointed ambassador at Constantinople, and held that office till after the accession of George the Third. He died at Venice, in his sister Elizabeth's† house, on his way home from Constantinople, and there he left three silver boxes marked respectively, "George I.," "George II.," and "George III.," containing the seals of his appointments as ambassador under those sovereigns. Two of these, together with his portrait, and that of his sister, are now in the possession of Mr. J. C. Crellin, of Ballachurry. He married the Dowager Lady Wentworth, but had no children. He had an estate called Landican in Cheshire.

MARK WILKS (b. 1759, d. 1831),

a son of the Rev. James Wilks (see p. 26) and Margaret Woods, was born at Kirk Michael Vicarage, being named Mark

---

* Malew Register; in the *Manx Note Book*, Vol. II., p. 136.
† John Murrey's sister's husband, Joseph Smith by name, was British Consul in Venice. It may be mentioned that he and his wife made a collection of books and articles of *vertu* which were sold to George III. for £20,000. They are now in the British Museum. The catalogue of these books is at Ballachurry.

after his godfather, Bishop Hildesley. His father endeavoured, in 1771, to get him on the Charter-House foundation, but he did not succeed in doing so. Being at one time intended for the ministry, he received a classical education, and, in consequence, went to India at a later age than was usual. He obtained a cadetship in 1781, and in 1782 he received a commission in the Madras army. In 1788, he was appointed fort-adjutant at Fort St. George, and in 1789 he was promoted lieutenant. From 1790 to 1792 he acted as brigade-major and aide-de-camp to Colonel James Stuart. In 1793, he was assistant adjutant-general. From 1795 to 1799, he was on furlough from bad health, and yet, in 1797, he joined the Royal Manx Fencibles, who were then serving in Ireland, as lieutenant. He had received his captaincy in his absence from India, in 1798, and, on his return there, he served successively as military secretary and private secretary to the governor, Lord Clive. He was next appointed town-major of Fort St. George. From 1803 to 1808, he was political Resident at the Court of Mysore, attaining the rank of major in 1804, and that of lieutenant-colonel in 1808.* He was invalided home in that year, being in the island for a short time between 1809 and 1811, when he was elected a member of the House of Keys. After another year in India he resigned the office he held there, and, coming home, he, early in 1813, married (as his second wife) Dorothy Taubman, daughter of the Speaker of the House of Keys, and was at once re-elected a member of that body. He had bought the estate of Kirby, and had just commenced building a house on it, when, in the spring of 1813, he was offered the post of Governor of St. Helena by the East India Company, which he accepted, but for three years only. He took up his duties there in June, and wrote from thence, on the 12th of August, resigning his membership of the Keys. "He had thus been out some two years when Napoleon landed, and, during that time, had succeeded in winning the devotion of the islanders by his improvements in agriculture and by inducing the Company to ameliorate the system of land tenure."† Though he received Napoleon on his arrival, Admiral Sir George Cockburn, who had brought him from England, remained in charge of him till Sir Hudson Lowe came, in April 1816. Napoleon evidently both liked and respected WILKS. Some notes of the interesting conversations they had together, which were taken by the latter, have been preserved by his lineal representative, the late Sir Mark Wilks Collet, Bart., and are now, for the first time, published.† These notes exhibit his strong interest in agriculture, science, and history, also "his power of interesting the bored Emperor."† It is unfortunate that he,

---

* He received the brevet rank of colonel in 1814.
† "Colonel Wilks and Napoleon," by Julian S. Corbett, in the *Monthly Review* (January, 1901), p. 65.

instead of the rough and tactless Sir Hudson Lowe, was not put in charge of him. This, at least, was evidently the Duke of Wellington's opinion since, according to Lord Stanhope, he said "that he thought the Government had been mistaken in removing the old East India Company governor, COL. WILKS." And he continued, "He was a very intelligent, well-read man, and knew everything that had been passing in Europe, and Napoleon had become really attached to him." After he was gone, Napoleon (as the Duke mentions) said more than once, "Pourquoi n'ont-ils pas laissé ce vieux gouverneur ? Avec lui je me serais arrangé, nous n'aurions pas eu de querelles !"* (Why have they not left that old governor ? I could have got on with him. We should not have had quarrels.)

It was said that St. Helena had never "been under the government of a man so judicious, so mild and affable, or so much beloved ;" also that "his kindness, firmness, and philanthropy caused his departure to be regretted by all ranks in that island, where he made so many wise and lasting improvements."† Soon after his arrival in England, he came to the Isle of Man and settled at Kirby with his wife. On the 20th of August, 1816, he was re-elected a member of the House of Keys, and, in 1818, he retired from the East India Company's service. In 1823, after the death of his father-in-law, he became Speaker of the House of Keys. On first taking the chair, he expressed the opinion that "some theoretical defects might be attributed to the mode of election to seats," but he said that he believed he truly interpreted the sense of every member "in declaring our deliberate intention to cure these defects, if such they be, by our own conduct—by determining to legislate on no subject that has not previously been submitted to the country ; by encouraging the free communication of their views—by opening the doors of this house to their petitions and representations presented through the medium of a member."‡ He had a wonderful knowledge of oriental languages, and, on being asked how he had been able to acquire them so easily, he replied that "he could not account for it otherwise than on the ground of his being the son of a Manx clergyman, who had been careful to give him a correct and extensive acquaintance with his mother tongue."‡ His knowledge of Oriental literature was no less remarkable, and he has made us partakers of this knowledge by his writings. The first of these, a History of the Mahratta War,§ has been described as "a work of great learning and merit."‡ The second was published under the title of

---

* Notes of Conversations with the Duke of Wellington, 1831—1851, by Philip Henry, 5th Earl Stanhope. London, 1888.
† Article in *Blackwood's Magazine*, January, 1834.
‡ *Manks Advertiser*.
§ This was perused by Napoleon at St. Helena, and was highly praised by him.—(*Blackwood's Magazine*, January, 1834.)

" Historical Sketches of the South of India, in an attempt to trace the History of Mysore." Sir James Mackintosh, then the greatest authority on India, pronounced it to be "the first example of a book on Indian history founded on a critical examination of testimony and probability, and from which the absurdities of fable and etymology are banished."* The third was an essay, printed in the Transactions of the *Asiatic Society*, of which Colonel WILKS was vice-president, which has been described as "a masterly analysis and statement of the philosophical work of *Nasir-ed-Din*, entitled *Akhlac-a-nasire*, a metaphysical treatise of great difficulty."† According to his obituary notice in the *Gentleman's Magazine*, MARK WILKS was a fellow of the *Royal Society*. In personal appearance he was, in 1815, described as "a tall, handsome, venerable-looking man, with white curling locks and a courtier-like manner."‡ In character he was straightforward, modest, and kindly.

(Information partly from The Dictionary of National Biography, and partly from the Rev. S. N. Harrison, M.A., besides the other sources indicated.)

MARK CUBBON, Knight (b. 1775, d. 1861),

seventh son of the Rev. Thomas Cubbon, vicar-general, and Margaret, daughter of the Rev. James Wilks, Rector of Ballaugh, and sister of Col. Mark Wilks (see p. 154), was born at Maughold vicarage, his father being then vicar of that parish. He was an active and daring boy, and greatly enjoyed scrambling over the hills and rocks which abounded close to his home. He attended the parochial school, and then went to the Rev. Henry Maddrell, in Ramsey, of whom he remarked in after life : " I wish he had taken more pains to thrash Latin into me." In 1801, through the influence of his uncle, Col. Wilks, he received an Indian cadet's appointment. He was first appointed to the 2nd Madras battalion, and then, in 1804, to the 2nd battalion of the 5th Native Infantry, in which he served with the force commanded by Col. Chalmers in Travancore. In 1810, he was appointed to the commissariat department. In the following year he received the post of assistant commissary-general, which he declared to be "a distinction far above my rank or claim on the service," though, at the same time, he said he had been unlucky in his regimental promotion. In 1827, he became commissary-general. In 1834, he was appointed sole Commissioner of Mysore, and such confidence was placed in him that he received

---

very large discretionary powers. He was made a K.C.B. in 1856.
During the Mutiny, Mysore remained perfectly quiet under his
wise rule. With reference to this the governor-general wrote to
him saying :

> The services you have rendered to the state in connection with the
> administration of Mysore for nearly a quarter of a century are, as
> they always have been, most highly appreciated by the Government.
> These services were a few years ago marked by the special appro-
> bation of the Queen, and the Governor-General freely and gladly
> concedes to you the high merit of having subsequently during the
> late crisis, and in the midst of difficulties which you have in no way
> exaggerated, kept the provinces under your charge in perfect tran-
> quility. The value of your services to those provinces, and the
> honour and esteem which, by your high character, as well as by
> your administrative ability and success, you have won from every
> branch of the community, European and native, stand on record
> and can never be forgotten by the Supreme Government.

In the following year an order was issued to transfer the super-
intendence of Mysore affairs from the governor-general to the
Government of Madras. When SIR MARK heard of this order he
sent in his resignation, but, when the people learned that he had
done so, they prayed Lord Canning not to accept it, and so the order
was withdrawn. Early in 1861, however, he felt compelled to
resign owing to ill-health. He left India in April, dying at Suez
on the 23rd of that month. His remains were brought home and
interred in Maughold churchyard on the 17th of May.* Let us
see what was thought of him in the country which had received
the benefit of his administration : —

> With the exception of Sir T. Munroe, we have never seen his
> equal as a statesman and ruler. He has solved the problem as to
> what kind of government best suits an Indian province, and what
> is most conducive to the people's interest in combination with
> revenual prosperity. He may be fitly designated the tutelar
> guardian of the country, and is looked up to and venerated as
> such. Were Mysore in rebellion to-morrow, his word would be
> sufficient to suppress it, and such has ever been the respect enter-
> tained for him and the influence of his salutary policy, that no army
> was required to overawe the millions subject to his rule.†

From another authority we learn that " in Sir Mark Cubbon were
rarely combined a cultivated intellect, a calm judgment, a firm
will, and an enduring patience, which was the more conspicuous
because associated with extraordinary penetration."‡ It describes
him as being " striking and prepossessing in appearance ; dignified
yet simple and unassuming in demeanour ; liberal to profusion,
with an exquisite tenderness of sympathy,"‡ and as possessing a

---

* The above is an abstract of the account by the Rev. S. N. Harrison in the
Manx Note Book, Vol. I., pp. 51-4.
† *The Bangalore Herald.*
‡ *The Madras Times.*

tact which extended to all the exigences of his position. It further states that "from many succeeding viceroys he enjoyed the greatest confidence ; from his many friends he won the warmest esteem ; from his assistants the most devoted attachment ; and from the people to whom he was for 27 years the friend and benefactor the profoundest gratitude."* When the tidings of SIR MARK CUBBON'S death reached Mysore all public offices were closed, and all public business throughout the Mysore territory suspended for three days. A large sum was raised to erect a memorial which took the form of an equestrian statue. But no such memorial was necessary to perpetuate the remembrance of the good work he did in Mysore, as the following extract from " The Nineteenth Century Magazine" for March, 1888, in a valuable article on "The Bankruptcy of India," will show :—

It so happens that there is a direct example of the effect of the two methods—the one of appointing a very few Europeans merely to superintend and improve the native administration, and gradually introduce an improved system suited to the people ; the other to pitchfork Europeans into every office of consequence, and force departments and public works upon the country almost without calculation as to their effects. In Mysore the two plans followed one after the other. Sir Mark Cubbon administered the province of 5,000,000 people with four Europeans, at a cost for the European agency of £13,000 a year. He used his influence as far as possible to check the abuses and foster the advantages of the native local administrations, encouraged the construction of public works by the natives themselves, insisted on light taxation, and abstained from continuous petty intermeddling. What was the result ? In 1861-62, though Mysore had suffered from short monsoons, and consequently bad average harvests since 1853, the people were, beyond all question, in a state of the greatest prosperity. Distraint for land-tax had become almost unknown. Notwithstanding all this attention to the people, the surplus for the year was £105,000, and there were no less than ninety-six lakhs of rupees, or nearly one million sterling, in the treasury. These were, indeed, the golden days of Mysore, and the cultivators were living in comfort, almost in wealth. There were drawbacks of course, but they were small compared with the benefits ; and to this day the people look back with bitter regret to the happiness they experienced under that light and considerate rule.

CHAPTER VIII.

The Merchant Service.

"The distinction," says Captain Mahan, "between the merchant seaman and the man-of-war's man, or even the naval officers, in those days of sailing ships and simple weapons, was much less sharply marked than it has since become. Skill in seamanship, from the use of the marlingspike and the sail needle up to the full equipping of a ship and the handling of her under canvas, was in either service the prime essential. In both alike, cannon and small arms were carried; and the ship's company, in the peaceful trader as well as in the ship of war, expected to repel force with force, when meeting upon equal terms." It is well to bear the truth of these remarks in mind, as regards the period up to 1815 at least, when reading about the gallant Manxmen who served in the merchant navy. It was the service, of all others, especially in its bye-paths of smuggling, privateering, and slave trading, which Manxmen took up most enthusiastically, because it was attended with excitement, danger, and, not its least attraction, excellent profits.

The first Manx merchant seaman we hear of is the EDWARD CHRISTIAN who has already been mentioned (see p. 60).

HENRY SKILLICORNE (b. 1678, d. 1763)

is the next. Nearly the whole of our information about him is
derived from the following long and curious epitaph in the old
parish church at Cheltenham :

> In Memory of Captain HENRY SKILLICORNE, deceased,
> born at Kirk Lonan
> In the Isle of Man in 1678, taught by Dr. WILSON,
> Bishop, and justly called
> the good Bishop of that Island. When young he
> went to sea and was many years
> in the employ of and concerned with JACOB ELTON
> Esq., Merchant in Bristol
> whose relation SARAH GOLDSMITH of that City he
> married. She dying in Childbed
> with two Children, He in 1731 married ELIZABETH
> MASON, then at Bristol,
> Daughter of WILLM. MASON of Cheltenham Gentle-
> man by MARGARET SURMAN
> Daughter of JOHN SURMAN, of Tredington in this
> County Esq.,
> He quitting the sea after 40 Years' Service, they
> resided together some years
> at Bristol, and in 1738 came to live upon their Estate
> in this Town,
> where he gave his Mind to increase the Knowledge
> and extend the Use
> of Cheltenham Spa, which became his Property. He
> found the Old Spring open
> and exposed to the Weather. He made the Well
> there as it now is, made the
> Walks, and planted the Trees of the Upper and
> Lower Parades,
> And by Conduct ingenuous & Manners attentive,
> He, with the Aid of Many worthy Persons of the
> Town and Neighbourhood,
> brought this most salutary Water to just estimation
> & extensive Use,
> and ever presiding with esteem in the Walks, saw it
> visited with Benefit,
> by the greatest Persons of the Age, and so
> established its Reputation,
> that the Present Most Gracious Majesty King GEORGE
> The Third,
> With His Most Amiable Queen CHARLOTTE, and the
> Princess Royal,
> AUGUSTA & ELIZABETH their Daughters visited it.
>
> .   .   .   *
>
> Captain SKILLICORNE was buried the 18th of October
> 1763 with his Son
> HENRY, by his last wife. at the West Door on the
> Inside of this Church,

---

* Here follow a number of lines not intimately connected with Captain
Skillicorne.

F

> Aged 84 years.   He was an excellent Sea-man, of
>   tryed courage.
> He visited most of the great Trading Ports of the
>   Mediterranean, up the
> Archipelago, Morea & Turkey, Spain, Portugal,
>   & Venice, and several of the
> North American Ports, Philadelphia & Boston
>   & Holland
> And could do business in seven languages.   He was
>   of great Regularity
> and Probity, and so temperate, as never to have
>   been once Intoxicated.
> Religious without Hypocrisy, grave without
>   Austerity, of a Cheerful
> Conversation without Levity.   A Kind Husband &
>   tender Father,
> Tall, erect, robust & active.   From an Ill-treated
>   Wound while a prisioner,
> After an Engagement at Sea, He became a strict
>   Valetudinarian.
> He lived and dyed an honest man.

The epitaph also informs us that his wife—

> Mrs. ELIZABETH SKILLICORNE a Quaker was buried
>   in the Quakers'
> Grave Yard, upon the 14th of April, 1779,
> A Virtuous Woman, A good Wife, & tender Mother.

From this we gather that he was practically the founder of
Cheltenham as a watering-place.   We know also that he did not
forget his native parish of Lonan, being a liberal contributor to
the erection of a new church there in 1733.

The only Manx pirate we know of is ROBERT CROW (b. 1679,
d. 1722) ; and let us say that, in the event of any objection being
taken to his being called a "Worthy," the "   " deprive the
epithet of all significance in his case !   He seem, however, as far
we can judge from a very obscure account, to have been a seaman
engaged in ordinary commerce, when, in 1720, he, with his vessel,
the "Happy Return" sloop, was captured by the notorious
buccaneer, Captain Bartholomew Roberts.*   But, for two years
after this, he served under his captor, in the pirate ship "Royal
Fortune," till it was taken by H.M.S. "Swallow," when he,
(briefly referred to as "Robert Crow, 44, Isle of Man") and
some forty of his fellows "were executed, according to their
sentence, without the gates of Cape Corso Castle, within the
flood marks."*

---

* "The Buccaneers and Marooners of America" (T. Fisher Unwin, London,
1897), p. 343.   My attention was called to this book, which is a reprint from
various old "chap" books, &c., by Mr. John Frowde.

Before giving an account of Captain Skillicorne's successors in the merchant service, we will briefly refer to Manx Smugglers, Privateersmen, and Slave-traders.

The Smugglers.

The most flourishing period of Manx smuggling was between 1715 and 1765, and it still continued, notwithstanding numerous revenue cutters, to be a profitable business between 1765 and 1798, and, to a less extent, between 1798 and 1815, or even later.

It is curious how little we know of the exploits of individual Manx smugglers, though those of such men as Yawkins, the Dutchman, are the subject of rugged verses. Manxmen were, however, his most successful rivals, and the fact that one of the best known smuggling creeks on the Kirkcudbrightshire coast is called the "Manksman's lake" indicates that they were well known in this trade. The verses, already referred to, record their presence :—

> Oft at the Ross, with Yawkins and with Doal,
> And Manksmen gabbling from the manor hole,
> What noggins I have drank of smuggled rum
> Just from the little "Isle of three legs" come.

We are only able to give accounts of three Manx smugglers, and they belong to the last of the periods we have mentioned.

It is for our readers to decide whether such Manxmen are "Worthies" or not.

The first, THOLLAN RADCLIFFE, of Cronk Breck, Andreas, attempted to run his lugger, with a whole puncheon· of French brandy* in her, over to Galloway, but was captured. The captain of the cutter put one of his crew on board the lugger, which he took in tow. Night came on, and, RADCLIFFE calling to his men in Manx, to "hoist the clout," a small square sail, the only sail which the lugger† carried, seized the cutter's man, threw him overboard, cut the tow-rope and stole away, ultimately disposing of the brandy as he had originally intended.‡

The second, JAMES MOORE, was lying in his lugger in Douglas Bay, where a revenue cutter happened to be at the time. In talking to some of the cutter's crew, MOORE boasted that his craft would beat theirs in a race. This reaching the captain's ears, he

---

* French brandy was, after 1798, openly imported into the island on payment of a small duty, and was then smuggled out again.
† The luggers at this time were no more than large open yawls without cabins.
‡ Fargher's "Annals of the Isle of Man."

accepted the challenge, as he thought it would be a good opportunity of showing MOORE and his fellow smugglers that the speed of his boat was such that they had but little chance of escaping. MOORE'S preparation for the race consisted in buying a crock of butter, and in smearing his boat to the water-line with its contents. The result, whether it was owing to this manœuvre, or the natural speed of the lugger, was that she not only out-paced the cutter, but actually sailed round her! The chagrin of the cutter's captain may be imagined.*

Of the third, QUILLIAM, the following story is told : "On one occasion his vessel, loaded with spirits, bound for Ireland, was chased and overhauled by a revenue cutter, but he paid no attention to the summons to bring to, and even when a blank shot was fired from the cutter, he sailed on without taking any notice. Then a cannon ball was fired, which fell into the sea not far from QUILLIAM'S vessel. On seeing this QUILLIAM ordered his crew to get below, but remained on deck himself and brought up his vessel in the wind. The revenue cutter then lowered a boat, which came alongside, and its officer angrily demanded why he did not bring his boat up when first signalled. QUILLIAM replied that out of his crew of six four were dead of cholera, and that the two remaining were dying. Horror-stricken by this news, the officer ordered his boat back to the cutter, which sailed off. When it was out of sight, QUILLIAM called up his men from below and made off for the Irish coast."†

Privateersmen and Slave=traders.

The businesses of "Privateering" and Slave-trading seem to have been intimately connected, as we find the same men and ships sometimes engaged in one and sometimes in the other. The most conspicuous Manxmen engaged in them were SIR JOHN TOBIN, WILLIAM LACE, and HUGH CROW.

JOHN TOBIN, Knight (b. 1763, d. 1851),

was a member of a family which settled in the Isle of Man, at Middle and Oakhill, in the parish of Braddan, about 1700. He was born in the island and entered the merchant service. One of his first adventures was being captured by a French privateer, but fortunately its captain, an Irish-Frenchman, called KELLY, knew his father at Douglas, and so released him. In 1793, we find him as captain‡ of the privateer "Gipsy," and in 1797 he was

---

* Fargher's "Annals of the Isle of Man."
† "From King Orry to Queen Victoria." p. 143.
‡ We give the courtesy title of "captain," the correct title of a merchant captain being, of course, "master."

captain of the "Molly," also a privateer and slaver. In both these vessels he made numerous captures. In 1803, he settled as a merchant in Liverpool, and entered upon the African slave and palm oil trade. But he also continued the lucrative business of privateering. One of his vessels, the "John Tobin," privateer, had, in 1812, a vigorous fight with an American, when the latter got the worst of it. We may mention that the chief mate of the "John Tobin," judging by his name, CANNON, seems to have been a Manxman. The captain, writing of his conduct in this fight, said he could not "speak too highly of him."* JOHN TOBIN next turned his attention to steam navigation, and built and launched at his own expense the largest steamer which had ever been launched on the Mersey before 1851. This fine vessel, which was called the "Liverpool," made several trips to New York, and was then sold to the Oriental Steam Navigation Co. JOHN TOBIN, who was Mayor of Liverpool when George the Fourth ascended the throne, was knighted on that occasion. He was one of the promoters of the docks on the Cheshire side of the river.

We may mention that it was on board one of JOHN TOBIN'S merchant vessels, the "William Heathcote," that a MR. KEWLEY, probably a Manxman, killed three men with his own sword, when she (in 1804) was captured by the French privateer, "General Augerau." The ": William Heathcote" was re-captured by an English vessel, but KEWLEY had been taken by the privateer, and it is not known what became of him.†

The following account of

WILLIAM LACE (b. 1763, d. 1850)

is given by Mr Williams in his interesting book on "Liverpool Privateers":— He "was the son of Mr. Ambrose Lace, merchant and ship-owner. of St. Paul's Square, and brother of Mr. Joshua Lace, the founder and first president of the Liverpool Law Society. He had a life full of adventure, for in the time of the war with France he fitted out privateers and took command of one himself. In 1797, when in command of the 'Lovely Lass,' he took part in beating off two French privateers. After taking many prizes, he was himself captured by the French fleet, and carried a prisoner to France, from which country he afterwards escaped, after enduring great hardships. On another voyage he lost his ship, and was fourteen days in a small boat, part of this time without water, and, when picked up, was one of the few survivors. He was one of the early African explorers, and, we believe, the first to give us an account of the gorilla, long before Du Chaillu. He was an enthusiastic botanist, and largely contributed to the

---

* Williams' "The Liverpool Privateers," p. 437.
† *Ibid.*, p. 393.

founding of the Liverpool Botanical Gardens, the freedom of which
[city] was presented to him in recognition of his gifts. Members
of his family repeatedly refused the office of Mayor, and the last
Bailiff of Liverpool was his cousin, AMBROSE LACE."*   Mr.
Williams gives illustrations of a fac-simile of an original sketch
made by CAPTAIN LACE of the palace and stockade of an African
king, of whom he purchased slaves ; also of the private signal
code of a slave-ship in his handwriting. These were lent him by
Mr. C. K. Lace, no doubt a descendant.

We come now to the most famous of our Manx merchant
seamen :

HUGH CROW (b. 1765, d. 1829)

was a native of Ramsey. He lost his right eye in infancy ; and
nearly lost his life by drowning at the age of twelve. He was
apprenticed in his native town to the trade of boat building;
spent two years at it; and then, at the age of seventeen, went to
Whitehaven, and was apprenticed to the sea. In those days
Whitehaven had a great foreign trade : and was as a port
relatively of more consequence than at present. CROW'S first
voyage was to the West Indies. The ship sailed with others
under convoy.   At Cork, where they joined the convoy, he
witnessed the impressment of seamen for the Royal Navy. All
his life he nourished hatred, and uttered rough denunciation, of
the press-gang.

In the West Indies the ship's carpenter deserted; and CROW,
with his boat-building knowledge, took the carpenter's place. He
came home to Whitehaven ; thence to Memel, and back to Whitehaven, where, through bad fare, he arrived in condition "thin as
a lath." His next voyage was to Charleston. He was aloft
handling a sail with a fellow apprentice, between whom and
himself some words occurred, and "the villain letting go the sail
exerted his utmost strength to throw CROW off the yard into the
sea."   In Charleston he became "a victim to the political
jealousies of the times ": was thrown by the police into a filthy
prison, among hundreds even more wretched than himself,—not to
be released but by the payment of jail fees to the amount of all
his voyage wages.

From Charleston he sailed to Liverpool ; thence to the Baltic;
back to Whitehaven ; away to Drontheim ; back to Belfast; and
off again to Memel.

At Elsinore the ship was got aground by a drunken captain ;
and got afloat greatly by CROW'S exertions ; then she was driven
by adverse winds into a Norwegian port, where she lay for eleven
weeks. When she got to sea again, captain and crew were drunk,
and the ship left to the apprentices, and by their good guidance,

---

" The Liverpool Privateers," &c., pp. 615-16.

and by much good luck, was brought into the port of Stornoway. The voyage was tedious and disastrous : "had the brandy and gin lasted they had never got home at all." Finally the vessel got on Lancaster sands. This voyage completed Crow's apprenticeship. He then sailed as carpenter to the West Indies ; and made some voyages to Ireland,—"by which time he had saved enough money to buy himself some articles of clothing and a quadrant." On the next voyage to the West Indies, "the captain placed in promotion over him a second mate certainly not better qualified than himself." Sense of injustice wrought in Crow's mind : he determined to leave his captain ; and did so at Kingston, by engaging himself as second mate on another ship. But the old captain with bailiff, constables, and soldiers boarded his new ship, and soon had Crow into noxious prison ; then into the workhouse ; and at last had him carried on board his ship by force, his "articles of clothing and quadrant" lost. He saved the ship from foundering on the home voyage ; and all the same was "fairly cut adrift in Lancaster without a farthing in his pocket."

Bent on recovering his "articles of clothing and quadrant" he went out again to Kingston ; by the hardy Norse blood in him, quite cheerful and even joyous. The voyage was stormy, "a succession of dreadful gales," and he did not find what he sought. But the tide of fortune had turned. He joined a Liverpool ship as second mate, then in Kingston, Jamaica, 1788. On the voyage home, in a tremendous gale in the night, the water rushed in upon the main deck, and "we had the utmost difficulty and toil to save her from foundering." "I was on the main deck up to the knees in water toiling and cheering on the men, and the chief mate slung in ropes over the bows endeavouring to stuff the hawse holes."

After his return, a ship grounded in the dock mouth at Liverpool. Crow volunteered his services. She was lightened in an incredibly short time ; got afloat and saved. It was considered a "smart achievement." Crow received from the underwriters "a sum of money," with which he bought "the first respectable suit of clothes he ever possessed." He was now twenty-four ; and at this time had several offers to go as second mate to the coast of Africa. He had what he calls "prejudices"; and went to Jamaica in unexceptionable trade. At sea he had a short effective method with the men who were backward to perform hazardous or difficult duty aloft. "I went to the mast-head myself and down by the lift." Of course "lie in ; and no grumbling" was then "the word."

In 1790 his friends overruled his "prejudices" against an African voyage. He was twenty-five ; and was appointed chief mate of a beautiful brig. They sailed to Rotterdam to take in spirits as cargo for the Gold Coast. Here begins the second epoch of his life. As mate, he made four African voyages ; but, on the fourth, was captured by a French ship, and brought to L'Orient.

He spent a whole year in France—at L'Orient, at Quimper, and in the hospital at Pontoise. At Pontoise he improved himself in arithmetic, and acquired a knowledge of logarithms from an English fellow-prisoner. At last, being well again, he contrived to escape ; wandered through the country with a tricolour cockade in his hat, answered in Manx all questions, and passed for a Breton ; at last got to Havre, and thence on a Danish vessel to England.

CROW was at sea again in 1795, as mate in the African trade. On the third voyage the ship was lost ; but immediately on his return to Liverpool, a mark of high approbation on the part of the employers, he was appointed captain of the " Will," and in 1798 sailed on his first voyage in that ship.

The confidence his employers felt in him is shown by the following story. A Liverpool shipowner complained to Mr. Aspinall, owner of the " Will ":—

" I give my captains very long instructions," said he, " yet they can hardly make any money for us . . what kind of instructions did you give your captain ?"——" Why . . we had a pint of wine together at Beat's Hotel . . and I told him ' *Crow ! mind your eye . . for you will find many ships at Bonny !*"——" Crow ?—I know the young man well . . he has only *one* eye."——" True ! but that's a piercer !" My instructions, in effect, were nearly as brief as " *Crow ! mind your eye.*"

Long before the suppression of the African trade, Mr. Wilberforce had obtained from Parliament in 1792, laws for its better regulation. One of his regulations was that a bounty of £100 should be paid to all captains who should land their cargoes without losing a certain percentage on the voyage. On his first voyage CROW received his bounty ; and again and again on subsequent voyages.

The Guineamen of those days went armed. On his second voyage " a fast sailing schooner brushed up alongside, hoisted French colours and began to fire ;" " we cooled his courage with a few broadsides and he sheered off before the wind."

When the " Will " was ready to leave Bonny for the West Indies, CROW's brother arrived in command of the " Charlotte," bringing intelligence that three French frigates were on the coast, and might be expected at Bonny. There were nine Guineamen in all there.

We ventured to drop down, and come to anchor in a line within four or five miles of the Frenchmen. There we lay seven days without their daring to attack us. They at length weighed anchor and stood from the coast, and when I thought all was clear I put to sea.

On the same voyage in the latitude of Tobago, the " Will " fought an action, lasting nine hours, with a French privateer brig.

All our top-gallant masts were shot away, our sails cut up, and our top-masts wounded ; three shots in the main-mast, four in the mizen-mast, our main-crosstrees shot away, our hull much injured, and our rigging so much cut up that we had hardly a brace or a stay left standing. One of the enemy's nine pound shot went into the men's room below and wounded twelve blacks.

Still he got his bounty of £100 for the condition of his cargo. Two more voyages in the "Will" were equally successful though less adventurous.

"CROW has come again, and as usual his whites and blacks are as plump as cotton bags," was a saying in Kingston, when CROW arrived. About this time he received two public presentations :— A piece of plate from the underwriters and merchants of Liverpool, for his meritorious conduct in the river Bonny ; and a piece of plate from the underwriters of Lloyd's Coffee House, for his gallant defence of his ship in the action at sea with the French privateer.

In 1803, he sailed in the "Ceres." The "Ceres" was well armed ; and CROW by mistake nearly fought an action at sea with an English Indiaman, who had mistaken him for French. On this voyage he fell ill ; and at its conclusion spent a year on shore.

In 1806, he was at sea in the "Mary," a fine ship, armed with 28 guns, and a crew of 60 seamen. On the middle passage, in the latitude of Tobago, the "Mary" fought a running action from ten in the evening till daylight, with two English sloops of war, the "Dart" and the "Wolverine," mistaking them for French privateers from Cayenne.

The man at the masthead saw two sail a long way ahead ; we hauled our wind to southward ; they both tacked . . I distinguished them to be powerful vessels of war. At 6 p.m. night came on, dark. with heavy squalls and rain . . at 9 p.m., a sail to windward . . we bore away westward, and made all sail . . he stood after us. and made signals to his consort . . he loomed large in the obscurity, came up astern and hailed us, ordering us to bring to . . well aware that French cruisers had a trick of hailing in English, I replied *"that I would not, and that no one should bring us to in those seas, and in the night."* (Admirable and honest Manxman.) He fired two shots, and we returned him one . . a few minutes after, I saw a *ship* close to us with her star-board tacks on board, evidently the consort . . she passed under our stern, and also hailed us . . I answered *"that no strange vessel should bring us to in those seas during the night"* . . she held on her course, and spoke the other vessel . . they both made sail after us. The first came up very fast . . she was a large *brig* . . she again hailed us . . I made the same answer as before . . she then rounded to and poured a broadside into our starboard quarter . . we returned her fire at close quarters for some time . . she then took her station at some distance, and we fought for an hour . . when her consort, the ship, came up, on our larboard side . . they both closed and simultaneously engaged us. I was employed

animating the crew by all the cheering language I could muster,
and in giving directions for the elevation of the guns . . while
thus engaged I received a violent blow from a splinter on the left
arm, near the shoulder, which staggered me a good deal . . my
crew stood boldly to their quarters and fought like heroes . . it
was now past midnight . . no fatality had yet occurred amongst
us . . then a large shot took off the boatswain's both thighs
. . another, entering the men's room below, wounded a great
number of blacks, five of whom died . . several of my crew were
soon wounded . . we continued to blaze away . . at length, after
nearly six hours, the *ship* all at once backed her topsails and dropped
astern . . but . . she made sail again . . came up to us and
resumed the action as fiercely as ever . . we engaged them both,
tooth and nail, till the grey of the morning . . when I was struck
violently on my left side by a splinter, then I fell breathless and
senseless on the deck . . the man at the helm sang out that the
captain was killed . . all began to leave their quarters and
gather round me . . before I could recover breath, the chief
mate said, "Sir, we have struck the colours!" . . I besought
them *again to hoist the colours* . . *three or four more broadsides* . .
we might carry away their masts . . my entreaties were in vain . .
a lantern was hoisted at the peak to signify that we had struck
. . I was carried from the deck and laid on a mattress in the cabin
. . When their boats came alongside, those who boarded us were
found to be our *own countrymen* . . we had been fighting all the
while two *English* men-of-war, the "Dart," sloop of war, 30 guns,
and the "Wolverine," 18 guns." Our main-mast was nearly gone,
and our bowsprit was in the same state . . three of our guns
were dismounted . . our sails and rigging were nearly cut to
pieces . . the lower fore-studding sail was burned to tinder . .

He arrived in Liverpool on the 2nd May, 1807 ; the African
slave trade had been abolished the day before his arrival. But on
landing he was solicited to take command of the "Kitty's Amelia,"
which had been cleared out previous to the passing of the Abolition
Act. It was his last voyage, like all the others successful, and
even more arduous. He rescued the crew and some of the cargo
of another ship that had been wrecked. They brought sickness
with them, which attacked Crow's cargo and crew. Fire broke
out in the middle passage :—

A dense cloud of smoke was issuing from below. I found the
people in the act of cutting away the stern and quarter boats . .
"Is it possible, my lads ! that you can desert me." . . I was the
first man to venture below . . the fire was blazing on the starboard side, there were forty-five barrels of gunpowder in the
magazine . . a thrill of despair ran through my whole frame
. . by a strong mental effort I suppressed my feelings . . and
only thought of active exertion *unconnected* with the thought of
imminent danger. . . Our spare sails were stowed at hand.
These were dragged out, and by extraordinary activity we
succeeded in throwing them over the flames, which they so far
checked that we gained time to obtain a good supply of water down
the hatchway . . .

On our arrival at Kingston I found sixteen sail of African ships, some of which had been there five or six months with the greater part of their cargoes unsold. . . The first thing I saw on landing was an advertisement in both the Kingston papers that "Captain CROW had arrived with the finest cargo of negroes ever brought to Kingston." On the fifth day after we began to sell not a single negro was left on board.

It was his last voyage. He sent the "Kitty's Amelia" to Liverpool in charge of another; and came home as a passenger.

The third epoch of his life remains to be told. He had got his son into the navy,—Dr. Kelly using his influence with his brother-in-law, Admiral Russell, to further his interests "Tell the war-like CROW to send me his son, that I may train him to be such a man as his father." The boy, however, turned out a disappointment. He died at Lisbon in 1812.

Meanwhile Captain CROW had retired from the sea. He bought a small estate near Ramsey; and set himself to improve it.

In 1812 he was proposed and appointed a member of the House of Keys, but declined that distinction. "After the melancholy death of my son, I continued to lay off and on, and to wander about seeking to divert my mind."

In 1817 he went to Liverpool again, where, among sights and society more congenial, he spent his remaining years. He is buried in Kirk Maughold Churchyard.*

Of less note were the privateer captains, QUIRK, GILL, CANNELL (2), BACON, CREBBIN, and QUALTROUGH; and the slaver captains, AMBROSE LACE, CHRISTIAN, WM. CROW, and EDWARD CLARKE. We will take the privateersmen first :—

In 1752, Captain QUIRK, of the "Prussian Hero," of 18 guns and 60 men, fell in, near Guadaloupe, with three French privateers, viz., a sloop of 10 guns, a sloop of 8 guns, and a schooner of 6 guns. After two hours' fight they sheered off, and, though joined by two others, took to flight. Before this cruise CAPTAIN QUIRK had commanded the *snow*, "Betty," a privateer, of 10 guns. She was taken on her passage to Jamaica by a French privateer, but was re-taken by the "Royal Hunter," privateer, of New York.†

In 1779, WILLIAM GILL, captain of the "Jenny," assisted by its namesake under Captain Walker, had a smart fight with an American frigate, of 28 guns, off the Banks of Newfoundland. The frigate, after getting the worst of the contest, was glad to escape.‡

---

* From the account by the Rev. John Quine in the *Manx Note Book*. For full particulars see the "Memoirs," from which the extracts given above are taken. See also Williams' "The Liverpool Privateers," pp. 626-90.
† "The Liverpool Privateers," p. 159.
‡ *Ibid*, pp. 278-9.

In 1793, Captain CANNELL, of the "Eliza," in company with
the "Tarleton," took the "Le Guerrier," a French privateer of
8 guns and 72 men.*

Another Captain CANNELL commanded the "Mary," of 14 guns,
her lieutenant being QUAYLE CREBBIN. In May, 1793, she
captured a "St. Domingoman," of 1,020 tons burden, laden with
sugar. Later in the same year a feat is recorded as having been
performed by Captain BACON and his crew, who sailed in the *snow*†
"Christian." The "Christian" was captured by a French frigate,
and Captain BACON and some of his crew were put on board another
prize which the Frenchman had also captured. On the voyage,
however, they rose upon the French crew, took the vessel, and
brought her into Penzance.

In the same year the "Phœnix," commanded by PAUL
CREBBIN,‡ captured the French Indiaman, "La Pauline," valued
at £30,000.

All these privateers seem to have been successful, but the most
curious account of Manx privateering is connected with an un-
successful privateer, the "Tyger," of which RICHARD QUALTROUGH
was captain and JOHN MOORE, lieutenant (see p. 101).

As her brief and unfortunate career throws some light on the
nature of the commercial speculations which our ancestors
occasionally indulged in, we will describe it at some length : —§

In March, 1778, the French ambassador was withdrawn from
London, and, shortly afterwards, war broke out between France
and England. The English Government proceeded to do as much
injury as possible to the enemy's commerce by issuing what were
called "letters of marque" which permitted merchants and others
to fit out armed ships, or privateers, and to retain any of the
ships or merchandize which they might capture.

Some Manx merchants thought that a venture of this nature
would be a very profitable one, and so they clubbed together
and purchased a ship called the "Tyger" for the sum of £3,465.
The chief owners were Messrs. HUGH COSNAHAN and LEWIS
GENESTE, of Douglas, but, according to the ballad, a number of
small owners and her captain, RICHARD QUALTROUGH, had
also a share in her. She had a crew of 70 men, 25 of whom were
able seamen, and carried 16 guns, fourteen of which were 6
pounders, and two 4 pounders. Such cannon in these days would
be considered mere pop-guns, but they then formed an armament
which would have rendered the "Tyger" a formidable opponent
to any vessel not a man-of-war.

---

* "The Liverpool Privateers." p. 316.
† Fargher's "Annals of the Isle Man."
‡ *Ibid.*
§ Our information about it is mainly derived from documents and letters,
formerly in the possession of the Rev. Philip Moore (see pp. 25-26).

In December, 1778, Captain QUALTROUGH wrote a letter, headed
"Tyger, Ramsey," to Lewis Geneste, in which he expresses regret
that he could not "verify the report of the 'Tyger' having made a
prize," and he continues," "the Dutch, or rather Prussian, ship, is
clear'd out of Wirewater and no cargo on board," a remark which
looks much as if he had in mind what was afterwards to get him
and his owners into trouble, *i.e.*, the pillage of a vessel belonging
to a neutral power. But he had designs also on a smuggler,
"alongside of which we were making ready to steal the next
morning, and did not despair of taking possession of her from our
own ship's height to command her decks, tho' she mounts 16
sixes, and 50 men, but she sailed that night. Should a similar
incident occur, your orders shall be strictly complied with. We
still find sufficient employment. but are now pretty ready, and
wish for a fair wind. If convenient I will call in your bay
(Douglas) by the way. The ship makes little or no water. I
have given the sides a good coat of tar. The crew are pretty
expert in their exercise and in good harmony. If it would be
agreeable I would prefer calling at Montaga (?) Bay prior to
Kingston, as at the latter place they would sweep away officers,
seamen and all." This refers to the impressment of merchant
seamen to the Royal Navy. He also suggested to Mr. Geneste
that the crew should not be informed that their destination was
Kingston (seemingly Kingston in Jamaica), because, if they were,
they would speedily "make off." On arriving off the Land's End
they encountered a terrible storm, which is graphically described
by John Moore, lieutenant, in his ballad :—

> The sea was big and foaming,
> Stormy beyond measure,
> Our cross-tree fell overboard,
> We could not keep our course.
> After a spell of blowing,
> The storm again took rest ;
> On Old Christmas Eve* we cast
> Our anchor in Mount Bay.†

A few days later they fell in with and captured the Dutch
galliott, "De Jonge Jessie Wittween de Lemmer," Captain Heere
Anskes, bound from Bordeaux to Dieppe, loaded with 289 hogs-
heads of tobacco. After a quick run the "Tyger" and her prize
arrived in Douglas, where they were greeted by the populace with
great joy, a joy, however, which was speedily turned into sorrow
as the governor declared the capture an illegal one, and at once

---

* 5th of January.
† In Cornwall.

sent John Cosnahan, son of Hugh Cosnahan, as representing the owners, together with Captain Anskes and three of his crew to Whitehaven, where they appeared before the Commissioners of the "High Court of Admiralty." An agreement was entered into between them and the commissioners that, on the owners of the "Tyger" paying £60 to Captain Anskes, and engaging to put him and his crew "free of expense into full possession" of his vessel, he should "exonerate and for ever quit all claims upon the captors and owners" of the "Tyger." The Dutch captain remained in Douglas refitting till the middle of February, when he sent in his bill of costs for 30 days, amounting to £45 8s. 8d., which was duly paid by Hugh Cosnahan. So ended the "Tyger's" first unfortunate venture.

Nothing daunted, however, her owners, in the following summer, commissioned her for a four months' cruise. Three days out from Douglas she fell in with the British fleet, under the command of Sir Charles Hardy, off the Scillies, and was brought to by the "Romney," Captain Johnstone, who tried, but in vain, to induce some of the crew to volunteer. On their refusal, he took all the able seamen except one, "who had been disabled by an accident," on board his own ship. These men he afterwards spoke of as "the finest fellows he ever saw." Captain Qualtrough, having thus lost the pick of his crew, found himself unable to navigate the ship properly, and so he returned to Douglas. This last disaster proved too much for the owners, who at once endeavoured to sell the "Tyger," and they at last parted with her for only £1,260, this being "the most money they could get for her." It would seem that they had some hope of recouping their loss by a lawsuit against Captain Johnstone, but they had to wait till that officer returned to England, which was not till October, 1780.

When the solicitors of the owners of the "Tyger" had an interview with him, Capt. Johnstone expressed his regret for "having been under the necessity, but the service of the state required . . . he admitted that the concerned had a claim upon the public for such a loss, but was not able to advise how to get it." He, however, recommended "a petition to Parliament," and said "he would with great willingness support it all in his power." The solicitors then advised that a statement of the "Tyger's" case should be laid before Mr Erskine and Mr Dunning for their opinion as to whether or not an action could not be supported against Captain Johnstone. The opinion of Mr Erskine, afterwards the famous Lord Chancellor, has not been preserved, but that of Mr Dunning was unfavourable. "Admitting the right of pressing," he says, "it seems a vigorous exercise of that right, taking all the seamen, a measure very likely to be attended with worse consequences to the property of the owners than those which it actually produced. On the whole I think it very doubtful whether the owners will recover in an action for consequential damages. Pressing seamen out of merchant ships is often very injurious to the interests of the owners, but I believe it to have been generally submitted to."

We do not know whether any lawsuit ensued or not, but we may note that Lord Eldon, then John Scott, who had been called to the Bar in 1776, was about this time engaged in a Manx case, which may just possibly have been the case of the "Tyger," to which he refers as follows : " Now I had been reading in Coke, and I found there that the people of the Isle of Man were no beggars— Lord Coke's words are : —' The inhabitants of the isle are a religious, industrious, and true people, without begging or stealing,' so in my speech I said, ' the people of the Isle of Man are no beggars ; I therefore do not beg their rights but demand them !' This so pleased an old smuggler who was present, that, when the trial was over, he called me aside, and said, ' Young gentleman, I tell you what, you shall have my daughter, and £100,000 for her fortune.' That was a very handsome offer ; but I told him that I happened to have a wife, who had nothing for her fortune ; therefore I must stick to her."[*]

It is not known what became of the "Tyger," and, as to her crew, all that can be discovered is that Callister was the name of one of the lieutenants, John Moore, already referred to, being the other ; that John Callow, who had been one of the petty officers, became master of the brig "Hope"; and that three of the crew were called Quayle, Kelly, and Harry Moore.

The following were more especially slavers :—

In 1762, Ambrose Lace, father of the William Lace already referred to, was master of the "Marquis of Granby," but, before 1773, he seems to have settled down as a merchant in Liverpool. Mr. Williams gives some amusing letters from "Grandy King George" to him in that capacity.[†]

The next captain on our list— Christian, of the "Othello"— had an unfortunate career. His ship, which in 1794 had re-captured an English vessel from the French, two years later caught fire at Bonny and blew up, several whites and about 120 blacks, among whom was a brother of King Pepple, perishing. His next ship, the "Parr," blew up at the same place, and on this occasion he lost his life.[‡]

William Crow, brother of Hugh, was chief mate on the "Othello" when she blew up. He afterwards commanded the "Charlotte."

---

* Life of "Eldon the Judge."
† " The Liverpool Privateers," pp. 541-7.
‡ *Ibid*, pp. 331, 631, and 634.

Another well known Manx navigator was EDWARD CLARKE, captain of the "Reindeer," who in 1806 was presented with a piece of plate by the Liverpool underwriters for his gallant conduct in beating off a French privateer, after a conflict of two hours, on his voyage from Africa to Jamaica, in 1805, with a cargo of slaves. He afterwards commanded the "Charlotte." The "Manks Mercury," in 1793, mentions that "Captain SHIMMIN is going out as commander of the 'Tom,' a Guineaman [or slaver] mounting 12 pounders."

The story of JOHN CLAGUE, of Douglas, who was taken prisoner by Algerine pirates and kept as a slave, shows one of the dangers to which navigators were then subject. He was employed at a slave factory on the coast of Guinea, from whence he came home as captain of a Guineaman. Unfortunately the "Mercury," which gives this information, does not explain how this remarkable change of fortune came about.

The three Manxmen whose names follow : THOMAS MOORE, JOHN QUANE, and JOHN GELL, do not seem to have been connected with either privateering or the slave trade.

General Traders.

THOMAS MOORE (b. 1750, d. 1808)

belonged to the family of that name which was settled at Pulrose in Braddan. He went to sea when very young, and in 1778 became master of the "Fame," an armed merchantman. It was in this vessel, two years later, that he performed one of the most remarkable and gallant feats during the war. He was sailing down the English Channel, when he made out five sail on the starboard bow. They were a long distance off when night came on, but at daybreak they were only about three miles away. He made straight for them and, when he was within gunshot, they hoisted French colours, and let fly their broadsides. He reserved his fire until he was within pistol shot of the largest, when he plumped shot after shot into her, until she struck, after having been engaged for three quarters of an hour. Without stopping to send any of his men on board, he proceeded to engage the second ship, and took her after a short resistance. An officer and seven men were placed in this prize, and ordered to keep an eye on the first ship till the "Fame" returned from pursuing the remaining three vessels, which were crowding sail to get away. MOORE overhauled two of them and forced them both to strike ; the third escaped. The rest of his career contains nothing remarkable.

JOHN QUANE (b. 1757, d. 1838)

was another successful merchant seaman. According to a quaint obituary notice in the "Manks Advertiser," "he left his home for sea quite young, with only a stocking full of clothes, and one quarter's schooling." He first served on a coal brig, getting a salary which only averaged 45/- per annum. During the American War he was taken prisoner, and no sooner was he released than he was "impressed" into the English Navy. From this service he was set free by the Peace of Versailles in 1783, and the prosperous part of his career began. He went to India, "where he became pretty successful in the private trade permitted in that country,"* by which is probably meant such trade as was not monopolized by the East India Company. But in 1796, "just as his business was beginning to be extensive," he was compelled by ill-health to return to his native island, where, as he had made a handsome little fortune,"* he was able to live in what the "Advertiser" considers to be "a state of genteel affluence."* He became a member of the House of Keys in 1812, and was noted for his great liberality to the poor. The obituary notice already referred to concludes with the curious statement that "a deep conviction was impressed upon his mind that the success which befel him was mainly to be a tributed to uprightness in his parents."*

JOHN GELL (b. 1761, d. 1845)

spent his early life at sea. He was the only son of the Rev. Samuel Gell, Vicar of Lonan, who sent him when he was seven years old to be taught at the Grammar School in Douglas by the Rev. Philip Moore. He remained there till he was fourteen, and was then sent to "Captain" Fannin,† by whom he was "perfectly instructed in navigation," and at sixteen he was "bound an apprentice" to John Joseph Bacon, merchant in Douglas, "to serve five years in the seafaring line" He relates his adventures at sea as follows :—

Upon Monday evening we sailed in a ship called the "Six Sisters," bound to Barbadoes ; on the Sunday following we fell in with a French privateer about two leagues off Cork, after two hours' desperate engagement our ship was obliged to surrender, our ammunition being exhausted, and she was made a prize by the enemy, and was ransomed for £1,500, and one month allowed us to proceed on our voyage. Owing to severe weather and contrary winds, and our ship being much damaged, the month allowed us

* *Manks Advertiser.*
† See p. 132.

was expired before we arrived at our intended port, and we unfortunately fell in with a large Spanish fleet homeward bound from
Buenos Ayres, and were again taken by them prisoners, and landed
in Cadiz, in Spain, and then imprisoned during nineteen weeks and
upwards, upon very short allowance.

There happened at that time to be an exchange of prisoners, and
we were marched, 240 in number, to Port Saint Lucas, a distance of
many miles, and put on board a Cartel* bound to Portsmouth.
When we arrived near to Cape Clear, in Ireland, we took by force
possession of the Cartel (for which there is no law), and brought her
into Douglas Harbour.

Some weeks afterwards I again sailed from Douglas in a large
cutter, the property of the said merchant, Mr. Bacon, and bound to
South Carolina, and within three leagues of that place we fell in
with three American ships, well armed, bound to France, and were
by them taken prisoners and landed in Lorion [L'Orient], in France,
and from thence marched to Donan [Dinan] prison, a distance of
scores of miles, and closely confined with hundreds of prisoners of
different nations, nearly in a way of starvation, having very little
to eat, and no beds, but merely a trifle of straw, without any
covering but our own clothes, some of the prisoners dying daily,
from eight to twelve in number.

Nine weeks we remained in this deplorable situation, until, to our
great joy, 200 of us were marched to a harbour called Saint Maloes
and put on board a Cartel bound to Plymouth, and we arrived there,
near the king's ship lying at anchor, the night being uncommonly
dark, four of us took the Cartel's small boat, and got on shore
unnoticed, and, being young and able, we made the best of our way
to Liverpool, travelling by night, through fear of being seen and
impressed, and keeping in *hidlands*† the most of the day.

Passing through Bath, Bristol, Kingswood, Accon, Salisbury,
Monmouth, Shrewsbury, Nantwich, Northwich, Chester, and Runcorn, and owing to our taking such roundabout roads to avoid press
gangs and soldiers, we travelled 414 miles from Plymouth to Runcorn, nearly exhausted with fatigue and hunger, having no more
than two shillings during the whole of our travels, which I procured
for a black silk handerchief which I sold off my neck. When we
were about an hour in a public-house in Runcorn, invited by a
boatman to take some refreshment, we were seized by a press gang
from Liverpool, consisting of six men, with whom we crossed
Runcorn river, patiently pretending to be perfectly satisfied to
enter into His Majesty's service; but when we had walked with
them more than a mile, and no others in sight, as we were well
provided with good sticks, we made a sudden stop, resolved to
conquer or die on the spot, and forthwith a desperate engagement
took place.   Two of them had cutlasses, and four of them
bludgeons, and we with our sticks, until one of them had his arm
broken, and another desperately wounded in the head, and the rest
sadly bruised by blows and falls.   None of us were very much

---

* A *cartel* was a ship employed in time of war to convey prisoners for
exchange, and was looked upon as a neutral vessel, and as such was considered
safe from molestation by all parties.

† *Hidlands* is a very expressive term, commonly used by Manx people,
meaning keeping out of sight, hiding; a debtor keeping out of the way of his
creditor, or a criminal out of the way of an officer of justice, is said to be
in hidlands.

hurted excepting me, who received a cut in my head with a cutlass, which caused the blood to flow over my eyes and down my cheeks, that with difficulty I could see to hit my mark as I wished. Well battered and bruised, they at last made off, and our bloody engagement ended leaving us the glory of the field.

We then with all speed set out in quite a contrary road, and concealed ourselves in a farmer's barn, by the farmer's liberty, until night, when he gave us a good supper, the only sufficient meal we had made use of during three weeks and more. The next morning he sent a man and horse with a letter from me to Mr. Leece, merchant in Liverpool, who sent for us to Liverpool in the night, and were put on board a Manx trader commanded by Edward Kegg of Castletown, and landed the day after in Derby Haven, when we were treated with great hospitality by Mr. Afflick and family, and he lent me his horse to ride to my father's in Kirk Lonon, as my head was so severely cut and bruised.

After I had been about a month at home Mr. Bacon sent for me, and informed me that he had employed Captain Barnes in Whitehaven to purchase a ship for him, and although I had two years yet to serve, that I should go mate of her, and as I was well instructed in navigation I consented to his proposals ; but on my return home, having made these proposals known to my parents, they very much disapproved of them, as I had been so unfortunate in the seafaring line, and they advised me to return to the Grammar School in Douglas, where I had been formerly, to which I consented ; and Mr. Bacon generously giving up my indenture, I repaired forthwith to school, and my former master, the Rev. Mr. Moore, being dead,* I was then under the tuition of the Rev. Mr. Quayle,† where I continued until I was twenty years of age.‡

At the end of 1783 he was appointed reader at St. Mark's, Malew, by the governor and archdeacon, there being then a vacancy in the bishopric. In 1786, he was licensed Chaplain of St. Mark's, where, in 1789, he is said to have written the foregoing account of his seafaring life. Some years later he seems to have resigned the chaplaincy, but to have been again appointed to it in 1797. This time he held it until 1809, after which, till 1835, when he was appointed Chaplain of St. John's, German, he was a curate in Liverpool. It appears that his early life had " unsettled him and rendered him rather unfit for the ministry."§

The " Manks Mercury," in 1793, states that " five of the finest ships in Liverpool were . . commanded by Manxmen," *i.e.*, the " Trelawney," by Captain HARRISON ; the " Ann and Susannah," by Captain QUILL ; the " James," by Captain WILKS ; the " Hope," by Captain TAYLOR ; and the " John," by Captain COWLE. We do not know what trade they were engaged in.

---

* He did not die till 1783, so this seems to be a mistake.
† The Rev. Thomas Quayle.
‡ From his own Journal, re-published in *Manx Soc.*, Vol. XXX., with an introduction by William Harrison.
§ This is the opinion of Mr. Harrison, who knew him personally.

Salt Fish Traders.

Another trade in which Manxmen had engaged for centuries was
that with Spain, Portugal, and Italy, in salt fish. Manx sailors
took out fish to these countries and brought back wine with them.
A story is told of one of the Manx skippers in this trade, named
PRESTON, being, when sailing in the Mediterranean, stopped by a
French man-of war. Her lieutenant came on board, insulted
Captain PRESTON, whose foot he pinned to the deck with his
sword. Captain PRESTON drew out the sword, and then knocked
the lieutenant down. He did not, however, suffer for this, since
the French captain, when the matter was reported to him, saw
that the Manxman was not to blame, and though, as there was
war between England and France, he and his crew were taken
prisoners, he was exchanged in due course.*

The Isle of Man Steam Packet Company.

Among Manx navigators of recent times those who have been
connected with the Isle of Man Steam Packet Company have
come most prominently into notice, though the first two captains
of that company, GILL and QUAYLE, had already established a
reputation as commanders of the Manx sailing traders, which
before 1830 were the chief means of conveying passengers as
well as goods between the island and England.

WILLIAM GILL (b. 1795, d. 1858)

was brought up in Ramsey to the trade of a ship carpenter, but
he soon took to the sea. He became a very skilful navigator,
and rose to be captain of one of the sailing vessels, the
" Duchess of Atholl,"† which carried the mails between Liverpool and Douglas. He was then appointed to a new and
larger vessel of this class, the " Douglas." In 1830,
the now famous Isle of Man Steam Packet Company was
established, and GILL was selected as captain of its first vessel,
the " Mona's Isle," which was 108 feet long, and of 90 horse
power. Under GILL's capable command she surpassed the rival
company's steamer, the " St. George," in speed, the contest being
terminated by the wreck of the latter vessel on Conister,
on the 30th of November, 1830. As the company gradually

---

* " Old Manx Sea Captains," in the *Isle of Man Examiner*, by the Rev. John
Quine.
† There is a picture of this vessel in the Peveril Hotel, Douglas.

purchased other vessels, GILL was always put in charge of the largest. He will be remembered as the discoverer of the Queen's Channel into the port of Liverpool.

EDWARD QUAYLE (b. 1803, d. 1862)

was equally distinguished in his profession, having sailed in many latitudes. He was in 1833 appointed to the command of the "Mona," of 100 tons, which had been purchased to take the place of the "Mona's Isle" during the winter, as the latter was considered too large and expensive a boat for that service. The "Mona's" average passage was about fourteen hours. The epitaph on his tombstone in Kirk Braddan Church-yard describes him as being "a prompt, fearless, faithful, and brave sailor, who felt and acted like a man." Another sturdy navigator,

JOSEPH SKILLICORN (b. 1811, d. 1877),

was for many years connected with the same company, but for some time he commanded the well-known steamer "Ellan Vannin," which belonged to Castletown. Let me quote a characteristic story of the Rev. T. E. Brown's about him :—"I remember sailing with him one day from Ramsey to Douglas. The captain was sitting on an inverted bucket, cutting some tobacco. We were passing under Kirk Onchan. ' Do you know the ould name ?' he said. ' Yes,' I said, ' Kionedroghad.' ' Do you remember Parson Craine ?' ' Of course I do,' said I, ' he was my godfather.' ' Well,' said the captain, ' that's the first man that ever hove the water in my face !' " (*i.e.*, baptized him.) He was, indeed, a grand old "salt." He lies near Captain Quayle under a stone erected to his memory by some friends.

When writing of the captains in the Isle of Man Steam Packet Company's service, we naturally think of the ships they commanded, and so, perhaps, it may be worth recalling the facts that the *first* "King Orry" was built in Douglas, at a building yard which afterwards became "Bath Place," and is now part of the approach to the Victoria Pier ; and that the *first* "Douglas," a vessel very remarkable for her speed, was bought by the Confederates, during the American Civil War, for the purpose of running the blockade. They painted her gray and re-christened her the "Margaret and Jessie." She was a successful blockade runner, but she at last succumbed when only fifty yards from the harbour at Nassau, having received one shot through her boiler and another through her bow from the guns of the Federal gun-boat "Rhode Island."

The Orange Traders, &c.

About 1840, a large and increasing demand sprang up in
England for oranges. To supply this it was necessary
to build swift vessels, and Manx builders, especially
those of Peel, were remarkably successful in doing so. This was
the great era of Manx ship-building, when vessels built in Peel,
Douglas, and Ramsey, not only for this trade, but for the
American cotton trade and the Chinese tea trade, were ordered
in large numbers by English ship-owners. It is curious, however,
that, though the Manx ships had a well deserved reputation for
swiftness, they did best when commanded by Manxmen. Many
tales are told of swift runs back from the Azores, Madeira, and
Spain. One of the most famous vessels launched in Peel at this
period was the "Vixen." We will quote the Rev. John Quine's
account of her : —

Gold was discovered in Australia about the year 1850, and of
course a good many Manxmen went abroad to try and get some of
the gold. The "Vixen" was a schooner of about 120 tons burden,
and was a very beautiful vessel. She was a sort of joint-stock or
co-operative concern. About 34 men, all in search of the Golden
Fleece. left Peel in the year 1853. She had a very interesting
voyage to Australia. One little incident had been related to him by
one of the crew. It appeared that whenever they sighted another
vessel and came close to, it was absolutely necessary for the crew of
the "Vixen" to lie down on the deck, for the schooner had such a
rakish appearance, and had such a large crew as 34 on board, that
she was taken for a pirate. On one occasion the crew wanted to
send letters home, and they sighted a large American brig off the
coast of South America The fast sailing of the "Vixen" and the
number of men that were on her deck, aroused the suspicions of the
Yankees, and they made all sail to get away. But the "Vixen"
overhauled the brig, and the Yankees were obliged to stop. Then
a boat with the letters was rowed from the "Vixen" alongside the
brig, and when the boat's crew reached the Yankee they found her
crew armed with guns, and ready to blow out the brains of the
desperate Manx pirates if they attempted to come on deck. The
fate of the "Vixen" was a very interesting one. Arrived at
Australia, they found large ships carrying cargo could not come
to within ten miles of Melbourne, and that there was a pot of
money to be made by any men who had a small vessel that could
be used as a lighter. So the "Vixen" went into that trade. Afterwards her speed caused her to be taken into the mail service for the
carriage of mails between Melbourne and Sydney, and while in
that service she invariably (?) beat the steamboats. Then the Manxman who had charge of the "Vixen" suddenly saw his way to
make a fortune. There was not such a thing as a potato in the
colony, so the "Vixen" was taken to New Zealand to get a cargo of
potatoes. In the skipper's haste he must have made some sort of
a mistake as to the quality or stowage of his cargo, for when he got
back to Australia his potatoes were in such a condition that they
were not worth anything. Years after the "Vixen" came home,

and this was her fate : One Saturday afternoon she was lying in Peel at the quay. It was blowing a gale, and the crew were all in the public-house waiting for high water to get out of the harbour. When they came on board they were certainly not in a fit condition to go to sea, and experienced men on the quay expostulated with them that in the state of the weather they should not go out of the harbour. The skipper of the "Vixen" was reported to have said that if the first port he arrived at should be in the other world he was going to sail. And so they went out of Peel in the height of the gale. The Peel men went across to the hill, and from the hill watched the "Vixen" until she was lost in the thickness that accompanied a squall, and she was never seen again. And so she went around the world to come back and go down almost in sight her own port.*

At the present day, when sails have had so largely to give way to steam, the number of Manx-owned vessels, apart from herring smacks, is not large, but numerous Manxmen are found in both the English Royal Navy and Merchant Service, where many of them have distinguished themselves. Amongst these Mr. Quine especially mentions Captain KERRUISH and Captain BELL, of Sydney, the latter of whom on two occasions, when the vessels he was connected with were wrecked, succeeded in saving every man of both crews from drowning. It may be mentioned that CAPTAIN OATES, of Mullin-y-cleiy, near Ballacraine (St. John's), who died in 1873, was in command of the "Northfleet" just before she sailed on her last fatal voyage.

We conclude this short and imperfect sketch of Manx merchant captains with a brief mention of two typical men of this class who have recently died :—

ROBERT EDWARD CHRISTIAN (b. 1817, d. 1891)

was born at Baldromma in Maughold, which belongs to his family. When a boy he was apprenticed as a ship's carpenter in Taggart's yard at Ramsey. He utilized the experience obtained in this way in repairing a schooner that had been damaged by having been run down by another vessel, and then ran ashore near the Point of Ayre, which he bought. This vessel he sailed as master for some years. He was afterwards master of numerous other vessels which were, for the most part, engaged in the North American timber trade. He was generally considered to be a most expert navigator. About 1876, he retired from the sea and conducted a ship-broking business. But Captain CHRISTIAN was remarkable in other ways than for skill in his profession. He had read and thought a good deal, and was an earnest student of his native language, having translated many of the old Manx songs and carols. Some of these translations of the latter appeared in the book of Manx Carols which was published in 1891. He was a tall active man, and his physical strength was very great.

* "Old Manx Sea Captains."

WILLIAM J. GELL (d. 1895)

was born in Patrick, and brought up in Peel. On leaving school he went to sea, and was for some time in the East India Company's service. About 1855, he became a mate on one of the vessels belonging to Messrs. Thomas and James Harrison, of Liverpool, and he served that firm for the greater part of the rest of his life, being one of their most trusted captains and, finally, their marine superintendent for many years. He had great skill and boldness as a navigator and had also some mechanical ability, having patented no fewer than five inventions for the preservation of life.

CHAPTER IX.

Reformers, Farmers, Merchants, Emigrants, &c.

Reformers.

Manx reformers have mainly concerned themselves with four questions : (1) The right of the House of Keys to a share in fixing the amounts of the customs duties ; (2) the right of the Tynwald Court to control the expenditure of the surplus revenue; (3) the reform of the House of Keys ;* (4) temperance.

Of these, the first dates from the end of the 17th century ; the others are comparatively modern. There were, of course, other important questions, mainly constitutional, which arose from time to time, and especially the land question, which was brought to an end by the Act of Settlement in 1704, with which the names of JOHN STEVENSON and EWAN CHRISTIAN (see p. 71) are connected, but, as, except in the case of the land question, little is known of the chief actors in them, they do not supply any material to an account of "Manx Worthies." This, indeed, also applies to the first of the four above-named questions also, which was sturdily contested in the Keys, headed by John Stevenson, till it was conceded in 1737, only to be again taken away in 1765. The second question was one which began to be agitated about the year 1802. With this period of its history the name of JOHN CHRISTIAN CURWEN (see p. 73) will always be honourably connected. It then fell into abeyance for a time, but was revived in 1837, and it resulted in at least partial success in 1866. The chief Manxmen

---

* See Edward Christian (p. 60).

connected with this movement at a later date were JOHN JAMES
MOORE, ROBERT FARGHER, JAMES G. GELLING, and WILLIAM
CALLISTER (see p. 76)

JOHN JAMES MOORE, of Baljean, Lonan, was one of the
deputation who went to London in 1837 to interview Lord John
Russell, and, though they did not gain their object, they were
successful in preventing an increase of the customs duties which
was then threatened.

ROBERT FARGHER (b. 1803, d. 1863)

was born in the parish of Maughold.   At the age of 14 he left the
island and went to London, where he occupied the post of
private secretary.   Three years later he returned and was
apprenticed to his relation, George Jefferson, then the printer
and publisher of the " Manks Advertiser " newspaper, an organ
with a very strong Tory and Church and State bias.   As ROBERT
FARGHER grew older, his views became those of an advanced
Radical, so that his work in connexion with the "Advertiser"
became more and more distasteful to him.   He, therefore, in 1833,
persuaded William Walls, a fellow printer in the same office, to
join with him in starting a newspaper, which they called the
" Mona's Herald."   They designed it to be the organ of political
reform, nonconformity, and temperance.   To promote these ends
ROBERT FARGHER never spared himself.   Passionate and impulsive
by nature, nothing would rouse him more speedily than cases of
tyranny and oppression.   Neither loss of popularity or of business
would prevent him from denouncing them, if he thought it his
duty to do so.   It is not surprising, therefore, that he made
enemies.   He was a true patriot, and his strenuous efforts to
improve the political and social conditions of the Isle of Man
should not be forgotten.

(From an account by Mr. James Cowin.)

The next question, that of the reform of the House of Keys,
which is now usually associated with the name of JAMES BROWN*
of the " Isle of Man Times " newspaper, has in reality had several
leaders, and dates from 1791, when a petition from most of the
principal people in the island, asking that they should have the
right to choose the Keys, was laid before the Royal Commissioners
who were at that time investigating the insular constitution and
revenue.   Petitions were also presented in 1834, 1838, and
1845.   The chief leaders from 1834 onwards were the five men we
have just mentioned, together with WILLIAM KELLY, who founded
the Union Mills ; JOHN W. S. CLUCAS, of Mary Voar, Santon,
who was a captain in the merchant service ; F. B. CLUCAS,

---

* He was not a Manxman.

advocate, Ramsey ; THOMAS KNEALE, merchant, Ramsey ; JOHN DUGGAN and JOHN DUFF, merchants, Douglas ; J. S. MOORE, of Lhergydhoo,* and WILLIAM CALLISTER. Except WILLIAM CALLISTER (see p. 76), the only one of them about whom we are able to give more than a mere mention is

JOHN STEVENSON MOORE (b. 1804, d. 1895).

He was a son of John Stevenson Moore and Catherine Clarke, of Peel, and was educated at the Peel Grammar School, under the Rev. Samuel Gelling, being intended for the Manx Church. He afterwards, however, decided to turn his attention to farming instead, and he managed his father's estate of Lhergydhoo, to which he succeeded in 1826. With his secular work he determined to combine that of a Christian evangelist, and so, at the age of 17, he joined the Wesleyans,† to which body he rendered great services by his preaching and religious fervour. Between 1840 aud 1855, his special reform work was the political instruction of those who resorted to the fairs and markets on the north side of the island ; it is said that there was no one during this period who possessed greater influence with the Manx country people. He was also a staunch total abstainer and one of the leaders of the movement. Elected a member of the House of Keys for Glenfaba sheading in 1867, he remained a member of that body till 1874. During his membership he distinguished himself by a rare independence of character, one instance of which was his vote against giving £13,000 to complete the Port Erin breakwater, contrary to the wishes of Governor Loch.

The last reform movement, that of temperance or total abstinence, has also had a very considerable measure of success. At the present day, fortunately, we are scarcely in a position to understand the terrible amount of drunkenness, chiefly the result of the consumption of rum, which prevailed in this island during the first forty years, or so, of the last century. Any one wishing to verify this statement has only to peruse the " Life of Hugh Stowell Brown," which affords the most easily accessible evidence on the subject. We believe that the earliest advocate of temperance (not total abstinence) in the island was the venerable Rector of Ballaugh, HUGH STOWELL (see p. 29). Then followed the teachers of total abstinence, among whom were the Rev. WILLIAM CORRIN (see p. 36), Vicar of Rushen ; the Rev. WILLIAM GILL (see p. 35), Vicar of Malew ; the Rev. WILLIAM CHRISTIAN, Chaplain of the Dhoon, the ever active ROBERT FARGHER ; J. S. MOORE, of Lhergydhoo ; and, at a somewhat later

---

* In *Manx Soc.*, Vol. XVI., pp. 112-117 will be found a clever satire on some of these reformers by John Kelly, late High-Bailiff of Castletown.
† It must be remembered that at this time there was no distinct line of cleavage between Churchmen and Methodists.

date, the Rev. THOMAS CAINE, Vicar of Lonan ; EVAN CHRISTIAN,
of Lewaigue ;   WILLIAM SAYLE, ROBERT CANNELL, and JAMES
TEARE.   Of these JAMES TEARE was, no doubt, the most
remarkable, but the greater part of his work was done outside the
island. We append brief accounts of him, EVAN CHRISTIAN, and
the Rev. THOMAS CAINE.

JAMES TEARE (b. 1804, d. 1868)

was the seventh son of John and Jony Teare, of Cronk-y-Shoggal,
Andreas. In 1812, his family removed to Ramsey, in which town,
after he had received a rudimentary education, he was apprenticed
to a boot-maker. Going to Preston in 1823, he followed the same
trade there. He had joined the Wesleyan Church before he left
Ramsey. In Preston he greatly distinguished himself by his self-
denying charity, by his visits to the sick, and his efforts to reclaim
drunkards. " I don't know," he writes, "that I was ever the
means of reclaiming one drunkard till I proclaimed the doctrine of
total abstinence from all intoxicating drinks." In March, 1832,
the Preston General Temperance Society was formed, and in
April JAMES TEARE made his earliest public speech on the subject.
In June, he, in the same town, publicly took the ground of total
abstinence from all intoxicating liquors as the only remedy for the
prevailing intemperance of the community, being the first to do
so, and, in August, he was one of the seven who signed the first
teetotal pledge. Shortly afterwards he became one of a band of
six missionaries who travelled about England and Scotland to
propagate the new gospel. In 1855, he visited his native island,
where his speeches led to the establishment of temperance societies
and the consequent lessening of drunkenness. The rest of his life
is simply a record of incessant missionary work throughout Great
Britain. Among other tokens of appreciation of his labours was
a testimonial, with a purse containing £788, which was presented
to him at Bristol, and on his tombstone in Harpurhey Cemetery,
Manchester, are the following words : — "As a pioneer of the
movement, he proclaimed the principles of total abstinence in
every county in England, in many parts of Wales and Scotland,
in the Channel Islands, and in the Isle of Man, of which he was
a native."[*]

EVAN CHRISTIAN (b. 1803, d. 1874),

of Lewaigue, was a descendant of the Ewan Christian (see p. 71)
already mentioned. In his early life he was a soldier, but
returned to his native island when quite young. He at once
became an earnest local preacher in connexion with the Wesleyans,

---

[*] The foregoing account is, for the most part, taken from a Memoir of JAMES
TEARE, by Dr. Lees.

and indeed he devoted so much of his time and energy to religious work that he somewhat neglected his property and died in very poor circumstances. Like many of his ancestors, he was captain of the parish of Maughold. Some time before his death he was presented with a testimonial in token of his unwearying exertions in the temperance cause. In one of the obituary notices of his career he is referred to as having spent fifty years "in relieving the troubles, losses, and trials of his fellow-countrymen, in warning the erring, in reclaiming the drunkard, in preaching the Gospel to the poor, in assisting the striving, comforting the widow, caring for the fatherless and orphan, in works of charity, mercy, and brotherly kindness ;" and, according to another account, "his uniform uprightness in business, his evident desire to sow seed by all waters, and to do good in his day and generation, will be remembered, and will surely bear good fruit."

THOMAS CAINE (b. 1809, d. 1878),

the son of Matthew Caine, an inn-keeper in Douglas, was a farmer in early life. He employed his spare time in educating himself with a view of entering the Church, which he accomplished in 1839. In the following year, he was appointed to the chaplaincy of St. Luke's, Baldwin, where he remained for thirteen years, till he became Vicar of Lonan. He was a good parish priest, and greatly endeared himself to his people by his quaint, hearty, kindly ways, and his profound sympathy with their chief pursuit (farming), of which he had a thorough knowledge. But it was as a leader in the Manx temperance cause that he will be best remembered. By his persistence and earnestness, he exercised a great and well-deserved influence, one proof of which is that it was declared in evidence before the Poor Relief Commission, which sat in 1878, that it was mainly due to him that the parishioners of Lonan had so greatly improved in sobriety. A stone was erected in Kirk Braddan Churchyard by the Manx Temperance Union, of which he was president, with the following inscription :—

> In memory of the Manx Apostle of
> Total Abstinence, the REV. THOMAS
> CAINE, Vicar of Lonan.
> Born December 21st, 1809.
> Died November 15th, 1878.
> Erected by friends of temperance
> throughout the Island as a tribute
> of respect and admiration of his
> consistent and self-denying labours.

Among other temperance reformers were ROBERT CANNELL, who did much to forward the cause of temperance among his English speaking hearers by his poetry ; while WILLIAM SAYLE, an excellent

Manx scholar, performed the same office by his tracts and poems in Manx for the Manx speaking section. Nor should we forget how nobly Colonel HENRY MURRAY, M.H.K., used his influence to induce the Legislature to pass the Taverns Act in 1857, by which public-houses are closed on Sunday.*

The most distinguishing characteristic of the two Manxmen, whose names follow, was their philanthropy.

PHILIP CHRISTIAN (d. 1652)

would probably have been forgotten but for his benefaction to his native town of Peel, since, except the fact that he was "a cloth-worker and citizen of London," absolutely nothing is known of him. By his will he, after the death of his "loveing wife Rebecca," "gave and devised two houses in Lovell's Inn, Pater Noster Rowe, in the Parish of St. Faith, to the master, wardens and cominalty of the art or mystery of clothworkers of the citey of London . . . and to their heirs and successors for ever ; to this intent and purpose that they and their successors shall pay out of the rents and proffits thereof yearly arising, or to them accruing, unto two poore youthes or boyes every year for ever, the somme of tenn pounds appiece, the said youthes or boyes to be natives of the Isle of Mann ; and if they be of my kindred or my name, my will is that they shall be preferred before any other . . . and if it shall happen that there be not a free school maintained for the teaching of children in the towne of Peel . . . then my will is that the twenty pounds a yeare by me formerly given for the putting out of two boyes to be apprentices shall cease, and the said somme to be paid by the said Company of Clothworkers towards the maintenance of the said schoole, of which somme my will is that the schoole master for the time being shall have eighteen pounds a yeare for his paines, and the other forty shillings to be paid and employed in buying and providing bookes, pen, inke, and paper, for poore schollers there."† There being no free school in Peel, a school was, about the year 1689, founded through the exertions of Bishop Levinz, who recovered "one hundred pounds for arrears of the said benefaction," and obtained "a Decree of Chancerie for the settlement of the annuall sallary of twenty pounds."‡ This school, known as Christian's School, is still in existence. In 1840, the Clothworkers announced that, if an improved school were provided, they would add to the annuity, the value of the premises in London having greatly increased. The present school house and teacher's house were

---

* See "Temperance in the Isle of Man," 1884 ; a pamphlet by James Cowin.
† Isle of Man Charities, pp. 63-4.
‡ MS. Letter in Episcopal Records.

erected by the Clothworkers in 1876, and the same beneficent
corporation has lately made large additions to the buildings. We
may mention that, in addition to this benefaction, PHILIP
CHRISTIAN also gave five pounds to " bee disposed of by twenty
shillings a year for five years . . . for buying of small books,
pen, ink, and paper, or what shall be thought most fit by the
minister and schoolemaster of the town of Peele . . . for
the use of the poorest men's sons and daughters of the said towne
of Peel, inhabiting there, and not otherwise."

PHILIP KILLEY (b. 1811, d. 1897),

son of William Killey, of Ballawilley-Killey, Marown, was
educated at various private schools in Douglas. Associated with
his father in the businesses of brewing and tanning, the latter of
which he continued to conduct for many years, he also, for some
years, successfully cultivated his landed property. He was a
useful member of the self-elected House of Keys, in which he sat
from 1855 till its dissolution, and, as captain of the parish of
Marown, he was a member of the Douglas District Licensing Court
for thirty years. He was also a director of the Isle of Man Steam
Packet Company. Nor should his valuable contribution to a
knowledge of the climate of Douglas, in the shape of a daily
record of the rainfall and weather for a period of thirty years,
be forgotten. But his chief activities, especially during later
years, were connected with philanthropic objects. It is no
exaggeration to say that any and every charitable movement in
Douglas was aided and abetted by him in the most energetic
and self-sacrificing way. Thus he was a strenuous supporter
of the hospital from its beginning in 1837, being one of its
administrative committee for many years. In all matters
relating to the relief of the poor his services were rendered even
more freely. He was one of the governors of the House of
Industry, in which he took a very great interest ; president of
the local branch of the Lifeboat Institution, and one of the
trustees of the Isle of Man Bank for Savings. " In short," says
the "Isle of Man Times," "his long career was filled with services
for the town of Douglas," and, it continues, " with superabundant
vigour and vitality, he possessed a warm and generous heart,
which would hardly allow him to refuse any request. A more
active friend to his fellow townsmen never lived. . . . He
was one of the best beloved men we had, and his memory will
long be green."

Farmers.

It is only at a comparatively recent date that Manxmen have
earned a reputation for ability in farming. At the end of the 17th
century, and during the greater part of the 18th century, smuggling
and fishing were the most attractive and profitable occupations,
leading, even when farming was not totally neglected, to its
occupying a very secondary position. At the beginning of the
last century the high price of corn induced a greatly increased
culture, but this was most successfully carried on in the island by
English and Scottish farmers, who had either bought or rented
land at lower rates than prevailed in their own countries.
Gradually, however, the Manxmen learned their methods, and by
steady economy and persevering industry have succeeded where
the Englishmen and Scotsmen, owing to their less careful and
economical methods, have, in many cases, failed. It is indeed
remarkable how much of the land, which fifty years ago was in
strangers' hands, has since then reverted to natives, both as
landlords and tenants.

COLUMBUS KEY,

of Kiondroghad, in Kirk Andreas, seems to have been
a typical specimen of the Manx farmer of the 17th
century. It is related of him that he paid a visit to William, Earl
of Derby, at Knowsley, in 1685, in return for one which the earl
had paid him at Kiondroghad. On his arrival at the front door,
the porter refused to admit him, saying that the earl was then
engaged in entertaining a party of gentlemen. It is probable that
Columbus was arrayed in the ancient Manx costume of long blue
tail coat, knee-breeches of homespun wool, *keear* stockings of the
same, and on his feet *carranes* of untanned cow-hide, with the
hairy side out, so that the porter, who had perhaps never seen
such a queer object before, mistook his social position. However
that may have been, the old man, for he was then in his seventieth
year, insisted on his name being sent in. As soon as he heard it,
the earl rose from the table and ushered him in himself. They
conversed for a time, and, when Columbus was about to retire, the
earl, wishing to make him a present, proposed to let him have his
estate free from lord's rent, which at that time was a much more
valuable gift than it would be at present. But he declined, saying;
" My lord, I cannot accept such a gift, for when my land will
not enable me to pay lord's rent, it will not be worth keeping by
myself or my descendants." On being pressed to say if
there was anything that he would like to have, he said he would
accept a dog and gun, with permission for himself and his

heirs to shoot over any land in the island. This privilege was accordingly granted. That he was both well-known and esteemed in his native island is evident from the following distich :—

> Columbus Key
> V'eh dooinney 'gyn moayrn ;
> Nagh ren braih curnagh
> Marish yn oayrn.

> Columbus Key was a man without pride ;
> He did not malt wheat with the barley.

i.e., he might be depended upon for giving an unadulterated article.

It must be remembered that it was not till towards the end of the eighteenth century that anything like scientific farming was introduced into the Isle of Man. Its pioneers should not be forgotten. They were Sir G. MOORE, of Ballamoore, Patrick (see p. 72); SENHOUSE WILSON, of Farm Hill, receiver-general; JOHN CHRISTIAN CURWEN (see p. 73); Deemster CRELLIN (see p. 84); J. J. BACON, the Rev. JOHN CRELLIN, the Rev. DANIEL GELLING, and BASIL and THOMAS QUAYLE (see p. 100).

A local newspaper* remarked, in 1793, that BASIL QUAYLE's land afforded "the best example of a complete farm carried on upon the system of the best cultivated counties in England, especially in turnips and other winter green food." Of our own time we may mention EVAN GELL (b. 1806, d. 1887), a useful member of the Legislature and Highway Board, both before and after 1867, who was the principal insular breeder of shorthorns, nearly all the best strains in the island, at the time of his death, being from his stock. He had an unrivalled knowledge of the value of land and was therefore appointed one of the valuers under the Tithe Commutation Act. He was a justice of the peace and captain of the parish of Michael, where he resided at the Whitehouse.

Merchants, &c.

The Isle of Man cannot boast of many sons who have made fortunes in commerce. Of trade there was practically none till smuggling began ; we know something of Manx merchants who made a good thing out of it, but their names are, perhaps, best left in oblivion.

---

* *The Manks Mercury.*

G

EDWARD CHRISTIAN (see p. 60) amid the varied occupations of his adventurous life, seems for a time to have been engaged in commerce.

PHILIP CHRISTIAN (see p. 190) was evidently a successful merchant.

Next in order of date is

JOHN MURREY (*circa* 1660),

who is famous as the issuer of the first Manx coinage, in 1668. We have evidence that coined money was very scarce in the island about that time, and so, no doubt, JOHN MURREY's pence were very welcome. They had the legend—"John Murrey ∴ 1668," with, in the centre, "His Penny, I.M." on the obverse, and *Quocunque Gesseris Stabit*, on the reverse. These pence were made legal tender by an order of the Council, and in 1679 an Act of Tynwald was passed which ordained that they should "still pass according to order." They did so till 1709, when they were superseded by the first Manx government coinage. They were then redeemed by his son, also named John, who married Susannah Patten, a first cousin of Bishop Wilson's wife. He was also a successful trader. In 1706, no less than 29 members of the Tynwald Court bound themselves to provide him with "20 tunns of strong beere," for export to the West Indies, he paying them eighteen shillings per barrel and finding the barrels. This bargain was actually arranged at a sitting of the Tynwald Court. In the same year JOHN MURREY presented St. Matthew's Church, in Douglas, with a clock which still (1897) bears the letters "J.M."* on its dial. He lived at Murrey's Court in Douglas. About the year 1720, he bought the estate of Ronaldsway from James Somerville, who had bought it from *Illiam Dhone's* grandson, William Christian, in 1716. This estate remained in the Murrey family till about 1817, when it passed by marriage to the late W. W. Christian's father (see p. 67.)

GEORGE QUAYLE (b. 1751, d. 1835),

of the Bridge House family, was conspicuous in a variety of ways. In 1777, he entered the first regiment of Fencibles that was formed, ultimately becoming a captain. But, not satisfied with this, he raised a corps of yeomanry, which he commanded until it was disbanded at the Peace of Amiens in 1802. In the same year,

---

* On the demolition of the church in 1899, the clock was placed in the tower of the new church, but it has not been set up.

he, in conjunction with his brother, Mark Hildesley Quayle, John Taubman, and James Kelly, opened the "Isle of Man Bank" in Castletown. In 1818, when the bank closed, he sold the Barony of St. Trinian's, in Marown, as well as other property, that the people should not suffer from the trust placed in his name, "Quayle's Notes" being considered as good as those of the Bank of England. He became a member of the House of Keys in 1784, his connexion with that body continuing till his death. He travelled extensively, and was the originator of several mechanical inventions, from which, however, he reaped no benefit.

LUKE WHITE (b. *circa* 1770)

is said to have left the island, about the year 1782, for Dublin, where he succeeded in obtaining a situation as assistant to a bookseller. On his master retiring he succeeded to the business, which he conducted with very great success, realizing a great fortune by it, and by dealings in State lottery tickets. He became a member of Parliament for an Irish county, and three of his sons were in the same position. The youngest of them. Henry, M.P. for Longford, and afterwards for Dublin, was, in 1863, raised to the peerage as Lord Anally, of Clonsilla, County Dublin, and Rathcline, County Longford. His son, the present baron, who succeeded in 1873, on his father's death, has residences at Lucan, Dublin, and Rathcline House, Longford.

ROBERT CORRIN (b. 1823, d. 1899),

of Knockaloe, Patrick, the eldest son of Thomas Corrin, was educated at the Peel Grammar and Mathematical School, and afterwards entered the grocery business. He was also interested in the fishing industry at Peel, to which, after a time, he entirely devoted himself. In connexion with this he established a net factory and, so excellent were his nets, that he obtained a large sale for them, not only in the island, but elsewhere. But his chief title to remembrance is his discovery, some forty years ago, of the value of the Kinsale mackerel fishery. He sent boats there at his own risk, and thus became the pioneer of a most valuable industry. Prior to this time the Manx fishermen only went to the fishery in summer and autumn. It will, therefore, be seen that the result of this discovery was, not only to employ capital more profitably, but to give increased and remunerative employment to thousands of people. His knowledge of all questions, whether practical or scientific, connected with sea fisheries, was very remarkable, and he was justly esteemed the greatest authority on them in the Isle of Man. As late as 1898, he sent a valuable contribution on the subject of the habits of the herring to the insular Industrial Commission, which was published by them in their report issued in that year. But his energy and ability were not confined to his own affairs. He took a great interest in public work, being, between 1870 and 1876, a useful and respected member of the House of Keys. In 1883, he was appointed a justice of the peace, and in 1892, captain of the parish of Patrick. His career has been " a distinguished one, and the manner in which he acquitted himself in whatever position he held gained for him the good will and esteem of his neighbours."*

JOSEPH MYLCHREEST (b. 1837, d. 1896),

the third son of John Mylchreest, a Peel smack-owner, and Christian Moore, was educated at Gawne's School in Peel, and, on leaving it, was apprenticed as a ship carpenter in that town. After five years of this employment he went to the West Coast of Africa, where he worked at his trade, but, being excited by the account of the gold discoveries in Australia, he went to that country in 1860. From thence he wandered to New Zealand, California, British Columbia, Bolivia, Peru, Chili, and back again to Australia, working off and on in gold and silver mines, but with no great success, till, in 1876, he went to the diamond mines at Kimberley, in South Africa. Here, at first, fortune was not kind to him, but, with his lease of the Royal Mining Company's Works, a change came, and he gradually acquired a most valuable property, which he disposed of to the De Beers Company for an enormous sum. In 1888, he returned to settle in his native country, where, till his untimely death eight years later, he did much for its good by the money he spent in charity and in encouraging agriculture. He was elected a member of the House of Keys for Peel in 1891, and was made a magistrate shortly afterwards. "The Diamond King," as he was usually called, was a man of magnificent physique, with a somewhat rough exterior, which concealed a kindly heart and great shrewdness. It can' be truly said of him that he never turned his back upon an old friend, however humble.

We may mention that the late Sir MARK WILKS COLLET, Baronet, whose father's name was Corlett, was a Manxman by descent, being connected with Colonel Mark Wilks and, we believe, with the Corletts of Loughan-y-yei, in Lezayre. He attained the distinguished position of Governor of the Bank of England.

---

* *Manx Sun.*

Oddities.

Perhaps the best heading for those who follow is that of "Oddities."

DANIEL TEAR (b. 1677, d. 1787),

a native of Andreas, was, during the latter part of his life, a vagrant, spending his time in "going on the houses," as the Manx phrase has it. Sir Wadsworth Busk, attorney-general, erected a stone to his memory in Santon Churchyard, and wrote the following lines which are engraved upon it :—

> Here friends is little Daniel's tomb,
> To Joseph's years he did arrive ;
> Sloth killing thousands in their bloom,
> While labour kept poor Dan alive.
> How strange, yet true, full seventy years
> Was his wife happy—in her Tears.

His age, as given on the stone, is 110, but he was generally supposed to be older.

THOMAS KEWIN (b. 1755, d. 1821),

commonly known as "Buck" Kewin. We extract the following notice of him from the "Kaleidoscope," vol. ii., " Trip to the Isle of Man, 1822 ":—

He directed me to Mr. Kewn, an adept at the pencil as well as the razor, and whose talent for caricaturing has once or twice put him to the expense of a broken head. On arriving at his shop, I was somewhat struck with the words "New Bond Street" painted in large characters over the door, while the following invitation was displayed in the window : "Kewn, superior hair cutter from Waterloo." Various specimens of his art in caricaturing, including his own likeness, taken by himself, were here arranged. I expected him to be communicative like his brethren of the razor, but he was not so. He rather drew attention to his own drawings ; but I learnt from him that the people here are much given to scandal. Mr. Kewn acquitted himself to my satisfaction, and after paying him, I asked to see more specimens of his talent. His portfolio contained some very old and rather clever productions. Among others, a sketch of a Manchester man belabouring a Manks porter, a scene that I had been present at the day before. It was well executed and with considerable truth.

Mr Kewin's talents for caricature upon at least one occasion caused him some inconvenience. The late Deemster Heywood had taken offence with the late Mr. Mark Antony Mills, a member of the bar, who is known to fame as the editor of an edition of the Statutes of the Isle of Man ; and the deemster, sad to relate, administered to Mr. Mills a sound beating in public. Within a day or two of the

chastisement there appeared in "Buck" Kewin's shop window a
sketch from Kewin's pencil descriptive of the assault, and underneath the drawing was written, "The man who took out a patent
for threshing mills." Deemster Heywood, who appears to have
been a quick-tempered judge, being apprised of the cartoon, paid
a visit to the barber-limner's shop, tore down the sketch, and
further expressed his disapproval of the exhibition by horse-
whipping Kewin.

ELIZABETH CHRISTIAN

first became notorious in 1843, when she, in company with a
man named Garrett, set up what she called a "Garden of Eden"
at the foot of Snaefell. She declared that she was the Virgin
Mary, and that her partner was Elias; that they were the first-
fruits of the Millenium, and that their office was to try all flesh as
to its eligibility for the millenial state. All, however, who could
not pass the naked ordeal were to be excluded. She stated that
she and her partner would appear weekly on the top of Snaefell
in a state of nature till the harvest was ready, when the wheat
would be separated from the tares, by the whole of the rest of the
island being submerged, but she does not seem to have carried out
her intention. In the following year she, with her two sisters,
one of whom was called JANE (b. 1801, d. 1871), took up her
residence at Laburnum Cottage, Castletown Road, and she assumed
the name of Elijah. Here they began to print a number of small
pamphlets and broadsides, which were issued from what they
called the "Millenial Office, Ballasalla." They were their own
compositors. ELIZABETH died about 1847, when the mantle of the
prophet fell on JANE, who carried on these publications for some
years longer. Their nature will be sufficiently indicated from the
following extract :—

"WHERE is the JEHOVAH EL SHADDAI, the LORD GOD of
ELIJAH?" See 2d. Kings, 2d. Chapter, 14th Verse.
"Behold, I give you power to tread on serpents and scorpions,
and over all the power of the enemy: and nothing shall by any
means hurt you."—See Saint Luke, 10th Chapter, 19th Verse.
"And, Lo, I am with you alway, even to the end of the world.
Amen."—See Saint Matthew, 28th Chapter, 20th Verse.
In the Name of the FATHER, and of the SON, and of the HOLY
GHOST. In the Name of GOD the FATHER, and of GOD the SON, and
of GOD the HOLY GHOST, the most HIGH GOD HELION ELSHADDAI,
Whose Name alone is JEHOVAH, and through the GRACE, and by the
POWER of our LORD JESUS CHRIST, I, a Baptised Papist, and a poor
unworthy Servant of the LORD JESUS CHRIST, do now command all
devils, and all dammed spirits, and all evil, wicked and bad spirits,
and all Fairies, and all Wizards, and all Witches, and every evil
eye, and each, all and every evil bad devilish satanick power and
powers of evil whatsoever, Not to hurt. Not to harm, Not to injure,
Nor do any devilish evil bad wicked mischief in anywise whatsoever
unto thee Margaret C—— alias C——, Nor unto thy Husband, Nor

unto any one of all your Children,] Nor unto anything that ever
did, or that now doth, or that hereafter shall and may both Justly
and Lawfully belong in any-wise whatsoever unto thee [Margaret,
or unto Thy Husband, or unto your Children, (And now especially) as
unto Thy Child Elizabeth Anna C——] so long as the *Almighty Lord
Jesus Christ, the Holy Son of God with Power*, Liveth and Reigneth *God
over all, God* blessed for evermore. Amen. even so, *Lord Jesus,*
Amen ; if it be Thy *Holy Godly Blessed Will ;* for the alone sake of Thy
most Holy Atoneing, Redeeming Propituous Blood, and justifying
Righteousness, and Holy Sanctifying saving Grace of *God* the *Holy
Ghost,* the Blessed gift of *God* the *Father Jehovah,* To them that
believe through saving Grace—Wherefore, none of all the powers
of evil shall not again be able to hurt thee [Margaret,] in anywise
whatsoever, so long as thou believeth in the *Lord Jesus Christ,* to be
the *Son* of *God,* with Power. Amen, *Lord Jesus,* Amen. For thy
great Almighty Name's sake.

May *Jesus* Help thee [Margaret, and Help all of Them.] May
Jesus Save thee [and Save all of Them ;] and, O, may *Christ the Lord
Jesus,* both Bless, Prosper, and keep thee, both now and forever
more, even forever. Amen. *Lord Jesus Christ,* our *God* and only
Saviour. Let it be so, according to Thy Promise, and our Faith
in Thee ; and give us Faith alone in Thee. Amen, Almighty *Lord
Jesus Christ.*

JAMES GARRETT (d. *circa* 1875),

mentioned in the foregoing account, was a very strange creature.
He had been wont to say that he had been three times in the
world. The first time, he came to it through the Red Sea with
the Children of Israel ; and the second time, he arrived in it on
the occasion of the miracle of the loaves and fishes. His third
advent was not marked by any special event, but, during the life
which followed, his experiences were so unpleasant that he had no
intention of coming back again. He remembered certain events
which occurred in all of the three periods during which he lived
in the world, and, when anyone doubted his accounts of them, he
always replied, " Wasn't I there, and you were not ?" Though a
plasterer by trade, his real bent was for mechanical pursuits.
With nothing but a file he made the endless screw and cog-wheels
for double-bass fiddles, and he also made American screw-bits with
the same implement.

(Information from Mr. Henry Corteen.)

ARTHUR CALEY (b. 1829, d. 1853),

was born at Sulby. Both his parents and grandparents were of
ordinary stature, and he had numerous brothers and sisters, none
of whom were remarkable for their height. At the age of 22 he
was 7ft. 6in., and weighed 21 stone, and it is said that he grew
slightly after that age. He was well built, and so strong that he
could lift a sack of flour with one hand and toss it into a cart.
Early in 1852 he went to London, where he was exhibited. Soon

afterwards he was engaged for exhibition in Paris for twelve months. It is said that the sumptuous living he indulged in in that capital had such a bad effect upon him that he died of surfeit. The man who engaged him had insured his life for £2,000.

CHARLES GELL (d. *circa* 1870),

generally known as *Chalse-y-Killey*, wandered over the island "going on the houses." But, though he begged, he performed many useful offices for his numerous friends and acquaintances, and for this and his power of quaint and humorous anecdote he was welcomed everywhere. He was supposed to be, and no doubt was, in some respects, rather "silly," but he nevertheless possessed considerable shrewdness. Truly devout, and to this he appears to have owed his nickname, which signifies "Charles of the Church," he was a fanatic where Roman Catholics were concerned. On one occasion, when asked where he had been, he remarked that he had been at the Union Mills with "Pazon Drury putting the Romans out." Another subject which greatly excited him was the people being deprived of their grazing on the "commons." At a meeting at Sulby, with regard to it, he said : "We muss put down this Popery, we muss hev a big grave made, and we'll hev the Pope in first, and then we'll hev Thomas Arthur."* A little later, when Governor Loch, with a possé of police and special constables, perambulated the southern commons to clear them of sheep belonging to the evicted commoners—the battle of *Cronk-ny-irree-lhaa* as this perambulation was called—Chalse made his appearance early in the day, and walked along "with measured tread and solemn look, carrying aloft a flag extemporised out of a pocket handkerchief. He said very little except that the 'great Captain' would in his own good time regulate all things and deal out equal justice to all."† Chalse, it should also be remembered, was a temperance orator. In this, as in other respects, he has been immortalized by the Rev. T. E. Brown, in the charming poem, "To Chalse in Heaven":—

> . . The ways were cold, the ways were rough—
> Oh Heaven ! oh home !
> No more to roam
> Chalse, poor Chalse.‡

THOMAS SHIMMIN (d. *circa* 1876),

commonly known as "Tom the Dipper," combined the functions of rag-gatherer and poet. During his early life his headquarters were at Port Erin, from whence he sallied forth with his

---

* The vicar-general of that name, who was then notorious as a purchaser of common lands from the Crown (quotation from Rev. T. E. Brown.)
† *Manx Sun.*
‡ "Old John and other Poems," pp. 16-22.

donkey cart, which bore his name and the legend "True
Manninagh" (True Manxman). In his later days he erected, by
permission of the High-Bailiff of Castletown, and with the help
of his wife, a small cottage on the mountain, near Ballakilpheric.
With reference to this dwelling he remarks in a foot note to one
of his poems :—

I will now conclude by saying, as the Queen of Sheba said, when
she came from the uttermost parts of the earth to see and hear the
wisdom of Solomon : "But a greater than Solomon was here," for
he with all his kingly power and riches never built a cottage in the
heather and left it to the poor (!)

His numerous doggerel effusions were occasionally in Manx, but
more often in English. One of the former is *Yn Coayl jeh'n
Lillee*, "The Loss of the Lily," a vessel which was blown up,
with loss of many lives, at Kitterland, in December, 1852. Of
his English poems the two most remarkable are those on the
"Happy Marriage of the Prince of Wales," and "The Royal
Manx Railway, or £5 of wit for a penny." A specimen of the
former will suffice to show his style :—

> But the despised metropolis,
> I call it Castletown,
> Although the Governor were amiss,
> In honour did abound ;
> 'Twas not alone the poor were fed,
> But tradesmen and there spouse,
> To the Town Hall were freely led,
> And quickly filled the house.
>
> *Chorus.*
> So long live good Queen Victoria,
> Likewise the Prince of Wales,
> May Britain prove victorious,
> And tell her wondrous tales.

It will be perceived that he considered the exigencies of rhyme
more important than those of grammar or sense.

Manx Women.

Manx women have quite as many "Worthies" in their ranks as
Manx men, but, from the nature of their chief vocations, they are
naturally less conspicuous, and so afford little material for the
biographer. Some of them have been mentioned under the head
of "Literature,"* and we now select three from their number, the
first of whom was conspicuous for courage, the second for beauty,
and the third for bountiful charity, qualities which may also be
found among many of their countrywomen.

---

* Nessie Heywood, Margaret Crellin, Mrs Kerruish, Esther Nelson, and
Bellanne Stowell.

ELINOR DRINKWATER (*née* LEECE),

daughter of William Leece, of Knockfroy, in Braddan, but who
was then settled as a merchant in Liverpool, particularly distinguished herself during a dangerous riot which broke out among
the sailors in that city in 1775. They visited the houses of the
merchants and, among others, that of Miss LEECE's father in
Water Street. She, " with a fearlessness and self-possession that
was completely wanting in the local authorities of Liverpool during
the riot, went to the door, and addressing the mob leader, who
was a sailor, enquired what they wanted. Jack, struck with
admiration at her courage and coolness, took off his hat and
remained uncovered while, in respectful language he solicited,
instead of demanding, a contribution. Having received it, he
thanked her, and drew off the rabble without doing any further
mischief."* The riot was eventually quelled by a troop of Light
Horse from Manchester. ELINOR LEECE afterwards married
William Drinkwater, who was Mayor of Liverpool in 1810. Her
eldest son, Sir George, held the same office in 1829 ; her second
son, William Leece, was a member of the House of Keys ; and
her third son, John, was the father of Sir William Leece Drinkwater. Her daughter, Margaret, married Peter Bourne, who was
Mayor of Liverpool in 1825.

LAURA, LADY BUCHAN, *née* WILKS
(b. 1797, d. 1888),

the eldest daughter of Col. Wilks by his first wife (see p. 154),
will be chiefly remembered on account of her interview with
the Emperor Napoleon just after his arrival in St. Helena.
She was then evidently a remarkably beautiful girl. Indeed,
when the writer saw her at her house in Portland Place,
London, some years before her death, she still had the remains of
great beauty. Our knowledge of the interview is mainly derived from
an article in "Blackwood's Magazine," of January, 1834, entitled,
"Reminiscences of Napoleon Bonaparte."† It was written by a
lady‡ who was staying with Col. and Mrs. Wilks at the time, and
who, by special request of Mrs. Wilks, accompanied her daughter
when she (Miss Wilks) and Col. Wilks called on Napoleon. "I
was delighted," she writes, "to chaperone so elegant, amiable,
and beautiful a young lady . . and felt proud that Napoleon
should see so perfect a specimen of my fair countrywomen. Miss
WILKS was then in the first bloom of youth, and her whole
demeanour, affability, and elegant, modest appearance, conspired
to render her the most charming and admirable person I ever

* Williams, " Liverpool Privateers."
† Kindly copied by Mr. Frowde.
‡ Her name is not given.

before or have since met with in all my peregrinations in Europe,
Asia, and Africa, for the space of thirty years." She then proceeds to describe their departure from Government—or Plantation
—House, as it was called, in a huge vehicle drawn by six bullocks
driven by three men.* After "some hours going across the most
dangerous narrow roads, or rather paths, sharp turnings and
precipitous horrors beneath, enough to terrify the stoutest heart,
and turn giddy the strongest head," they arrived at Longwood.
They found Napoleon "fully dressed and standing to receive
Governor Wilks with etiquette." He was "arrayed in a green
coat, with all his stars, orders, and ribbons—silk stockings, small
shoes with gold buckles, and a *chapeau-bras* under his arm." His
secretary and interpreter, Count Las Cases, stood by his side.
The governor then presented his daughter to Bonaparte, who,
"looking at her with a pleasing smile, addressed her in these
words : ' I have long heard from various quarters of the superior
elegance and beauty of Miss Wilks ; but now I am convinced
from my own eyes that the report has scarcely done her sufficient
justice.'† Saying this, he bowed to her politely." From another
source,‡ we gather that Napoleon also said : "You must be very
glad to leave the island ;" to which she replied, "Oh ! no, sire, I
am very sorry to go away," to which Napoleon very naturally
answered : "Oh ! mademoiselle, I wish I could change places with
you." He then presented her with a bracelet. Some years after
her arrival in England she married General Sir John Buchan,
K.C B., whom she survived. She was a considerable landowner
in the Isle of Man, having succeeded to her father's properties
of Kirby, Castleward, &c.

EMILY MARIA GAWNE, *née* MURRAY
(b. 1814, d. 1889),

the second daughter of Colonel Richard Murray and Catherina
Bacon, and great granddaughter of John, the third Duke of
Atholl, was born at the Hill's House, in Douglas, but spent
most of her young life, till she was married to Edward Moore
Gawne (see p. 75) in 1835, at Mount Murray. Till her father-
in-law's death in 1837, when they removed to Kentraugh, she and
her husband lived at Ardairey in Arbory. When once settled at

---

* The writer explains that on account of "the steep precipitous roads . . .
to proceed in a carriage drawn by horses would be dreadfully dangerous, nay
almost impossible."

† O'Meara, in his "Napoleon at St. Helena," gives the date of this interview
as April 21, 1816, saying that it took place just before Col. Wilks left for England
in the "Havannah." In describing it, he uses the following words: "He
(Napoleon) was highly pleased with Miss Wilks (a highly accomplished and
elegant young lady), and gallantly told her that she exceeded the description
which had been given of her to him."

‡ A note in the *Isle of Man Times* of May, 1888. The writer of it refers to the
article in "Blackwood," but does not say where he got his further information
from.

Kentraugh, she inaugurated the systematic plan of almsgiving
which she carried out during the rest of her life. Her charitable
deeds, though munificent, were never spasmodic, being thoroughly
well directed, and organized in a business-like way. An instance of
this is afforded by the benefit society in the parish of Rushen,
which she instituted in 1843. Again, during the time of the Irish
famine, when there was great destitution in the island, she started
a shop where tea, groceries, and other necessaries were sold at cost
price, and she also gave employment to a number of people in
spinning and weaving wool. Before the introduction of public
elementary education in 1872, she largely supported the girls' school
in the parish of Rushen, and she was mainly instrumental in
building the new church at Port St. Mary. A true lady bountiful,
she was regarded with affection, mingled with profound admiration
and respect for her pious and amiable life. In her relations to her
husband, her family, and her friends, she was in every respect
admirable, and she performed the duties of hostess with
dignity and affability. To commemorate her goodness and kindness to the poor, a stained glass window has been erected in
Rushen parish church, the subject of which is very appropriately
"The Raising of Dorcas." Of a fourth Manxwoman,

MARGARET CHRISTIAN, *née* TAUBMAN
(b. 1748, d. 1778),

daughter of John Taubman, of the Bowling Green, and wife of
John Christian, of Milntown and Unerigg, we can only say that,
judging by her epitaph in Malew Church, she must have indeed
been a paragon !

Tho' called away in the prime of life from the fairest prospects of
human felicity ; from the delighted hopes of most indulgent
parents ; from the tender affection of a loving husband ; from the
early promise of an only son, and from an affluent fortune ; yet did
she not repine. Innocence, virtue, and unaffected sanctity, enabled
her to meet the awful summons with devout resignation. The
esteem and admiration of the wise and good ; the dearest love of
those that knew her best; the agonising sorrows of disconsolate
friends, pleaded in vain for her longer stay ; yet was not her death
untimely. Blessed with wisdom above her sex, and virtue beyond
her years, her task she soon finished. A specimen was all that was
required, and now with the dead that die in the Lord, she resteth
from her labours, and her works do follow her.

Emigrants.

No account of "Manx Worthies" would be complete without some reference to the Manxmen who have emigrated to America and the British Colonies. The large proportional number of able and distinguished men among them is very noticeable. It is, indeed, remarkable how wonderfully Manxmen have developed and succeeded in larger fields than are afforded by their own little island. Nor is their strong feeling of love, even after the lapse of many years, for their old home less remarkable. This feeling has been strongly shown recently by the liberal contributions to the Snaefell Disaster Fund by Manxmen in South Africa and Australia.

The earliest Manx emigrants, if we may believe tradition, were

ROSE and BARBARA STANDISH,

wives of the famous Myles Standish (b. 1586, d. 1656), the military leader of the Puritans who left England for America in the "Mayflower" in 1620. They are said to have come from Lezayre, and it is probable that their maiden, as well as their married, name was STANDISH. A branch of the Standishes, of Standish Hall,* in Lancashire, had settled in the Isle of Man, first at Pulrose, in Braddan, and then at Ellanbane, in Lezayre, since the beginning of the sixteenth century ; and one of them, John, perhaps ROSE and BARBARA's father, was a member of the House of Keys in 1593. William Standish of Ellanbane,† who was perhaps his son, was a member of the House of Keys from 1629 to 1656, and was concerned in the rising against the Stanleys in 1651. He was evidently a leading Manxman, since he was one of those who went on board Colonel Duckenfield's ship to arrange terms with him in October, 1651. Between 1661 and 1665, John Standish, probably William's son, was an M.H.K., and was one of those who tried *Illiam Dhone.*

These Standishes held a quantity of intack property in Lezayre besides Ellanbane, and, though the family has long since disappeared, there is to this day a curragh called Standishes' Curragh in that parish. Whether this property, or any part of it, belonged to Myles in his own right, or through his Manx wives, we do not know, since, though he left certain estates both in Lancashire and the Isle of Man to his son Alexander on his death in 1656, and though Alexander by his will, dated 1702, also claimed these estates, a diligent search in the Manx manorial records has failed to discover

---

* Myles belonged to the same branch of this family; so that he and his Manx wives were probably cousins.
† Another William Standish was Vicar of Lezayre in 1630.

the names of either ROSE, BARBARA, Myles, or Alexander. As regards the two latter, however, it may be accounted for by the remark in Myles' will that these estates had been "surreptitiously detained"* from him, so that it is possible that his son never obtained possession. Myles had been engaged in the war of independence in Holland, after which, when he was one of the garrison at Leyden, he became intimate with some of the Puritan emigrants from England, though he was never a member of their Church. He is said to have paid a visit to the Isle of Man shortly before 1619 and to have married† ROSE when there. On returning to Holland with her, he was elected military leader of the emigrants, and left England with them in the autumn of 1620, in the "Mayflower," arriving in New England at the end of the year. ROSE was one of the first to succumb to the privations and diseases which almost overwhelmed the new community, dying three months after the first landing at New Plymouth. In 1623, BARBARA, who is said to have been ROSE'S sister, and to have been "left an orphan in England"‡ when the "Mayflower" sailed, went out in the ship "Ann" to Myles, and soon afterwards married him. They had six children§ and lived happily together for thirty years.

In 1871, a monument was erected to Captain Myles Standish, and at the dinner, which took place after it was unveiled, a tribute was paid to ROSE STANDISH, she being designated as "the type of womanly sacrifice." "It was a graceful act," writes Mr. Johnson, "thus to remember the woman who had thrown in her lot with the captain, and shrunk not at crossing the seas to a strange land . . . and who was one of the first of the gallant company to drop from the ranks a victim to privation and hardship."‖

The next Manx emigrants we hear of left the island in 1655, their destination being Virginia. They consisted of two brothers, WILLIAM and JONATHAN CHRISTIAN, from the parish of Maughold, and a family named COTTIER from the parish of Lezayre. One result of their emigrating together was that the brothers Christian married two of the Cottier girls. WILLIAM received a grant of land from the Crown, which is still in the possession of his descendants.

* "I give unto my son and heir apparent Alexander Standish all my lands as heir apparent in lawful descent in Ormskirk, Boscough, Wrightington, Maudsley, Newbury, Croxton, and in the Isle of Man, and given to me as right heir by lawful descent, but surreptitiously detained from me, my grandfather being a second or younger brother from the house of Standish of Standish."

† Unfortunately there are no church registers in the island of sufficiently early date to contain her marriage. The Ballaugh register, the earliest, begins in 1598, but, at first, contains only births and deaths, and there is neither a Rose nor a Barbara mentioned under the first category.

‡ Abbott, in "The Puritan Captain."

§ Information from Belknap (orig. ed. Boston, 1794), per Mr. Frowde; Carlyle in Dict. of Nat. Biog.; and the Rev. W. Ball Wright.

‖ "The Exploits of Miles Standish." Henry Johnson (London, 1897).

The first of the Christians who became prominent was ROBERT, a descendant of William's. `` He was a colonel in the Revolutionary War, a devoted friend of Washington, an ardent federalist in politics, and an Episcopalian in religion. He was possessed of an ample fortune, and his home was the seat of that genuine Virginian hospitality which was so famous in his day, and is still the charm and crown of our civilisation."* Another writer states that `` he was long a member of the Virginia Assembly, and a member of a family which has for quite two hundred years been honourably and usefully represented in the judiciary and varied local trusts in Virginia."† His judicial position was that of presiding justice of his county—New Kent. By his wife, a daughter of Commissary-General John Browne, of the continental army, he had issue JOHN BEVERLEY and LÆTITIA. JOHN BEVERLEY CHRISTIAN (b 1796, d. 1856) was educated at William and Mary College, the *alma mater* of many of the most distinguished sons of Virginia. As soon as he reached his majority he was admitted to the bar, and soon built up a large practice. He was `` about six feet high, handsome, a good speaker, and of exceptionally fine bearing before the courts and juries. His splendid manner, imposing presence, and persuasive style of argument, made him a most effective advocate, as well as dangerous opponent at the bar."‡ When comparatively young he was appointed judge of the Williamsburg circuit, and, till the circuit was `` changed under the constitution of 1852,"§ he presided over its courts `` to the satisfaction of the suitors, and with a dignity, ability, learning and integrity rarely equalled."§ He also presided over the appellate court of the State in criminal cases, from 1835 to 1848. `` His deportment on the bench is said to have been singularly fine, combining *suaviter in modo* with the *fortiter in re* to a degree rarely met with."§

His sister, LÆTITIA, married John Tyler, at one time Governor of Virginia, then United States Senator, then Vice-President of the United States, and finally President, on the death of General William H. Harrison, who only lived one month after his inauguration.

GEORGE CHRISTIAN (colonel) was on the staff of General—afterwards President—Washington, and took a conspicuous part in the revolutionary war. His brother JAMES was in the army at this time, and was killed in battle during Burgoyne's invasion of New York. George's son, THOMAS, served on the Canadian frontier during the war with England in 1812-14. One of Thomas's

---

* From an address by the Hon. George L. Christian, of Richmond, formerly judge of the Hustings Court, published in 1900.
† Quoted by G. L. Christian.
‡ From Geo. L. Christian's address.
§ *Ibid.*

sons, WILLIAM HENRY, went out to California as a lieutenant in
Stephenson's regiment.   He afterwards had command of the old
" Presidio " at San Francisco   He aided the state surveyors in
laying out the city of Sacramento, and he kept the first English
school on the Pacific slope.   At the beginning of the civil war he
returned to New York and raised the 26th New York Volunteers,
being made colonel of that regiment.   He was brevet brigadier-
general at the battle of Antietam, where he received injuries that
caused his death.   Another relative of Thomas's is WILLIAM
CHRISTIAN (colonel), who gained fame in fighting against the
Indians.   Christian County, Missouri, was named after him.*
This family is now a very numerous one, and has spread into the
states of Mississippi, Missouri, Kentucky, Colorado, and Alabama,
having no less than seven judges among its members, as well as
numerous representatives who are either doctors, lawyers, or
clergymen.

The only information we have about the COTTIERS is that the
present representative of the family is a judge, he being a son of
the late Hon. ROBERT COTTIER.

The next emigration took place in consequence of the potato
tithe in 1825.   It was, for the most part, to the United States,
Cleveland, in the State of Ohio, being the headquarters of the
emigrants.   It is said that they went there in consequence of the
favourable report of the country given by Dr. HARRISON, brother
of the well-known Manx scholar and divine, the Rev. JOHN
EDWARD HARRISON (see p. 32), who had visited it before 1820.

Dr. HARRISON, who had been on the medical staff of the army,
was a great traveller.   He crossed the Arabian Desert disguised as
a Mussulman.   He then came to America, visited the Falls of
Niagara, and passed along the southern shores of Lake Erie.
Mr. W. S. KERRUISH, one of the most distinguished American-
Manxmen at the present day (from whom this information is
derived), says that Dr. HARRISON foresaw and predicted the
splendid destinies of the district to the south of Lake Erie.
The first Manx family came to it in 1824 ; then, in 1826, followed
two families called KELLY and CRAINE, the latter being connected
with the Caine's of Ballaskyr, Kirk Michael.   In 1827 and 1828,
about 140 families arrived.   Amongst those who came in these
years were PATRICK CANNELL, THOMAS QUAYLE. the parents of
Mr. W. S. KERRUISH, and the Rev. THOMAS CORLETT, who was
then a child, with several brothers and sisters.   PATRICK CANNELL
(b. 1754, d. 1839) was a Wesleyan local preacher, and continued
his ministrations to his fellow-countrymen in their new home.

---

* Information from Mr. Nathan Morse Christian Fletcher, of Jefferson
County, Missouri, grandson of the Colonel George Christian mentioned above,
and from Judge Joseph Christian, late of the Supreme Court of Appeal of
Virginia.

A faithful friend, shepherd, and counsellor, it was, according to the Rev. Thomas Corlett, to his "good practical sense and Christian influence" that they owed "no small part of their success . . . and the high tone of Christian morals which they have maintained."*

THOMAS CORLETT (b. *circa* 1815, d. 1891) son of William Corlett, known as "Billy-Bill-Beg," was a native of the parish of Michael. He was educated at Oberlin College, Ohio, obtaining the degree of B.A. therefrom in 1844, and that of M.A. at a later date. He then went to Kenyon Theological College at Gambier, and, about 1848, was admitted to holy orders in the Episcopal Church. He was a scholarly man, an effective preacher, and a great favourite socially.†

THOMAS QUAYLE (b. 1811, d. 1895),

founded a large and very successful shipbuilding business; he is said to have done more towards establishing the inland mercantile marine of the States than any other man. "If he could not build a boat on terms that would enable him to do it well, he would not undertake the contract at all,"‡ so that "no cheap or shoddy work was ever turned out at his yard. The result was that when one of his boats was mentioned, men knew its quality." He built no less than 150 ships of various kinds. There were few men in Cleveland who commanded a wider degree of public confidence and respect than he did, and few who have so well and honestly performed the duties of life.

Since 1828 there has been a steady emigration to Ohio and other States in America, though not on such a large scale as at that time.

Many Manxmen, whether born in Man or in America, served in the Civil War, and one of them, CASEMENT, attained the rank of general. Another, GEORGE BROWN GELLING (b. 1841, d. 1864), second son of Edward Gelling, of Douglas, merchant, went to New Orleans in 1857 to enter the counting-house of an uncle there. When the war broke out he volunteered his services and joined the Hampton Legion of South Carolina as a private. He was in twelve general engagements, among which were Bull's Run and Antietam. At the latter battle he was wounded and taken prisoner. He was soon exchanged, and continued in active service, attaining the rank of lieutenant and adjutant, till he, with three brother officers, was killed by a shell when in the trenches at Petersburg, Virginia, in 1864.

---

* "Annals of Early Settlers Association," p. 32.
† Information from Mr. W. S. Kerruish.
‡ "The Early Marine Interests of Cleveland," p. 461.

JOHN QUAYLE CANNON (b. 1827, d. 1901),

late President of the Mormons, and their representative in
Congress for many years, emigrated to Canada with his father.
Three years later he went to the State of Illinois, and embraced the
Mormon faith.   The following account of him is taken from
an article on Mormonism contributed to the "Contemporary
Review" by the late Rev. H. R. Haweis, in January, 1894 ·*—
"John Quayle Cannon is certainly . . one of the ablest, if not
the ablest, of the Mormon rulers. In Congress they used to call
him ' smooth-bore Cannon ' on account of his singularly persuasive
manner, and a certain quiet, stately, and restrained eloquence,
which seemed to deprecate rather than silence opposition. He is
never hurried into a rash adjective or an extreme statement, and
his severe composure, and at times almost pathetic seriousness,
make his conversation as impressive as it is charming." When
plural marriage was declared illegal, he called his wives together
and explained the law to them.   "They were now free, I said,
to depart, and to marry if they chose ; but I was morally
bound to provide for them if they did not do so. We had lived
long and happily together ; I could never suffer them to want and
I should still provide for the education and maintenance of my
dear children and wives. They all replied they accepted the
sacrifice imposed, but they would not leave me unless compelled to
do so. It was hard, very hard—a terrible rending of family ties
all round ; but I had to decide what I would do. My first wife
was dead. I would henceforth have no wife—there should be no
jealousy—and I now live apart with the children of my first wife.
But we could not break up the family social circle, and I try for
the sake of all to keep it together. I built a large room. Every
morning the ladies with their children meet me there as usual for
reading of the Bible and prayer. We dine in the same hall.
Each mother sits at a table with her own children, and that it may
not be said that I sit down with my ' wives' to dine, I have a
table set apart for me with the children of my first wife."

We may mention that JOHN CANNON was succeeded as delegate
to Congress from Utah by JOHN CAINE, a native of Kirk Michael.

Numerous Manxmen have also emigrated to Canada, to the Cape
of Good Hope, and to Australia, where many of them have distinguished themselves. Among those who have passed away the
most remarkable career was that of

---

* See also "Travel and Talk." Vol. I., pp. 250-5 and 299-300; by the same
author.

WILLIAM KERMODE, The Hon. (b. 1775, d. 1852),*

a native of Port Erin. He went to sea as a boy, and soon became
a skilful navigator, being distinguished by great ability, energy, and
undaunted courage. During the early part of the present century
he had command of large ships trading to India and Australia,
and, in the course of these voyages, he visited the country then
known as Van Dieman's Land (now as Tasmania), which was at
that time a penal settlement. The English Government, however,
wishing to encourage colonists, offered large tracts of land, at a
nominal price, to those who would undertake to settle there and
cultivate them, with the assistance of convict labour. In 1822,
WILLIAM KERMODE accepted a grant of land on these conditions.
At first he had what he termed a "rough" time of it with his
convict labourers, but he was just the man to manage them, as
is shown by the following incident : It is well known that at one
time bushrangers were a terror in Tasmania. During one of their
outbreaks, WILLIAM KERMODE was being driven to Hobart Town,
a distance of 80 miles from his farm, through what was in those
days a dense bush, in a closed carriage, when two of the bushrangers suddenly thrust their heads in at the window and
demanded his money or his life. His reply was to knock their
heads together, which so stunned them that he, with the aid of
the driver, was able to tie them up before they recovered their
senses. They were then placed in the carriage and driven into
town, where they were recognized as two of the most dangerous
of their class. For this action he received the thanks of both
Houses of Parliament. By 1828, he had his land laid out
and brought into order. On this land he grazed an enormous
number of sheep, and he amassed great wealth by the sale of their
wool, which was well known in the London market by its brand,
the "Three Legs of Man." He always took pains to get the best
possible stock, whether it was of merino sheep or of the "Suffolk
Punch" horse, for the breed of which he was equally famous. A
man who knew him, another Manx colonist, writes of him : "He
was known to all classes of the community. He introduced some
of the best stock ever brought into Tasmania, notably the Suffolk
Punch horse, and also one of the best classes of merino sheep."
He was for many years a member of the Upper House of
Parliament in the colony, called the Legislative Council, a
position which carried with it the right to the title of
"The Honourable." All the governors during his time were
on intimate terms with him, especially Sir John Franklin,
the Arctic explorer, who was a frequent visitor at his

---

* In 1810, he married Ann Quayle, daughter of the Rev. John Moore, vicar of
Braddan and vicar-general, and his wife Margaret, a daughter of Robert and
Catherine Quayle, of West Hill, Castletown.

large and handsome residence, called "Mona Vale," where the
subject of this sketch and his wife dispensed a lavish hospitality.
He was no doubt one of the ablest, most influential, and popular
men who had ever sought a home in the colony.

(Information mainly from Mr. L. Q. Kermode, grandson of W.
Kermode ; Mrs. Jeffcott, and Mrs. James Watterson, Port Erin.)

ROBERT QUAYLE KERMODE. The Hon. (b. 1812, d. 1870),

the only son of William Kermode and Anne Quayle Moore, was
born in the Isle of Man, being educated in Castletown, but,
when quite a boy, he went out to Tasmania, where, except for two
short visits to the "old country," he spent the rest of his life. Of
the many public services which he rendered his adopted country
perhaps the greatest was his share in bringing about the cessation
of the transportation of convicts to it. In acknowledgment of
this, he was made a member of the Governor's Legislative
Council. Under his careful management the fine estate of
"Mona Vale" was much enlarged, and he erected a mansion on
it which was considered the finest private residence in Australasia.
Distinguished men from all parts of the world visited · him.
Among them we may mention the Prince de Joinville and the
Duke of Edinburgh. R. Q. KERMODE also, in common with his
brother-in-law, GEORGE MOORE (a Manxman and a brother of the
late Thomas Moore of Billown), owned one of the largest properties
in New Zealand, and was, at that time, said to be the wealthiest
Manxman. His life was one of great activity, and he was regarded
with affection and respect by all classes. This is well shown by the
following extract from a Tasmanian newspaper at the time of his
death : "All who know Tasmania know the name of Robert
Quayle Kermode, and have been accustomed to associate with it
the ideas of spotless honour, affectionate kindness, warmth of
heart, and unsparing benevolence. . . It will be remembered
by prince and peasant, by the rich and poor ; for by the lowest
beggar as well as by the prince of the blood royal, he was known
as a Christian gentleman."

(Information from his son, Mr. L. Q. Kermode.)

BENJAMIN MICHAEL FREER, M.A. (b. 1837, d. 1898),

was the fourth son of Lieutenant Thomas Freer (see p. 140). He
was educated at King William's College, and from thence he
proceeded to Oriel College, Oxford. He then went out to Canada,
where he obtained his degree. He was distinguished by his great
literary taste, and was, therefore, admirably fitted for the post of
public school inspector, which he filled with great ability and

success for many years. "Wherever," says the "Minden Echo,"
"the late Mr. Freer has resided, he has, with his geniality,
culture, and straightforwardness, been a general favourite.
Since his advent in Minden he has been most faithful and diligent
in the discharge of his official duties, being eminently successful
in promoting the educational interests of the county, his demise
being felt as a public loss."

INDEX.

* Date of Episcopate.

---

* Date of episcopate.

---

* Date of episcopate.

---

* Date of episcopate.

SUBSCRIBERS.

	No. of Copies.
His Excellency the Lieut.-Governor (Lord Henniker) ...	4
The Lord Bishop (Dr. Straton)	2
The Clerk of the Rolls (Sir James Gell)	1
The Deemster Kneen	1
The Deemster Moore	1
The Venerable Archdeacon (Rev. H. S. Gill)	2
The Vicar-General (S. Harris, Esq.)	1
The Attorney-General (G. A. Ring, Esq.)	1
The Receiver-General (Colonel Anderson)	1

Alldritt, Mr. John	Castletown	2
Allen, Mrs. Robert	Douglas	4
Allen, Mr. Thos.	Maughold	2
Booth, Mr. William	Wakefield	1
Boyd, Mr. John T.	Ramsey	2
Backwell, Mr. M. J.	Castletown	12
Briscoe, Mr. F. W.	Douglas	1
Beck, Mr. Thomas...	Colorado	1
Broadbent, Mr. S. K.	Douglas	10
Brown & Sons, Ltd., Messrs.	Douglas	10
Bridson, Mr. M. M.	Douglas	1
Callow, Mr. D. T.	Castletown	1
Cubbon, Mr. T.	Douglas	2
Craine, Mr. James...	,,	1
Crennell, Mr. W. T.	Ramsey	1
Cregeen, Mr. A.	Liverpool	1
Clarkson, Mr. H. C. ... ... Norwich, near Bolton		1
Clucas & Fargher, Messrs.	Douglas	6

Cubbon, Mr. R. H.	Douglas	1
Cowell, Mr. J. T.	Douglas	1
Craige, Mr. S. C.	Douglas	1
Casement, Battery Sergeant-Major H. ...	Liverpool	1
Craine, Mr. Thomas	Douglas	1
Cubbon, Mr. John	Burnley	1
Clarke, Miss...	Peel	1
Clague, Mr. J.	,,	1
Cannell, Mr. John E.	Ramsey	1
Clague, Mr. W. D....	Cheshire	1
Cowin, Mr. William	Douglas	1
Cashin, Mr W.	Peel	3
Cubbon, Mr. W.	Douglas	4
Clague, Mrs.	Crofton, Castletown	3
Craine. Mr. W. C.	Douglas	1
Cowin, Mr W. D.	Douglas	2
Corteen, Mr. E.	Douglas	1
Clarke, Mr. H. S.	Sulby	1
Cowley, Mr. R.	Ramsey	1
Crellin, Mr. J. C.	Andreas	2
Cowen, Mr. J. Stanley	Union Mills	1
Casement, Mr. J. W.	Douglas	1
Cook, Mr. Charles T.	Manchester	1
Corlett, Mr. J. J. ... ... Prestwich, near Manchester		1
Cannell, Mrs. J.	Douglas	1
Corlett, Rev. John	St. John's	2
Curphey, Mr. Robt. T.	Liverpool	1
Clucas, Mrs.	Thornhill, Ramsey	5
Cosnahan, Mr. James	Douglas	1
Clucas, Mr. G. Fred.	Douglas	1
Cowin, Mr. John Thos.	Laxey	1
Costain, Mr. John	Liverpool	1
Do. for Members of Liverpool Manx Association		100
Callow, Mr. Thomas	Liverpool	1
Clucas. Mr. J. D.	Douglas	1
Casement, Mr. John	Douglas	1
Cowin, Mr. R. D.	Douglas	1
Clucas, Mr. W. J....	Liverpool	1
Cannell, Mrs. J.	Peel	1
Christian, Mr. W. W.	West Kirby	1
Callow, Mr John	Liverpool	1

Cregeen, Miss	Chester	1
Cowin, Mr. W.	Maughold	1
Duke, Mr. Henry	Tynemouth	1
Dickson, Mr. E. D. L	Cheltenham	2
Ellison, Mr. T. P.	Douglas	1
Fargher, Mr. William	Indiana, U.S.A.	1
Frowde, Mr. J.	Bermondsey	1
Faraker, Dr. W. Cregeen...	Peel	1
Farrant, Mr. R.	Douglas	3
Faraker, Rev. R.	London	1
Faraker, Miss	Douglas	2
Goodwin, Mr. Edmund	Peel	2
Gell, Mr. J. S.	Castletown	1
Gell, Sir James	,,	1
Gill, Mrs. J. F.	Killiney, Ireland	1
Gill, the Ven. Archdeacon	Andreas	2
Goldsmith, Mr. W.	Douglas	1
Goldsmith, Mr. Josiah	,,	1
Harrison, Mrs. J. A. ...	Furness Vale, Stockport	1
Hogg, Mr. John J....	London	1
Hodson, Mr. J. J.	Douglas	1
Hough, Mr. Alexander	Douglas	1
Hodson, Mr. T. H.	Douglas	1
Hall, Mr. J. (Mayor of Douglas) ...		1
Hincksman, Major W. H.	Lytham	1
Heaton, Mr. R. W.	London	1
Joughin, Mr. D. C.	Ramsey	1
Joughin, Mr. W. J. Clucas	Peel	1
Kewley, Mr. Thomas	Douglas	1
Kennish, Mr. William I.	,,	1
Kewley, Rev. J.	Arbory	1
Kissack, Mr Charles	Ramsey	1
Keown, Mr. Joseph K.	Peel	2

Robinson, Mrs. M....	... .	Liverpool	1
Randall, Mr. J. ...	... ...	Sheffield	1
Ridge, Mr. A. J. ...	... ...	Douglas	1
Rothwell, Mr. A. E.	... ...	Douglas	1
Robertson, Mr Alex.	... ...	Douglas	1
Screech, Mr. P. T....	... ...	Douglas	1
Sherlock, Mr. J. ...	... .	Ladysmith	1
Shimmin, Miss J. A.	... ...	London	1
Savage, Mr. E. U.. .	... ...	Liverpool	1
Stephen, Mr R. S.	... ...	Spring Valley	1
Stead, Mr. A. ...	... ...	Douglas	1
Stevenson, Mr. W. A.	... ...	Castletown	1
Sissons, Mr. F. B.	... ...	Douglas	3
Stowell, Mr. P. F.	... ...	Douglas	1
Symons, Mr. T. G.	... ...	New York	1
Teare, Mr. Henry ...	... ...	Douglas	1
Taggart, Mr. William	... ...	Manchester	1
Teare, Miss... ...	... ...	Port St. Mary	1
Taylor, Mr. Henry...	... ...	Rushen	1
The Lord Bishop (Dr. Straton) ...	...	Bishop's Court	2
Tellet, Dr F. S. ...	... ...	Ramsey	2
Tyson, Mr. Thomas	... ...	Douglas	1
Teare, Mr. A. H. ...	... ...	Ramsey	2
Wragg. Sir Walter, D.C.L.	... ...	Port St. Mary	1
Wood, Miss M. L. ...	... ...	Douglas	1
Warman, Mr. Henry W. ...	... ...	London	1
Wattleworth, Mr James ...	... ...	Birkenhead	1
Woods, Miss R. O.	... ...	Malvern	2
Woods, Miss Caroline M.	... ...	Malvern	1
Woods, Mr. R. Ambrose ...	... ...	Glenville	1
Ward, The Hon. J. K. ...	... ...	Montreal	1
Wicksey, Mr. J. T. W. ...	... ...	Castletown	1
Webb, Mr. S.	... ...	Douglas	1

Douglas :
S. K. Broadbent & Co., Ltd.,
" Isle of Man Examiner " Office.